MYTHS AND REALITIES:
Studies in Biblical Theology

John L. McKenzie Reprint Series
(in order of original publishing)

The Two-Edged Sword

Myths and Realities: Studies in Biblical Theology

The Power and the Wisdom

Mastering the Meaning of the Bible

Authority in the Church

Second Isaiah (Commentary)

The Gospel According to Matthew (Commentary)

Did I Say That?

Light on the Epistles

Light on the Gospels

Theology of the Old Testament

The Old Testament Without Illusions

Source (on contemporary issues)

How Relevant is the Bible?

The New Testament Without Illusions

The Civilization of Christianity

MYTHS AND
REALITIES: STUDIES
IN BIBLICAL THEOLOGY

JOHN L. McKENZIE, S.J.

WIPF & STOCK · Eugene, Oregon

Wipf and Stock Publishers
199 W 8th Ave, Suite 3
Eugene, OR 97401

Myths and Realities
Studies in Biblical Theology
By McKenzie, John L.
Copyright©1963 by The Estate of John L. McKenzie
ISBN 13: 978-1-60608-050-4
Publication date 12/11/2008
Previously published by The Bruce Publishing Company, 1963

IMPRIMI POTEST:

    IOANNES R. CONNERY, S.I.
    Praepositus Provincialis
    Provinciae Chicagiensis, S.I.

NIHIL OBSTAT:

    JOHN A. SCHULIEN, S.T.D.
    Censor librorum

IMPRIMATUR:

    ✠ WILLIAM E. COUSINS
    Archbishop of Milwaukee

July 22, 1963

Series Foreword

M ARK TWAIN ONCE RUMINATED, "It ain't the parts of the Bible I can't understand that bother me; it's the parts I do." John L. McKenzie, commenting on the same subject from another perspective, wrote, "The simple see at once that the way of Jesus is very hard to do, but easy to understand. It takes real cleverness and sophisticated intelligence to find ways to evade and distort the clear meaning of what Jesus said."

But McKenzie, like Twain, was himself a person of exceedingly high intelligence, distinctively witty, with a double-edged sword's incisiveness. As the first Catholic elected President of the Society of Biblical Literature, President of the Catholic Biblical Association, fluent in ten languages, sole author of a 900,000-word Bible dictionary, of over a dozen books and hundreds of essays, John McKenzie attained worldwide recognition as the dean of Catholic biblical scholars.

But again like Twain, McKenzie possessed a cultivated reservoir of abiding empathy—cognitive and emotional—for ordinary people and what they endure, millennia-in and millennia-out. He insisted: "I am a human being before I am a theologian." Unlike many who become entrenched in a hermetic, scholarly world of ever-multiplying abstractions, McKenzie never permitted his God-given faculty of empathy to atrophy. To the contrary, he refused to leave his fellow human beings out in the cold on the doorstep of some empathically-defective theological house of cards. This refusal made all the difference. It also often cost him the support, or engendered the hostility, of his ecclesiastical and academic associates and institutional superiors—as so often happens in scholarly, commercial and governmental endeavors, when unwanted truth that is the fruit of unauthorized empathy is factored into the equation.

John McKenzie produced works of biblically "prophetic scholarship" unlike anything created in the twentieth century by any scholar of his stature. They validate, with fastidious erudition, what the "simple see at once" as the truth of Jesus—e.g., "No reader of the New Testament, simple or sophisticated, can retain any doubt of Jesus' position toward violence directed to persons, individual or collective; he rejected it totally"—but which pastors and professors entrenched in ecclesiastical nationalism and/or organizational survivalism have chronically obscured or disparaged.

In literate societies, power-elites know that to preemptively or remedially justify the evil and cruelty they execute, their think-tanks must include theologians as part of their mercenary army of academics. These well-endowed, but empathically underdeveloped, theological hired guns then proselytize bishops, clergy, and Christians in general by gilding the illogical with coats of scholarly circumlocutions so thick that the opposite of what Jesus said appears to be Gospel truth. The intent of this learned legerdemain is the manufacturing of a faux consensus fidei to justify, in Jesus' sacred name, everything necessary to protect and augment an odious—local, planetary and/or ecclesial—status quo.

John McKenzie is the antidote to such secular and ecclesial think-tank pseudo-evangelization. Truths Jesus taught—that the simple see at once and that Christian Churches and their leaders have long since abandoned, but must again come to see if they are to honestly proclaim and live the Gospel—are given superior scholarly exposition via McKenzie. This is what moved Dorothy Day to write in her diary on April 14, 1968, "Up at 5:00 and reading The Power and the Wisdom. I thank God for sending me men with such insights as Fr. McKenzie."

For those familiar with McKenzie this re-publication of his writings offers an opportunity to encounter again a consistent scholarly-empathic frame of consciousness about Genesis through Revelation, whose major crux interpretum is the Servant of Yahweh (Isaiah 42). Ultimately embodied in the person of Jesus, the Servant is the revealer of Abba almighty—who is "on our side," if our means each person and all humanity. For all Christians, John L. McKenzie's prophetic scholarship offers a wellspring of Jesus-sourced truth about the life they have been

Series Foreword

chosen to live, the world in which they live, and the Christ in whom they "live and move and have their being."

(Rev.) Emmanuel Charles McCarthy
September 2008
Brockton, Massachusetts

Foreword

A NUMBER of friends and colleagues have expressed a desire that the papers contained in this volume be made more easily available for a wider circle of readers. This desire attests anew the lively interest in biblical studies exhibited by both clergy and laity. The book is published with the hope that it will serve those who wish to pursue these studies.

It is a pleasure to acknowledge assistance received in preparing the papers for publication. Miss Anita E. Weisbrod has furnished invaluable editorial assistance. The Reverend Robert J. Fox, S.J., has helped in selecting the articles to be published here. My secretary, Miss Carolyn Cuccia, has served cheerfully and competently. Mr. William May of The Bruce Publishing Company has seen the manuscript through the press with an expeditiousness which makes publication a pleasure for the author. The Very Reverend John R. Connery, S.J., has given unique support and assistance to this work and to future projects. The Reverend John Amberg, S.J., has furnished substantial assistance. To these and to many others whose encouragement has been more meaningful than I can tell I am deeply grateful. I offer them this book as a token of my sentiments.

JOHN L. McKENZIE, S.J.

Loyola University
Chicago, Illinois

Preface

THE collected papers of scholars are usually published posthumously or after retirement. The Reverend John L. McKenzie is neither dead nor retired. Therefore one may wonder why this collection appears. In Europe this book would cause no wonder; a number of distinguished scholars have published collections.

The scholar writes because he feels that he has something of value to say which has not been said before, and because his colleagues concur with his conviction. Most of what the scholar writes appears in professional journals; it is in these journals that the scholarly endeavor takes place, that advances are made. Those who have read and enjoyed *The Two-Edged Sword* and have appreciated its candor and brilliance should recognize that it was a popular work — the French *haute vulgarisation* — which restated the conclusions of scholarship. The articles which appear in this book represent the advance of scholarship and exhibit the creative study from which the author and others can produce popular works.

The idea of the book arose from several conversations and suggestions over the past year. Father McKenzie's associates and students felt that the success of *The Two-Edged Sword* warranted more from the same author. More can be expected: Father Mc-Kenzie is now engaged in the production of three books and has plans for two more. This might seem to satisfy his most avid readers. But an author writes not only because he has something to say but also because he believes he has readers. We assembled this collection because we thought it would appeal to several audiences. Biblical scholars, for whom the articles were first written, will be grateful to see these papers collected in one volume. Many of those who read *The Two-Edged Sword* became interested in biblical studies, and we hope that this collection will satisfy their desire to know more about the methods of the most recent biblical scholarship. Students and teachers in colleges and universities who have sought bound volumes in vain will be happy to have these papers within reach; the professional journal is too often hard to obtain, and selection of articles is difficult for the beginner. It is worth noticing that students wish and need this type of material as they never did before. The same desire and need can be seen in the numerous programs of biblical and theological study now open to the laity or being instituted specifically for the laity. The interest is not regional but nationwide; and while each region is different in its approach, each region has expressed a wish for more of this type of work.

The Two-Edged Sword was completed in 1953, although it was not published until 1956. In the ten years that followed its writing, biblical studies have matured, as this book witnesses, and an entirely new audience of both clergy and laity has emerged with an interest which simply did not exist fifteen years ago. The interest of the audience has been heightened by the Second Vatican Council. Developments before and during the Council have made it clear that biblical studies, warmly encouraged by Pius XII, are central in the *aggiornamento* proclaimed by John XXIII. It is to these groups, then, that we present this work.

The articles which appear in this book were chosen from some fifty titles which Father McKenzie has published during the past fifteen years. These were selected not necessarily because they are better but because they seem to have more to say to more people. No unity of theme appears, and we did not search for rigid unity. The unity is primarily the unity of authorship. The book exhibits the freedom of the scholar in action, searching the wisdom of the Church in the past to see what her position is in the present. The two articles on free scholarship in the Church are quite recent and were written because Father McKenzie felt the need, in encountering the problems of freedom in his own work, for a reasoned statement of scholarly freedom. This topic does belong to biblical theology, but not exclusively; it belongs to every scholar and every area of learning. The publication of these articles established Father

McKenzie as a leading spokesman for freedom of speech in the Church, particularly here in America.

Students of the Bible will recognize that inspiration, revelation, and messianism are topics of intense current interest. The interest in inspiration and revelation is not a result of the Council; rather the interest of the Council reflects earlier theological work. The work which is being done on messianism will also no doubt produce new theological ideas.

The significance of Father McKenzie's work on myth and the Old Testament can hardly be overstated. Mythopoeic thought is basic to the understanding of the Bible, and it has often been neglected. Modern biblical interpretation proceeds from an explanation of ancient mythopoeic thought and a presentation of this view of the cosmos to the modern mind, which has its own species of mythopoeic thought. It is perhaps this section which will be most interesting both to the scholar and to the layman, and from which they will draw material for future use.

I thank those who helped in the preparation of this book, particularly the Reverend Robert J. Fox, S.J., Miss Carolyn Cuccia, and Mr. William May.

Permission is hereby acknowledged for use of the following published material:

> *Ancient Near Eastern Texts*, edited by J. B. Pritchard (Princeton University Press).
>
> *The Complete Bible: An American Edition*, edited by J. M. Smith and E. J. Goodspeed (The University of Chicago Press).
>
> *Intellectual Adventure of Ancient Man*, edited by H. and H. A. Frankfort (The University of Chicago Press).
>
> *Physics and Philosophy*, by Sir James Jeans (Cambridge University Press).
>
> *Inspiration and Revelation in the Old Testament*, by H. Wheeler Robinson (Oxford University Press).
>
> *Archaeology and the Religion of Israel*, by W. F. Albright (Johns Hopkins Press).
>
> *Forgotten Religions*, edited by Vergilius Ferm (Philosophical Library).
>
> *Ezekiel*, by G. B. Cooke (Charles Scribner's Sons).
>
> *El in the Ugaritic Texts*, by Marvin H. Pope (E. J. Brill. Leiden).

The Philosophy of Symbolic Forms, by Ernst Cassirer (Yale University Press).

The Old Testament (CCD translation) (St. Anthony's Guild).

ANITA ELIZABETH WEISBROD

Loyola University
Chicago, Illinois
September 30, 1963
Feast of St. Jerome

Acknowledgments

"Intellectual Liberty in the Church," *The Homiletic and Pastoral Review*, LXI, 4 (Jan., 1961), pp. 350–359. Reprinted with permission.

"Faith and Intellectual Freedom," *The Critic Magazine*, XX, 1 (Aug.–Sept., 1961), The Thomas More Association. Reprinted with permission.

"The Word of God in the Old Testament," *Theological Studies*, XXI, 2 (June, 1960). Reprinted with permission.

"The Social Character of Inspiration," *Catholic Biblical Quarterly*, XXIV, 2 (April, 1962), pp. 115–124. Reprinted with permission.

"Pastoral Apologetics and Modern Exegesis," *Chicago Studies*, I, 2 (Fall, 1962). Reprinted with permission.

"God and Nature in the Old Testament," *Catholic Biblical Quarterly*, XIV, 1–2 (Jan.–Apr., 1952). Reprinted with permission.

"The Hebrew Attitude Towards Mythological Polytheism," *Catholic Biblical Quarterly*, XIV, 4 (Oct., 1952). Reprinted with permission.

"The Literary Characteristics of Genesis 2–3," *Theological Studies*, XV, 4 (Dec., 1954). Reprinted with permission.

"Mythological Allusions in Ezekiel 28:12–18," *The Journal of Biblical Literature*, 75 (1956), pp. 322–327. Rtprinted with permission.

"Myth and the Old Testament," *Catholic Biblical Quarterly*, XXI, 3 (July, 1959). Reprinted with permission.

"Royal Messianism," *Catholic Biblical Quarterly*, XIX, 1 (Jan., 1957). Reprinted with permission.

"Messianism and the College Teacher of Sacred Doctrine," *Proceedings of the Society of Catholic College Teachers of Sacred Doctrine* (1960). Reprinted with permission.

Abbreviations

AAS — *Acta Apostolicae Sedis*
ATD — *Das Alte Testament Deutsch*
BA — *Biblical Archaeologist*
BASOR — *Bulletin of the American Schools of Oriental Research*
BHK — *Biblische Handkommentar*
CBQ — *Catholic Biblical Quarterly*
EA — A. Knudtzon, *Die El-Amarna Tafeln*
ERE — Hastings' *Encyclopedia of Religion and Ethics*
ETL — *Ephemerides Theologicae Lovanienses*
GHK — *Göttinger Handkommentar*
HAT — *Handbuch zum Alten Testament*
HSAT — *Die Heilige Schrift des Alten Testaments*
HUCA — *Hebrew Union College Annual*
ICC — *International Critical Commentary*
JBL — *Journal of Biblical Literature*
KHK — *Kurzer Hand-Kommentar zum Alten Testament*
OTS — *Oudtestamentische Studien*
PEQ — *Palestine Exploration Quarterly*
RB — *Revue Biblique*
RGG — *Religion im Geschichte und Gegenwart*
RSR — *Recherches de Science Religieuse*
TS — *Theological Studies*
VD — *Verbum Domini*
VDBS — Vigouroux, *Dictionnaire de la Bible*, Supplément
ZATW — *Zeitschrift für die Alttestamentliche Wissenschaft*
ZKT — *Zeitschrift für Katholische Theologie*

The books of the Bible are abbreviated according to the style adopted by the Catholic Biblical Association of America. The following exceptions, however, should be noted: 1–2 Kgs (1 and 2 Kings) is used in place of 3–4 Kgs; 1–2 Chr (1 and 2 Chronicles)

in place of 1–2 Par (1 and 2 Paralipomena); Hos (Hosea) in place
of Os (Osee). The spelling of biblical names uniformly is that of
the King James version, the spelling used in the literature of the
English-speaking people, in place of the spellings found in the
Douay or CCD versions of Scripture. Thus *Isaiah* is found instead
of the *Isaias* of the Douay or the *Isaia* of the CCD, *Ahab* instead of
the *Achab* of both the Douay and CCD, *Hosea* instead of the *Osee*
of the Douay and CCD.

Contents

PART IV

MESSIANISM

PART I

FREE SCHOLARSHIP IN THE CHURCH

. 1 .

Intellectual Liberty in the Church

IN A thoughtful article published in the *Homiletic and Pastoral Review*,[1] the Rev. John J. King, O.M.I., has discussed intellectual liberty in the Church. The problem is not and cannot be stated as a question whether there *is* intellectual liberty in the Church; it can be stated only by defining what "intellectual" means, and by establishing the principles upon which intellectual liberty and its restraints are based. As a working definition I understand that intellectual liberty is freedom of speech in intellectual matters: freedom of the scholar not only to think, but to publish his thoughts in print and in public and academic lectures. This freedom rests upon the certain or probable truth of what is said, affirmed as certain or probable. I see no principle restraining intellectual liberty except the principle which limits all freedom of speech: the intellectual, like everyone else, is not free to utter something which he believes to be untrue, or which offends prudence, justice, or charity. The discussion can only be confused by treating intellectual liberty as a special case where the general principles of morality are not effective. Within these terms so explained, I wish to expand some of Father King's observations; no polemic is intended, although there are obviously some differences in opinion or in manner of formulation.

I. AREAS OF TENSION

Father King notices a certain tension between some Catholic intellectuals and the teaching authority of the Church. My own

3

acquaintance among intellectuals is limited, and I shall, as he does, refrain from generalization. I should have preferred that he state some concrete instances of the tension, delicate as the subject may be, for I must state that I have not observed this tension within the limited circle of intellectuals of my acquaintance. "The biblical movement," I suppose, would be included among contemporary Catholic intellectual activities. I speak of it because it is the activity with which I am most familiar, and here I can risk a generalization. Catholic biblical scholars feel no tension whatsoever with the teaching authority of the Church. When they count their blessings they are inclined to thank the *magisterium* each day for the liberty they enjoy; if their intellectual liberty were left to the private enterprise of some individual members of the Church it would have disappeared some years ago. The gratitude of these scholars to the hierarchy for protecting them from extinction is another bond which strengthens their loyalty to the teaching authority of the Church.

Who Speaks for the Church?

If the question of tension is to be raised, it should be located precisely where it exists. Limiting myself again to the area of my own studies, I observe tension between exegetes and some ecclesiastics who, without any canonical mission to do so, claim to speak for the Church. Biblical scholars know that these men are qualified neither by specialized learning nor by appointment to speak for the Church with any more authority than biblical scholars themselves possess. Exegetes are ill at ease in a discussion in which one of the parties assumes from the beginning that he alone is loyal to the Church and concerned about safeguarding orthodox Catholic doctrine, since this assumption can neither be demonstrated nor refuted. They are willing to discuss their opinions with anyone, but no discussion is possible where one of the disputants assumes the judicial function. It is disturbing, as John Courtney Murray once remarked, to find, when one expects to enter a theological discussion, that one is invited into the confessional. It should be conceivable that two men may sincerely and totally differ in their theological opinions and still be, both of them, within the area of orthodox Catholic belief. Refusal to admit that this is possible seems to be an effective denial of the principle of intellectual liberty within the Church.

If the principle of intellectual liberty is to be protected, then it must be conceded once and for all that no private individual nor group of individuals may pretend to be an authoritative source of Catholic doctrine. To refuse to admit that one's opinion is subject to discussion and review is to claim an infallibility which belongs to the Church alone. In the Church no one but the Holy See and the bishops assembled can speak with authority for the whole Church, and in the diocese only the bishop. No one else can utter anything but a personal opinion. It is assumed — or is it? — that any theologian spares no efforts to see that he is always faithful to Catholic doctrine; it is also assumed that no individual theologian is protected from a misstatement of Catholic doctrine by anything except his native intelligence and his habits of research. Professions of loyalty to the Holy See are not a substitute for these two conditions. The scholar who expects the Church to do all his thinking for him is shirking his own task; if he comes to believe that his thinking is the thinking of the Church, he is not only a laggard but a menace.

Who Is Infallible?

I submit that the principle of intellectual liberty is not properly stated unless it grants the liberty to make an honest mistake. There are occupations, I understand, where one mistake is one too many, such as the dispatching of trains and aircraft. Infallibility is the ideal proposed and maintained at the cost of one's job. Without implying that the train dispatcher is a more important servant of the human community than the intellectual, I do not see how we can apply this rigid standard to intellectual work. Intellectuals would say that a man who never arrives at an erroneous conclusion is not thinking, and that abandonment of thought is the only way to be sure of inerrancy. If one wishes personal infallibility, he can have it at this price. Intellectuals are disturbed by the assumption that any erroneous conclusions which they may reach must at once be attributed to a lack of submission to the *magisterium* and not to the limitations of human wit and industry. They are even more disturbed when their conclusions have not been proved to depart from the *magisterium* of the Church, but only from what some one *thinks* the *magisterium* has said.

Intellectuals are also concerned because of the unfounded assertion, so often implicit in criticism of their work, that only the errors of "advanced thinking" are dangerous, and that there is no danger in retaining erroneous opinions of the past. Does an erroneous opinion give security because it has been wrong for a long time? If I am wrong in teaching that the deluge of Noah is not presented in the Bible as an historical event, is my error any more or less pernicious than the error of one who affirms that the deluge is so presented, in the hypothesis that his opinion is wrong? Has the position of the Church become so feeble that it cannot tolerate the existence of conflicting theological and exegetical opinions? "No," I can imagine the disputant responding, "but not on this point." Yet is not the definition of the areas where different opinions can be tolerated itself a matter of opinion, as long as the Church herself has not defined the area?

It must be remembered that there always has been, is now, and ever shall be a vast amount of theological error current in the Church among both clergy and laity; I speak of *theological error,* a false theological opinion. Yet the Church manages to survive this human defect; ignorance and concupiscence are two defects which the Church always fights without ever achieving a complete victory. Was the affirmation of the Ptolemaic astronomy on a biblical basis a theological error? If it was, the Church has survived it. A few years ago a theologian made a survey of theological manuals written in 1880–1900. He found that of some twenty-five manuals all but three or four censured the theory of evolution as heresy. Did these men serve the Church better than those who denied that the theory is heresy? These good men were trying to defend the truth; but the truth cannot be defended by falsehood. Their misjudgment of the theory of evolution can be pardoned; their assurance in their misjudgment cannot.

How to Live With Error

The *magisterium* of the Church does not and cannot give any or all individual members of the Church a personal guarantee against theological error. If she could not give this guarantee to Thomas Aquinas, I doubt very much that she can give it to me. Now when differences in theological opinion arise, at least one of the opinions is obviously a theological error. The intellectual has confidence in the body of scholarship; he is convinced that scholarly discussion and criticisms are the best means to reduce the number of errors and to prevent really serious errors from gaining headway. The scholar knows that progress in learning begins with false starts, which some scholar must be lucky or unlucky enough to make; a false opinion can be a fertile point of departure. The scholar believes that the Church and scholarship are strong enough to preserve intellectual liberty and the growth of learning at the price of tolerating the circulation of some erroneous opinions. He is all the more convinced that this must be done because he knows that suppression of intellectual freedom will not guarantee immunity from theological errors; it can only canonize existing errors by removing them from discussion.

The confidence of the intellectual in free discussion is not shared by everyone. It does not occur to the intellectual that anyone who differs from him is by that fact a proved adversary of Catholic orthodoxy, and it shocks him when he learns that anyone can be so arrogant as to make this presumption. Where he desires to have a hypothesis tested by the criticism of his colleagues, he discovers that others wish to summon the Inquisition at once. Is it not fairer and kinder to presume that our adversary is in good faith until it is proved otherwise? If his opinion is wrong, it can be shown, and the honest scholar will accept the demonstration. Is the cause of truth served by slanderous gossip, by whispering campaigns in high quarters and in low without any serious discussion of the opinion in question? Anyone who has followed recent intellectual currents at all knows that I am not talking in the abstract.

We can be candid; the one real obstacle to intellectual liberty is ignorance, fear of knowledge. Conclusions or opinions or hypotheses of scholars are indignantly repudiated by those who have taken no pains whatever to examine the often complex questions which the scholar discusses. But the scholar's opinions imply that what we were taught in the seminary or the college or by Sister Mary Dolorosa in the eighth grade is wrong and therefore his opinions are subversive of orthodox doctrine and disrespectful to the teaching authority of the Church. The possibility that learning has advanced since we were in college or seminary or the eighth grade, or that our instructors in these institutions actually were wrong does not seem to be considered. Not everything that is taught in these institutions is an eternal verity.

In summary: there is no tension which I have observed between intellectuals and the teaching authority of the Church. There is tension between intellectuals and some who fear that the teaching authority of the Church is unable or unwilling to do its duty. This tension, like most tensions, can be resolved by charity.

II. INTELLECTUAL LIBERTY AND THE MISSION OF THE CHURCH

The principle of intellectual liberty in the Church cannot be understood outside of its place in the general mission of the Church. Father King has said: "The mission of Church is to preserve the deposit of faith which she has received from Christ and to bring this faith to all men of all times."[2] It may be unfair to take this statement out of its context; the teaching office of the Church must of necessity enter into a discussion of intellectual liberty. With all due apologies, I must say that this conception of the Church seems too narrow even for this discussion. I would say that the mission of the Church is to unite all men to the Father through incorporation into Jesus Christ. One of the things the Church must do to accomplish her mission is to teach; but she will never accomplish her mission by teaching alone. And I fear that Father King appears to reduce all larger concepts of the Church to some form of neo-Kantianism or pietism. I trust I am not unfair in drawing this conclusion from what he says; perhaps it is an impression rather than a conclusion. But surely Jesus Christ lived, died, and rose from the dead to confer upon men a new life and not a new set of theses.

In a broader concept of the Church — which I believe is a more profound apprehension of her mysterious reality — she does not become less a teacher. But if her teaching office is overemphasized at the expense of her functions of government and sanctification, or if her governing and teaching offices are merged into one so that they become obscured, then the defender of the Church feels compelled to enlarge the front upon which he must defend the teaching mission of the Church. What is the Church empowered to teach? Father King is in a line of assured theological orthodoxy when he says "not only matters of faith, but all things in so far as they are connected with faith." It is a rather easy jump, and I wish Father King had refused it more explicitly, from "all things in so far as they are connected with faith" to "all things." Is the Church honored and vindicated when she is turned into an educational institution? The fullness of Catholic life, we believe, is within the reach of all the members of the Church who desire to share it, and her teaching is and must be such that it is within the understanding of even her least educated and least intelligent members. Surely no one wishes to lay down minimum standards of intelligence quotient and academic achievement for full participation in the life of the Church. And this shows us the place of her teaching office within her general mission: she teaches all men of all conditions the truths they must know in order that Jesus Christ may live in them, and they in Him. A distorted perspective of the teaching office of the Church can lead to a distortion of the concept of Catholic life; it can be an expression of the eternal Gnostic tendency which believes that life, salvation, and perfection come from knowledge.

To say that the Church is empowered to teach in all things "in so far as they are connected with faith" does not imply that all things are connected with faith. The Church is like any other teacher in this respect, that she can teach only what she has learned; and she has not learned "all things" by revelation. We know what things are connected with revelation only by what the Church teaches concerning them; and it seems evident from the nature of things that she can add nothing to the human knowledge of "all things" except what she has learned. It seems evident also that she can enlarge the sphere of human knowledge only indirectly, unless she sets herself up as a research institute. "This alleged learning," she can say, "is false because it cannot stand with what I know to be true." But she was not instituted either to advance or to retard human learning, which of itself is neither a means of grace nor an occasion of sin: *"Non in dialectica placuit Deo salvare animam eius."* The remark seems ferociously anti-intellectual, but it is a paradoxical statement of a profound truth.

The theologian will scrutinize the teachings of the Church to see what application they have to questions which do not appear to lie within the scope of her mission; but he can err by extending her teaching too far as well as by restricting it too narrowly. Again, there seems to be no particular virtue in erring in one direction rather than in another. Theologians who have tried to tell masters of other sciences how to do their work have always fallen flat on their faces.

III. The Limits of Intellectual Liberty

I am not sure that Father King and I agree on the limitation of intellectual liberty. I said above that it is limited by the truth as the scholar perceives it, and by factors of prudence, justice, and charity. I should add that the scholar, with or without counsel, must form his own judgment concerning these other factors. I fear Father King might find this statement somewhat "subjectivist" and neo-Kantian. But I cannot attest truth myself except as I see it; I cannot take it out of my mind and lay it on my desk in its naked objectivity. If too many people do not see it as I do, I am forced to ask whether I see it at all; but where they seem to have no more assurance than I have, I believe we must keep searching.

Father King uses the word "fact" rather than the word "truth" to define the limit of intellectual freedom. It is this term which betrays the difference between us, for a "fact" seems to have that desired objectivity. It is like Dr. Johnson's rock, which is there whether you kick it or not. Now the Church, he says, is a fact, and her teachings are facts; and the scholar has no freedom where facts are concerned. Omitting the Church from the discussion for a moment, I observe that Father King's implications concerning scientific methodology are inexact. If it is raining at this minute, this would seem to be an irrefragable fact; but what happens to this irrefragable fact after the rain stops? The only reality it then has is its persistence in the notoriously fallible human memory, and after a few days most of us could not affirm on oath that it did or did not rain at 8:10 p.m. on a given date. We should have to consult the records of the weather bureau, which we would acccept because these records are carefully checked and are scarcely ever in error. The fact becomes an observed phenomenon; we can never get away from the observer and the reporter, and the "hard facts" turn out to be very soft in spots. In the sciences, a fact is always subject to examination and verification, and the scholar has all the freedom he wants where facts are concerned. I suggest that in calling the Church and her teaching "facts" Father King is giving them much less than they deserve. If they are "facts," then they impose hardly any restraint on intellectual liberty.

The Intellectual Lives in the Church

And I would remark that the genuine reality of the Church and her teaching is not a "fact" in any sense. The Church is a phenomenon which can be observed; she has a visible organization and visible members and can be distinguished from other phenomena. Does observation of the phenomenon show that she is the kingdom of God and the body of Christ, the source of supernatural life and the communion of saints? Does one know what the Church is unless one — horrid word — experiences her living reality? I accept the Church by faith and not by what I observe, as I believe all her members do; observation confirms my faith, but only God gives faith. And I accept her teachings also by faith and not by observation. These teachings are not "facts" which can be observed and verified; they are transcendental truths which are known in themselves and in their impact on thought and life by the infused virtue of faith and the gifts of the Holy Spirit. They are not "facts" even in the improper sense of conclusions which can be reached by deduction, the sense in which a scientist might speak of the "fact" of evolution or of nuclear fission.

Therefore I prefer to think of the Church and her teachings not as facts which limit my range of thinking, but as the element in which thinking is done. The Catholic thinker as a thinker does not see the Church merely as a teacher. In his thinking, as in his entire life, he feels the total impact of the whole Church in its offices of teaching, ruling, and sanctifying. The Catholic thinker lives in his faith as mammals live in the atmosphere and fish live in water. If he leaves his proper element, he dies, not only as a thinker but also as a man. All human activities are predicated on the hypothesis that the agent can ingest oxygen; but the oxygen does not determine that he pursue one activity rather than another. The Catholic thinker must be familiar enough with his atmosphere to recognize danger, as the human being instinctively senses the lack of oxygen. But he is not a fully developed human being just by breathing, and the Catholic intellectual is not a fully developed intellectual just because he has not departed from orthodox Catholic doctrine. This much was achieved by Pasteur's Breton peasant woman.

IV. The Mission of the Intellectual in the Church

Ultimately the conception of intellectual liberty leads us to the position of intellectuals in the Church; or shall we call it a mission? Father King is ambiguous on this. He observes that the Church needs her intellectuals,[3] but he remarks that the Church is not dependent upon them.[4] I cannot myself see that the Church needs her intellectuals. The Church needs things like the papacy and the hierarchical structure and the sacramental system; but she can fulfill her mission without intellectuals, and has often done it. She may not fulfill it as fruitfully without them, but that is another question; there are always factors which tend to inhibit the full vigor of the life of the Church. A few years ago I spent a summer as substitute chaplain in a public hospital in one of our large cities. The chaplain is the only priest serving an institution of 7000 patients, and the work is demanding; the archdiocesan authorities have been accustomed to relieve the incumbent of this office after two or three years, which are all that flesh and blood can bear. In some ways it was more difficult than intellectual work, but in other ways it was easier. One of the elements which rendered it easier was that I never had to ask myself whether what I was doing was necessary and useful. No one ever suspects that such work generates tension with the teaching authority of the Church. There can be no doubt that the parish priest and the hospital chaplain are more necessary to the Church than the intellectual, and I can add that they receive, as they ought, better cooperation.

So the intellectual is not *necessary;* is he *useful?* I suspect that there are many people, both in higher echelons and in lower, who are not really convinced that he is. No one, of course, ever makes a flat statement that intellectuals are useless; but actions and policies speak more loudly than words. If this kind of silent pressure is sustained long enough, the intellectual himself begins to wonder whether, considering the immense needs and the limited resources of the Church, he is entitled to continue his parasitic symbiosis, living off the energy of those who really do some work and who do not imperil Catholic orthodoxy. In actual and sorry fact the number of intellectuals who are discouraged by this pressure into giving up their intellectual ambitions is large enough to be distressing, and this is a "fact" which it does no good to conceal.

What Makes the Intellectual Run?

What supports those who persevere? Clerical intellectuals, at least, are sustained by a canonical mission. They are appointed to an office and freed from other responsibilities — although often not freed enough — and there is really nothing else for them to do. Their work may not be thought as important as *they* think it is (a common human failing), but it is their work, and they must be judged on how well they perform it, not on how well they do other men's work. The point deserves emphasis, since it seems to be assumed at times that the scholar is working for himself. He may be, but this is due to his failure as a man, not to his mission as scholar, which is of itself no more conducive to pride, vanity, and selfishness than the mission of bishop, pastor, or university president. Single-minded devotion to the tasks of any of these offices is an ennobling discipline. Scholarship, like these offices, can be a tool of self-aggrandizement, although the rewards are not so great.

If the intellectual wishes to understand his position more concretely, he contemplates the scholars whom the Church venerates for their learning and holiness; here he finds examples of what he can hope to accomplish. The Church expects to find among her scholars the modern Augustine or Thomas Aquinas. No scholar is so vain as to think himself another Aquinas; but he knows that the modern Aquinas must come from the ranks of men like himself if he is to appear at all. He knows that he has the mission to do now what Aquinas did in the Middle Ages, if he is man enough to do it; and he thinks he deserves the chance to succeed or to fail. If he does not have what it takes, he knows that Thomas Aquinas was not an isolated flash of genius or of grace; Thomas Aquinas is inconceivable except as the high point of an intellectual movement which was carried forward by a large number of men. The scholar is humble enough to know that we cannot have great scholars unless there be a multitude of little scholars upon whom the great scholar may rise. He is willing to do this work, if it is all that he can do.

Freedom of Movement

Thomas Aquinas and others of his stature did not achieve greatness by refusing to advance beyond traditional learning. We venerate them not for their conservatism, but for what some call "creative scholarship," and others call "innovation." Innovation may be good or it may be bad; but if there is no innovation at all, there is no creative scholarship and no growth in learning. We often forget that the canonized opinions of our day were the dangerous, radical innovations of the time of their origin. To reject innovation is to render it impossible for any one of the stature of Thomas Aquinas to arise, and surely such a step should not be taken hastily. Is this the price we wish to pay for the *securitas infallibilis* which Father King proposes as an ideal?

The scholar, studying the life and the work of the great scholars of the Church, observes that they insisted that the scholar must be left to do his own work in his own way. The scholar is devoted to the Church, and as a rule he is at least as well acquainted with the teachings and the directions of the Church as are those who throw these teachings and directions at his head. But the Church cannot give him the techniques of scholarship, and still less can private individuals who have neither the mission to speak with authority nor the authentication which comes from their personal scholarship. Intellectual liberty means nothing unless it is generally conceded that the scholar and his colleagues know their business better than amateurs, and are better equipped to protect themselves from mistakes.

What Can the Scholar Do?

What can the scholar contribute to the Church? Again he must look to the great scholars of the past. The scholar never makes remarks of the type which Father King attributes to nameless individuals to the effect that the Church is failing to meet modern needs. The Church is always contemporary; and the scholar knows that the Church uses men like himself to formulate her message to the contemporary world. In the providence of God and in ordinary practice this is the work which only the scholar can do; he would like to do it, imperfect as his achievement may be, because no one else is likely to do it. Those who present the message of the Church to a wider public, whether the Catholic laity or the general public, depend upon sound scholarly work that their presentation may incorporate the finest and freshest fruits of learning, may answer the questions which the present generation asks, and may speak in a language intelligible and attractive to contemporary listeners. These results, accessory as they may be to the mission of the Church, are sufficient to reward the scholar for his work.

The Costs of Scholarship

Eternal vigilance is the price of intellectual liberty just as it is of political liberty. The intellectual knows from the history of scholarship that the results of scholarship have always been the fruits of adversity. Scholars are trusted only when they have been dead long enough for us to be sure that they will no longer trouble us. The scholar smiles when he hears that he is regarded as a contemporary nuisance at best, a menace at worse. "If a little man like myself can cause so much alarm," he thinks, "what would these people do if Thomas Aquinas or Jerome or Augustine were here to disturb them? Those firebrands would make the contemporary intellectual ferment look like an Altar Society picnic."

If the scholar is unwilling to pay the price of a degree of unpopularity and distrust, he should not attempt to carry on scholarly work. He must refuse to be diverted from his responsibility by irrational panic. If a theologian of national reputation should write that the modern biblical movement is suspect because biblical scholars are not men of prayer, the biblical scholar is annoyed not so much because the remark is unkind as because it is unscholarly. Should men attempt to suppress his work rather than submit it to discussion and criticism, he must continue in the confidence that while one man or a few can be suppressed, intellectual freedom and intellectual work cannot be. He must be satisfied with the degree of freedom which is his. But he must be vigilant and never abuse his freedom; he must work so carefully that he will furnish no real handle for prejudice to seize. He must protect his intellectual freedom in the only way possible, by producing results which will convince the clerical and lay public that intellectual freedom deserves to be cherished.

My friend and colleague Canon Joseph Coppens of Louvain once wrote that exegetes have little to say in the Church, but they ought to have the courage to say it. One may properly extend this remark to all intellectuals. The exercise of freedom demands not only vigilance but courage. It is the duty of the intellectual to take the risks of "advanced thinking." May he not expect, as the late Pius XII said of exegesis, that other members of the Church will judge his work not only with equity and justice, but also with charity, and abhor that intemperate zeal which imagines that whatever is new should be suspected or opposed?

The scholar is too much of a realist — I hope not too much of a cynic — to expect that these wise and kindly words of his late Holiness will ever be universally effective. But he is grateful that they were uttered; they show him the mind of the Church concerning himself and his work. In the long run, he is grateful to his critics too; they keep him alert, compel him to examine his methods and to write with clarity and accuracy, and they assure him that his labors are not in vain. If his conclusions never disturbed any one, the scholar would have good reason to fear that he is not doing his work.

.2.

Faith and Intellectual Freedom

INTELLECTUAL freedom, by the definition of the words themselves, means freedom to think; in common usage, however, people understand it to mean freedom to think out loud. It is not merely a synonym for freedom of speech; intellectual freedom means the absence of constraint upon those processes which are usually called *intellectual* and the expression of ideas issuing from those processes. In common usage, again, the name *intellectual* is given to those activities which revolve about learning, and learning is the professional business of scholars. By implication, then, common usage seems to suggest that intellectual freedom means not only the absence of restraint upon thought and expression in intellectual questions, but also the competence to speak on these questions. One is not free to drive a car unless one has the competence to drive. If intellectual freedom is the freedom to speak in matters of learning, this freedom can scarcely belong to the unlearned; and by the unlearned I mean those who lack specialized learning in the area which comes under discussion. The attitude which prevents people from attempting what they are incompetent to do is called responsibility. There are laws which prevent the incompetent from driving a car; there is nothing but personal responsibility, aided by a vague and not always active social pressure, which prevents the incompetent from expressing opinions when they are not informed. Where such incompetence is a threat to society, as it is in the practice of medicine, law, and some other professions which are called learned, society restrains such incompetence by

18

law, and surely no one thinks that society is unduly restraining intellectual freedom.

If we are to reach an understanding of intellectual freedom and responsibility, we must admit that intellectual freedom and responsibility are not the business of the scholar alone, but of everyone. Each individual person has the freedom to think and to speak upon matters in which he is competent, and he ought to have the responsibility to keep silent on matters where he has no competence. I realize, of course, that rigid observance of this principle would be a fatal blow to most casual conversation, and would reduce the speech of all of us to an alarming degree; one wonders whether this would be an unmixed disaster. But we all recognize the difference between the casual light conversation of our hours of relaxation, when it amuses us to play with ideas which are too large for us to handle, and earnest discussion, especially if earnest discussion includes public utterance orally or in writing. Unguided ideas can be as dangerous as unguided automobiles. Every genuine scholar is aware of this, and of the responsibility which it imposes. The acquisition of competence in any field of learning comes only through prolonged and patient submission to a demanding discipline. One who has acquired competence does not insult his colleagues by intruding into a field which is not his own. In this way the discipline of scholarship imposes a certain humility upon those who practice it; I say a certain humility, for it would be ridiculous to say that scholars are any more or any less proud, vain, and self-opinionated than the rest of men. But I have found that they are not likely to exhibit these defects in their professional work, because they know that their colleagues will not stand for it.

The humility which ought to ornament the scholar can and ought to be the fruit of a genuine liberal education; the values of liberal education seem to consist less in teaching students what they know than in teaching them what they do not know — and how to find out the truth which they do not know. From such a genuine education should come a balanced judgment which enables its possessor to define his own areas of competence very clearly and to act with responsibility outside his areas of competence. The educated man respects truth by not assuming that it can be reached cheaply. I do not imply that this humility and respect for truth are exclusively the fruits of a liberal education; they are character traits, and unfortunately education is not a character-building process. Among my acquaintances there are some who without a liberal education have an excellent sense of intellectual freedom and responsibility, and there are some who have spent half or most of their lives in academic institutions without learning that when one has nothing to say, it is the best thing to say.

Intellectual freedom and responsibility of the scholar, then, are not isolated phenomena in human society; the scholar shows them in his life and work and in the manner demanded by that life and work. The scholar's competence assures him a greater freedom than others may claim; it is an axiom of social ethics that responsibility grows with freedom. We must look for the reasons which justify the freedom of the scholar. Now the existence of scholarship rests on the assumption that man does not know everything. The scholar is freed from other engagements and supported by society so that he may organize and communicate the knowledge which we have and discover if he can the truths which we do not know — which is to say in longer words that society expects from the scholar the two functions of teaching and research. In our Western society the customary seat of scholarship is institutions of higher learning, but the location is merely accidental, particularly the location of the work of research.

It is easy to make a false distinction between teaching and research. For reasons which are hard to analyze, it is the common experience of scholars that one who devotes himself entirely to investigation and abandons teaching is in danger of producing barren research; there are exceptions, but there are also well-established probabilities. It is likewise a common experience that research within the degree in which it is possible to the individual generally improves his teaching. For the teacher who is not a student is not a teacher; and even if, as so often and so unfortunately happens, he is not granted time for research, his own personal control of current research in his field is the indispensable price of maintaining competence as a teacher. And it is risky to attempt to establish a primacy of one or the other; perhaps it is best to say simply that a university is an institution populated entirely by students, some of whom teach. While some men give more time to research and others more time to teaching, it is misleading to think of these as two distinct and opposed activities; they are two elements in a single activity, which is most simply and accurately described as learning.

If research and teaching are a single activity, then neither should a false distinction be made between freedom of research and freedom of teaching. Both research and teaching are resolved into the investigation and the proposition of knowledge, and differ not in their material so much as in their intended audience; the investigator addresses primarily his colleagues in teaching and research, the teacher primarily addresses students who have not yet received the fullness of academic training. I have said elsewhere that there appears to be no restraint upon intellectual freedom beyond the restraints which lie upon all freedom of speech; this remark has been discussed and criticized, but it seems to stand up. No one is free to say anything which he knows to be false, or which is offensive to prudence, justice, or charity. The judgment of the truth of what he says in his own field is primarily the responsibility of the scholar as scholar; but he knows he does not work alone, and if his judgments have not been submitted to his own criticism and the criticism of his colleagues, he is not a genuine scholar. The judgment of the prudence, justice, and charity of what he says is the area where the scholar's personal responsibility as a member of society is operative. I see no reason why his responsibility to maintain these virtues in his work should differ from the responsibility of anyone — by which I mean that he must make his own decision, remembering here also that the wise man takes counsel.

It is here that I raise the ugly question of the possibility of suppressing the truth, which scholarship regards as the cardinal sin against the mind — and it is. To be honest, no reason appears why the truths of scholarship should enjoy a sacred immunity which is not enjoyed by truths in other human affairs, for no one questions the principle that at times the truth may be and ought to be suppressed. We should add that it is dangerous to suppress the truth, that it is impossible to suppress it permanently, and that one may suppress it for a time only when there are compelling reasons which demonstrate that more harm will be done by revealing it than by suppressing it. For when a point has been reached where suppression of the truth is a recommended action, we can no longer think of what will do more good, but only of what will do less harm. Normally the suppression of the truth is an exceptional means of reaching an end; and scholars generally are convinced that the occasion for suppressing the truth arises more rarely in scholarship than it does elsewhere.

More frequent and more urgent is the problem of suppressing not the truth, but opinion and discussion. Since scholarly opinion and discussion are the only means by which the scholar hopes to arrive at the truth, the compulsion which would demand their suppression can scarcely be less. We must admit, I think, that the scholar's dedication to the truth can sometimes mask motives which are less noble; and the need for personal responsibility becomes evident. Scholars believe that they should enjoy the liberty which all men concede each other of saying something which they think is true but which because of their ignorance is false; scholars, like other men, must pay the usual penalty if they make a habit of doing this. Responsibility imposes upon the scholar the obligation of employing every resource of method and technique, every criticism of his own and of his colleagues, to secure him against proposing falsehood. If he is careful, he will propose opinion as opinion and not as established truth; if he is responsible, he will not cry that academic freedom is raped because someone questions his right to propose half-baked untested opinions. If he is responsible, he will often realize that an opinion which is sound in the scholarly sense of the word is premature; he will then wisely attempt to lay the ground for the proposition of his opinion rather than rush into print, almost baiting his readers. Scholars are often accused by laymen of a pathological desire to publish; I think the charge is grossly exaggerated, and among the competent scholars of my acquaintance I do not know one who has not suppressed more of his own opinions than he has published. These men know that freedom demands responsibility, and they honor the learned profession by a respect for the truth which forbids them to toy with unformed and uncriticized opinions.

It seems to me that the same principles govern teaching. Teaching, except on the highest graduate levels, addresses a group to whom the most advanced scholarship is almost by definition premature. The good teacher will leave his students aware that at best he can give them the current work of scholars and prepare them to accept further advances without shock or surprise. Between the teaching of safe and secure and antiquated falsehoods and the most recent and novel and venturesome hypotheses the good teacher must steer a careful course. He is wise if he remembers that learned hypotheses have scarcely ever been erected into principles without substantial modifications; to give his students no more than the most recent hypotheses serves them as poorly as to pretend that nothing has been discovered since the teacher himself was in graduate school. The good teacher does not raise in the minds of his students questions which he has not helped them equip themselves to answer; and he never forgets that, while the teacher teaches, it is the students who learn.

You will observe that I have not presented an ideal of intellectual freedom without restraint; you will observe also that I have presented the personal responsibility of the scholar as the only effective restraint. By this is meant not only the personal responsibility of the individual scholar, but the responsibility of the body of scholarship. Scholars are able to submit the hypotheses of their colleagues to rigorous testing and criticism which is beyond the ability of those who are not scholars; and the nonscholarly public can be assured that opinions which survive this process have been as well examined as is humanly possible. The public can also be assured that scholars find this examination a pleasure as much as a duty.

The collective responsibility of scholars answers the question which one might raise: If the scholar fails in his responsibility, should not some other agency intervene, as it does in the practice of medicine and law, to prevent the irresponsible scholar from doing harm? It should be noticed that the body which polices the practice of medicine and law is proximately the professions themselves; public authority supports and authenticates their judgments, but it does not attempt to form them. An external agency could intervene, it seems, only on the assumption that scholarship as a body had proved its lack of competence and responsibility; and if this assumption were ever verified, it is doubtful whether anyone could be sure what he is doing. It is the conviction of scholars that some degree of incompetence and irresponsibility must be tolerated in scholarship, as it is tolerated in all human affairs, in order that the activity itself can be maintained. Freedom of opinion and discussion are the essential means by which scholarship achieves its ends; scholars believe that in academic examinations, learned societies, and the exchange of opinion in learned books and journals, adequate means exist to prevent the incompetent and the irresponsible from abusing the freedom of scholarship. They are convinced that the investigation and communication of truth cannot be promoted by the suppression of free discussion and opinion. When scholarly activity is suppressed, when the carefully considered opinions of scholars are rejected by those who have not examined these opinions critically, scholars wonder whether it is they or the external agency which is acting irresponsibly.

I have set forth the principles of intellectual freedom as I understand them without reference to the Church and the Catholic scholar. Do these principles have validity for the Catholic scholar without further modification? Many people, both inside and outside the Church, think they must be modified, and substantially. It would surprise many Catholics to find that they agree with many non-Catholics that the Catholic scholar does not enjoy intellectual freedom. The easiest way to show how utterly false this belief is would be to review the history of Catholic scholarship, but this is not possible here or very often elsewhere; the most practical demonstration of the intellectual freedom of the Catholic scholar is its exercise, and this is the demonstration which scholars prefer to employ. In exercising their freedom they also show their responsibility. Whether Catholic scholars have always and everywhere enjoyed full intellectual freedom is another and a historical question; it scarcely differs in principle from the historical question whether scholars of any description have always and everywhere enjoyed full intellectual freedom. Of course they have not. Freedom, whether intellectual or political or religious or anything else, must be affirmed and exercised; far from being the naturally instinctive condition of man, freedom must be achieved and maintained. My thesis that the Church as such imposes no restraint upon intellectual freedom beyond the general principles of restraint is possibly enough of a surprise to many to require some elaboration. This restraint, if it were to exist, could be found only under two heads: dogma and discipline. Dogma is the belief of the Church as she herself has defined it, and it is the faith professed and accepted by everyone who calls himself a Catholic. The scholar does not submit dogma to criticism and examination because it is neither his office nor does it lie in his power to define what the Church believes; only the Church herself can do this, and she does it only through quite well-identified organs. No one speaks for the Church except the Holy Father and an ecumenical council and the bishops together, and only these speak for the Church as a whole. In the individual diocese the bishop and no one else speaks for the Church, although the statements of the individual bishop are not irreformable, as are the statements of the Holy Father and the ecumenical council when they are made with due solemnity. When the scholar accepts the faith, he, like all members of the Church, accepts it as a dogmatic faith; like other members of the Church also, he does not accept it as a scholarly conclusion. Through the Church the scholar apprehends those truths which no scholarship ever attains and on which a way of life is founded. The Catholic scholar, like all scholars, has to accept his way of life from another source than himself.

Catholic scholars would prefer that their fellow Catholics do not think of them as existing in a state of tension with the teaching of the Church by their very profession of scholarship. To the Catholic scholar the Church is life: the life communicated from God through His Son Jesus Christ, who is one with the Church which is His body, a life integral with God and one's fellowman, an assurance that one has grasped the ultimate reality which gives meaning to all reality. The scholar whose work lies in areas closely related to the reality of the Church considers himself fortunate that his investigations never fail to show him anew the grandeur of the Church and to confirm him in his faith in the Church as the extension of the Incarnation. Far from feeling tension with the Church, he finds that she is a principle of freedom because she is a principle of confidence and not of fear. For the Church is a principle of life, and freedom is the fullness of life.

But the scholar does examine the meaning of the dogma which he accepts; when he does this, he is enjoying a freedom canonized many centuries ago as faith seeking understanding. Here tension can arise not with the Church but with some of her individual members. For his investigations may disclose that a very old and popular understanding of dogma is a false interpretation. He may find that the progress of learning in other areas requires a different interpretation from the one commonly accepted. Since dogma does not stand in isolation from human knowledge and human activity, he may discover new relations of dogma to knowledge and life. When he proposes these conclusions, he is surprised to find that they are frequently met with shock, hurt, and resentment. Here he must be aware of a basic difference between his own scholarly attitude toward knowledge and the attitude frequently exhibited by others. To the scholar knowledge is a constantly growing understanding. The front of the advance of knowledge he conceives as extremely fluid, moving forward here, reversing itself elsewhere, modifying and abandoning earlier positions; but the movement is always forward. Truth is as inexhaustible as reality itself, and the scholar believes that comprehension is an impossible ideal. Generally, when one learns something new, one must also unlearn something old. The scholar has made this his way of life and thinking, but he should not be surprised if others are shocked by this, seeing in it a subjectivistic and relativistic attitude toward truth — which, of course, it is not.

Yet what is the mission of the scholar in the Church? I conceive it to be the mission of the scholar in society at large: the investigation and communication of knowledge. The Church is by her divine mission equipped neither to pursue knowledge nor to retard its pursuit. But she should pursue her own mission under more favorable conditions if those who do her work are as free of ignorance as contemporary learning can make them; if her members do not suffer difficulties in understanding their faith which arise from ignorance, and do not cherish opinions which learning has shown to be false; if she is able to speak to the contemporary world with a deeper familiarity with its language and a more secure grasp of its ideas and its problems. The scholar can serve the Church by helping to create these conditions for her ministry, and the Church traditionally has left this to her scholars. Again this can be best shown by a simple enumeration of her scholars, which cannot be done here. By what principle can anyone affirm that these great men did their work so well that they have left nothing for contemporary scholars to do? Is it likely that they themselves would approve the erection of their work into a kind of pseudo dogma, which permits modern scholars to do no more than repeat traditional learning? It is inconceivable that the need and the possibilities of creative scholarship are any less now than they were at any time in the past; and it is also inconceivable that the Church no longer produces men capable of creative scholarship. It should not be surprising that one cannot think of a single scholar who deserves the name of creative in modern times who has not been under attack precisely for his originality; it should not be surprising because one can say the same thing of every creative scholar in the Church during the past eighteen centuries. Time has vindicated the services of the scholar to the Church, but it has not dulled the attack.

The second head under which restraint of intellectual freedom in the Church may be conceived is discipline. It must be understood that the Church does not claim and does not possess in her discipline the infallibility which she has in defining her beliefs. No Catholic doubts that the Holy Spirit works in the discipline of the Church, but He does not work in the same way as He does in her teaching. The Church is not protected by a specific charisma against imprudence and unfairness in her discipline; she is protected by the prudence, intelligence, justice, and supernatural charity of the men to whom her discipline is committed. The historian is free to point out instances in the past when her discipline has not been exercised with the fullness of these virtues; and their absence at definite times and places in the past is no assurance that they are always exhibited in the present. That we are much slower to point them out in the present is not mere cowardice, at least not always; our reluctance to do so arises from caution founded in the knowledge that we are incompletely informed. I dare say many share my conviction, for example, that there can never be a good prudential or pastoral reason for the Church in the United States to remain silent on interracial justice or to permit its practice to reflect the patterns of segregation. I suppose that we who are so convinced believe that a Church which preserves itself by accepting segregation is not preserving itself as the Catholic Church. And I would point out that the hundreds of people who have said things like this are a living testimonial to the Catholic belief that discipline is not above criticism.

It would be altogether dishonest to say that ecclesiastical discipline has never been a restraint upon intellectual freedom; it would be equally dishonest to say that the imposition of restraint by ecclesiastical authority has never been unwise, imprudent, or unfair. The Catholic scholar recognizes this, but it does not alarm him. He knows that none of his non-Catholic colleagues in scholarship expects to find a world where intellectual freedom is never endangered by imprudence, unfairness, and folly, nor is the Catholic scholar so simple as to expect to find such a world. He is encouraged by a long collective experience which shows that the discipline of the Church is better secured against imprudence, unfairness, and folly than any other administrative discipline known to history. After so long a time and so many turns of fortune, it becomes clear that intellectual freedom survives in the Church, as it survives today, only because the discipline of the Church, while it may fail in judgment or even in virtue in isolated instances, ultimately cherishes and defends the freedom of its scholars. If he takes the long view, as a scholar ought, he knows that freedom of discussion and opinion will never perish in the Church, even though it may seem to be under suspicion in his own time.

The discussion up to this point has turned upon principles; we live in a real world, and it would be unrealistic in the extreme to omit what is now and has always been the greatest threat to intellectual freedom. This threat is not peculiar to the Catholic community, for it springs from some deep and atavistic and not very attractive human passions. The one word which I think best defines this threat is fear of knowledge, which is ultimately fear of truth. Man seeks truth, although I think Aristotle overestimated his desire to know; but his more primitive impulses move him to seek security first, and truth insofar as it contributes to his security. Security is attained by the conviction that one possesses the truth, whether one possesses it or not. To point out error is to threaten security, and it arouses another atavistic passion besides. For man finds security also in a life of ordered routine; few men are adventurers. He prefers that his activities fall into a pattern to which he can become accustomed, and he prefers that his thinking also fall into a pattern which will not be disturbed. The scholar disturbs the pattern and demands that man revise his thinking, and thus he is a threat both to security and to routine.

Nowhere does man cherish security and routine more than in his religious life; for security and routine liberate him from the necessity of thinking about religion. I fear that Catholics are more open to this habit of mind than others, for the Church makes a total demand upon its members, and the members are ready to ask for a total return — now. They like to think that the Church has answers to all questions and solutions to all problems and directions for all situations; and if she has not, some will create them and present them as her teaching. Thus they are secure in their thinking, because the Church has done it all for them; they are secure in their decisions, because the Church has made them all for them. I am aware that I present a caricature rather than a portrait; but it is really difficult to describe without caricature an attitude of mind which is a flight from reason. I think that no one will deny that there is a reality which I have caricatured, unless he is ready to claim that never in his life has he fled from reason; and I make no such claim for myself.

The scholar therefore is considered a threat to the faith of the unlearned because he proposes opinions and conclusions which cannot be reconciled with popular beliefs. For some reason, it seems to make no difference that these popular beliefs have never been examined either by the faithful or by many of their instructors; and I suspect the reason is fear of knowledge, fear that examination might impose a change in the routine which gives security. Nevertheless, since even the most serene faith cannot entirely wall itself from the world of reality, a reason can be found why the scholar should not disturb popular belief even when it is in error, for it is alleged that it is better to leave people in an error which they have so long cherished and from which they have reaped so much devotion, rather than shock and disturb them. This principle by logical dexterity can be maintained together with another favorite principle, the principle that error has no right to exist. When the principle is applied, it means that the scholar may propose nothing which might possibly be erroneous, while the faithful are free to retain errors as long as they are old errors and not new errors. Equivalently the principle means that error has no right to exist unless it is my error.

The fear of disturbing the good faith of the laity is regarded as a sufficient motive for invoking the hierarchy with petitions to arrest those scholarly discussions and opinions which the petitioners judge to be disturbing. Whether it be wise or prudent or not, the hierarchy is likely to think that if many people say they are disturbed, they are disturbed; they may even think that if a few people say many are disturbed, then many are disturbed. The hierarchy is aware that the Church does not answer all questions and solve all problems; but it may judge that scholarship, which is a long-term project after all, can in a concrete situation be deferred until the panic dies. The scholar cannot make decisions which belong to the hierarchy, but he thinks the hierarchy can profit by consulting him; if the scholar is consulted, he will submit respectfully that the history of the Church shows no instance where the suppression of intellectual freedom did not work as much harm as good, and he doubts whether it can be presumed that any situation will be resolved by these means with any other result.

For the suppression of intellectual freedom is a practical vote of no confidence in scholarship; it carries with it an assumption, which cannot be rationalized away, that scholarship no longer exhibits competence and responsibility. Such imputations are found in statements in the popular press made by clergymen and laymen who do not qualify by training and achievements as scholars and who, to be candid, seem quite ready to speak with authority in areas where they have no competence. I have said earlier that such behavior is irresponsible, and I say it again. That many scholars or most scholars have abandoned their loyalty to the Church and their professional integrity as scholars is a charge so sweeping and so profound in its implications that it demands more evidence than I have seen adduced. And it is a charge which cannot be refuted; frankly, I have no idea how I would demonstrate my loyalty to the Church and to the standards of scholarly integrity. I doubt whether those who make such charges could demonstrate their own loyalty any more easily.

The idea that the Church is a living encyclopedia of all knowledge is such a desperate distortion of her genuine reality that one scarcely knows where to take hold of it. This misconception can arise, it seems, only from a fairly comprehensive ignorance of what genuine knowledge and the processes of scholarship are, and an unwillingness to admit that professional scholars understand these processes any better. The Church is a way of life for the unlearned and the learned. She teaches what she has learned, which is not the sum total of all possible knowledge. She cannot give the scholar sound methods and techniques of investigation, nor has she ever pretended to give them. To attempt to solve problems by an appeal of the teaching of the Church where her teaching is not relevant is as much a disservice to the Church as to ignore her teaching where it is relevant, for her teaching is distorted by both the one and the other. The faith of many has been shaken when the teaching of the Church was reduced to less than its full truth; the faith of just as many or more has been shaken when unenlightened teachers imposed upon them as beliefs of the Church things which are not true.

What I am describing is a threat to intellectual freedom arising from a kind of mob panic. Witch hunting is an ugly word, but it describes an ugly phenomenon which will not vanish if we pretend it does not exist. The hunters will hunt until there are no more witches, and then they will hunt each other. Outbreaks of this kind are prevented only by firm leadership, and scholars themselves must be willing to assume their part in leadership; they cannot sit in their ivory towers and weep because others do not defend them. I conceive the part of scholars in leadership to be precisely their scholarly work; by producing the best and finest fruits of learning they must convince the general public that scholarship is worth cherishing. They will preserve their intellectual freedom best by its responsible exercise.

This means first of all that they are meticulous in their scholarship; that they proceed by sound method and thorough investigation; that their exposition is well reasoned; that they propose conclusion as conclusion, opinion as opinion, fact as fact, and hypothesis as hypothesis. Where there are hostile observers ready to pounce on careless scholarship, the scholar must take care to give them no occasion; and this may mean that the scholar will postpone his publication until he can ground it more firmly and set it forth with more conviction.

It means also that the scholar must never forget that he is a member and a servant of the society which frees him from other responsibilities and supports him in the investigation and communication of knowledge. I have no desire to get bogged down in a discussion of useful research and useless research, which have become bad words among scholars; useful research has come to mean research which produces a better face cream or a better tire. But I remind my colleagues in scholarship that we have all learned the difference between research which we think will be a genuine advance and research which has no merit except that it gives us something to publish. What is a genuine advance, of course, must be judged by scholars and not by the general public, which is less likely to see the value of a critical edition of the fragments of the exegetical work of Theodore of Mopsuestia. Genuine research finds its way quickly enough into the structure of knowledge; scholars who never get beyond the fringe of a discipline ought to engage in self-examination.

The responsible exercise of intellectual freedom means that scholars are willing to talk to others besides their fellow scholars and to show the general public the value and meaning of scholarly work. This is a delicate area; all the learned disciplines with which I am acquainted are infested to some degree with headline hunters whose excesses often drive their colleagues into the opposite direction. We cannot forget that if the public sees no public service in the work of scholars, it may lose interest in supporting them; whatever may be true of other cultures, our contemporary society seems unwilling to support a college of mandarins. Hence scholars ought to regard the interpretation of their work to the general public as a legitimate and necessary part of their profession. If they are to do this, they must strive for more lucidity and persuasion in their style than one usually finds in learned journals; literary craftsmanship, like solid research, comes only through prolonged hard work. They must be aware that the general public is not prepared for what they have to communicate, and they must without patronizing dispose their readers or hearers to a sympathetic understanding. If scholars are too busy or too proud to communicate their research to the public, they leave this communication to the mountebanks, who are ready and willing to do it. Hence I cannot agree with those who believe that scholars should form a secret society and conceal their deliberations from the public, lest the public be shocked; an honest and careful presentation of scholarly work will not shock any except those who want to be shocked, and others will be pleased that scholars are doing what they are paid to do.

By such means the scholar may demonstrate that intellectual freedom does not belong to him alone nor is it given him for his own personal convenience and advancement; it is a social good which belongs to the entire society, whether we mean the political society or the culture or the Church. The society, recognizing the social importance of intellectual freedom, will protect it. Intellectual freedom involves risk, of course; freedom of any nature involves risk, to be a living human being involves risk. There is no more reason for diminishing the risk by suppressing intellectual freedom than there is for suppressing political freedom or, were it possible, moral freedom. Whatever man accomplishes he accomplishes because God has made him a responsible free agent; whatever man accomplishes as a scholar he accomplishes because he is a responsible free scholar. If he loses his intellectual freedom, his intellectual potentialities will be destroyed just as surely as his moral or political potentialities are destroyed by the loss of moral or political freedom. Faith can never be preserved at the cost of the mind.

PART II

INSPIRATION AND REVELATION

. 3 .

The Word of God
in the Old Testament

VINCENT TAYLOR has written: "By general consent 'the Logos,' or
'the Word,' is one of the greatest titles applied to Christ in the
New Testament. Many would say that it is the sublimest title of all.
The name is used only by St. John, in the Prologue to the Gospel
1:1–18 and in the opening words of the First Epistle, 1:1–4; but its
ideas color the teaching of St. Paul in Colossians 1:15–20 and of
the writer of Hebrews in Hebrews 1:1–3."[1] The purpose of this
article is to synthesize the Old Testament usage of the divine word
which is the background of the application of the term of Jesus; it
is hoped that theologians and others will find such a synthesis
useful. I believe that the background, while complex, is extraordinarily rich and fruitful.[2]

THE DIVINE WORD IN THE ANCIENT NEAR EAST

In tracing the pattern and growth of any Old Testament idea, it
is necessary to see whether the idea has roots in the older cultures
of the Near East; from such a comparison alone is it possible to
determine the degree to which the Hebrew idea is original. Oskar
Grether and L. Dürr have called our attention to Mesopotamian
uses of the phrase which are similar in conception and form to some
Old Testament passages.[3] This is illustrated in the texts below.[*]

---

[*] From a hymn to the moon-god Sin:
"Thou! When thy word is pronounced in heaven the Igigi prostrate themselves.
Thou! When thy word is pronounced on earth the Anunnaki kiss the ground.

37

The Mesopotamian texts show that the divine word is conceived as an entity laden with power; both gods and man are moved by it and find it irresistible. It is a principle of life and of fertility, a

---

Thou! When thy word drifts along in heaven like the wind it makes rich the feeding and drinking of the land.

Thou! When thy word settles down on the earth green vegetation is produced.

Thou! Thy word makes fat the sheepfold and the stall; it makes living creatures widespread.

Thou! Thy word causes truth and justice to be, so that the people speak the truth.

Thou! Thy word which is far away in heaven, which is hidden in the earth is something no one sees.

Thou! Who can comprehend thy word, who can equal it?"
— Translation by Ferris J. Stephens, in J. B. Pritchard, *Ancient Near Eastern Texts* (Princeton, 1955), p. 386

From the creation epic *Enuma Elish;* Marduk, invited to take up the combat of the gods against Tiamat, demands the right to decree the fates:

"If I indeed, as your avenger,
Am to vanquish Tiamat and save your lives,
Set up the Assembly, proclaim my destiny!
When in Ubshukinna jointly you sit down rejoicing,
Let my word, instead of you, determine the fates.
Unalterable shall be what I may bring into being;
Neither recalled nor changed shall be the command of my lips!"
— Translation by E. A. Speiser, in Pritchard, *op. cit.,* p. 65

The gods grant his request and he displays his power:

"Having placed in their midst a piece of cloth,
They addressed themselves to Marduk, their first-born:
Lord, truly thy decree is first among gods.
Say but to wreck or create; it shall be.
Open thy mouth! The cloth will vanish!
Speak again, and the cloth shall be whole!
At the word of his mouth the cloth vanished.
When the gods, his fathers, saw the fruit of his word (outcome of his mouth),
Joyfully they did homage: Marduk is king!"

— *Ibid.,* p. 66

From a hymn to the goddess Baba:

"My lady, thy word is true,
Thy lofty utterance is not brought down.
Thy holy word comes before the god,
It rises upon the king like the dawning day.
Baba, thy holy word comes before the god,
It rises upon the eager king like a day."
— This selection and those which follow are translated from the German rendition of the original in A. Falkenstein and W. von Soden, *Sumerische Hymnen* (Zurich, 1953), p. 72. The "eager king" is Ningirsu, spouse of Baba; "eager" is a more polite rendition of the word which expresses his desire for his consort.

creative utterance. Once spoken, it partakes of the eternity of the gods themselves. An even greater power is attributed to the divine word which determines the fates. Mesopotamian thought on the

---

From a hymn to the goddess Inanna:
"Before thy word, which, like a double strand, no one can break, the whole heaven trembles."

— *Sumerische Hymnen*, p. 75

From a hymn to the god Enlil:
"The utterance of thy mouth cannot be brought low —
Who can resist it?"

— *Ibid.*, p. 78

From a hymn to the moon-god Nanna:
"When thy word descends upon the sea, the sea surges,
When thy word descends upon the marsh, the marsh groans."

— *Ibid.*, p. 80

To these may be added lines from a hymn to the god An: "The utterance of An is firmly established; no god resists it"; from a hymn to the god Numushda: "The lofty word will never be overturned"; from a hymn to the god Enki: "The utterance of Enki cannot be overturned; it is established forever."

— *Ibid.*, pp. 103, 113, 135

The divine word appears also in Egypt in connection with the creative action of the gods in the theology of Memphis. The text of this document is preserved on the Shabaka stone of 700 B.C., but the original is to be placed in the First Dynasty, about 2700 B.C. Part of it reads as follows:

"There came into being as the heart and there came into being as the tongue (something) in the form of Atum. The mighty great one is Ptah, who transmitted life to all the gods, as well as (to) their *ka's*, through this heart, by which Horus became Ptah, and through this tongue, by which Thoth became Ptah.

"(Thus) it happened that the heart and tongue gained control over every (other) member of the body, by teaching that he is in every body and in every mouth of all gods, all men, all cattle, all creeping things, and (everything) that lives, by thinking and commanding everything that he wishes.

"His Ennead is before him (in the form of) teeth and lips. That is (the equivalent of) the semen and hands of Atum. Whereas the Ennead of Atum came into being by his semen and his fingers, the Ennead (of Ptah), however, is the teeth and lips in his mouth, which pronounced the name of everything, from which Shu and Tefnut came forth, and which was the fashioner of the Ennead.

"The sight of the eyes, the hearing of the ears, and the smelling of the air by the nose, they report to the heart. It is this which causes every completed (concept) to come forth, and it is the tongue which announces what the heart thinks."

— John A. Wilson, in Pritchard, *op. cit.*, p. 5

The following notes of John A. Wilson will help to the understanding of this passage:

"Ptah thought of and created by speech the creator-god Atum ("Totality"), thus transmitting the divine power of Ptah to all other gods. The gods Horus and Thoth, a commonly associated pair, are equated with the organs

relation of the will of the gods to the course of events was vague and undefined. A part of the ritual of the New Year's festival, which reenacted the annual renewal of creation, was the determination of the fates for the coming year. Nothing could happen unless the word of the gods decreed that it should happen; once this was decreed, nothing could alter the fates.

The power attributed to the divine word in Mesopotamia was similar to the power attributed to the human word in the formulae of magic. This power did not belong to every word, but to those formulae known by occult revelation. The magical word, the exact pronunciation of which was of vital importance, had the power to compel; it was more than a mere imperative, as the divine word was more than a mere imperative. By the very existence which it received in utterance it was able to reach the intended object and there overcome any opposition. The divine word and the magical word created what they symbolized.

A similar background appears in the Egyptian theology of Memphis. Once one penetrates beneath the obscure and tortuous cloak of Egyptian mythological language, one perceives that the purpose of this document is to extol the creative power of Ptah over the power of Atum, who created by grossly obscene masturbation. The "theologians" of Memphis attempted to rise to a higher plane, and they did so by recurring to the metaphysics of the name. The name gives reality; that which is nameless is unintelligible and therefore unreal. When the god utters a name, the reality which the name signifies springs into being. The conception, however, is more than a primitive nominalism. The name is formed by the heart (the organ of thought, not of feeling) on the data furnished it by the senses, and the organs of speech announce that which the heart has formed. When the conception is uttered by the creative deity, it receives reality.

---

of thought and speech. . . . A distinction is made between the act of creation by Atum through onanism and the creation by Ptah through commanding speech with teeth and lips. Pronouncing a name was creative. Shu and Tefnut were the first deities to be spoken. . . . The senses report to the heart. With this reported material, the heart conceives and releases thought, which the tongue, as a herald, puts into effective utterance."

— *Ibid.*

THE ISRAELITE CONCEPTION OF THE SPOKEN WORD

The attribution of speech to the deity is an analogy; and in order to comprehend the full meaning of the analogy, it is necessary to understand the analogical term. When the analogy comes from a culture and a language different from our own, it is easy for us to miss its full force and its true emphasis. When the Israelites spoke of the word of God, they intended to affirm that it differed from the word of man; but whatever definition we may give it depends on what they thought the word of man to be.

The Israelites, in common with most of the ancient world and with many peoples all over the world, attached a power to the word which has been lost in modern civilized thought.[4] It is tempting to see in this conception a survival of belief in magic, but the conception is not so easily explained; one should rather say that the belief in magic is a perversion of the power of the word. The belief in the power of the word seems to reflect a preliterary culture in which there were no written records to preserve the spoken word. Yet the word has a permanence, especially when it reaches from the present into the future, as it does in promises, threats, wishes, commands. Here the word posits the reality which it signifies and endures in the process which it initiates. Once uttered, it cannot be recalled. The word so conceived is evidently not the *verbum* of Scholastic metaphysics but the externalization of the reality conceived in the heart, the desire. If the will is strong enough, the reality which is posited by the word will infallibly come into being. This is apparent in the words of those whose power is known and recognized, such as kings; but who knows the power which any individual person may possess and communicate to the words which he utters? In this world of thought harsh words may hurt me far more than sticks and stones.[5]

The power of the word is most clearly seen in those human utterances in which law and custom demand that a man speak from the heart, such as covenants, in which a man promises to keep certain obligations. Such utterances are solemnized by witnesses, but the witnesses do not add to the reality of the word; they simply

attest that they saw this reality come into existence. In the Old
Testament the power of the word appears in particular in the blessing and the curse, which are solemn utterances spoken from the
depths of the heart. Here, as van der Leeuw has put it, the person
externalizes himself and looses the power which he possesses. The
power is seated in the word. When Isaac was deceived into blessing
Jacob instead of Esau (Gn 27), neither Isaac nor Esau thinks of the
modern *error circa personam* which invalidates a contract. The
blessing is a release of psychic energy which cannot be recaptured
and delivered to the proper destinatary. The one who blesses has
put something of himself into this solemn word. A similar instance
of the enduring reality of the word even when there is an *error circa
personam* occurs when Jacob is deceived by Laban and receives
Leah instead of Rachel as his wife (Gn 29:20–27). The compiler
of the Jacob stories has matched these stories. The man who secured
his blessing by misdirecting the solemnly spoken word is himself
deceived when another misdirects the solemnly spoken word of the
marriage covenant. When Isaac was deceived, he could do nothing
but give Esau another and inferior blessing, for it was thought that
a man had only one such blessing in him. When Jacob was deceived,
he could do nothing but serve another seven years for the wife he
desired; his spoken word of acceptance stood against him.

The mother of Micah of Ephraim cursed the thief who stole her
silver (Jgs 17:1–2). When Micah in fear of the curse restored the
stolen silver, his mother could not withdraw the curse; all she could
do was to send a blessing after it to neutralize it. When David heard
Nathan's parable of the poor man's ewe lamb, he declared that the
man who took it was worthy of death. The king had spoken a word
of power, and when Nathan said, "You are the man," the king had
pronounced his own death; and nothing but a prophetic assurance
that Yahweh would spare him could deliver him from the sentence.
But death had been pronounced, and it fell upon the child of David
and Bathsheba; the death-bearing word could not be recalled (2
Sm 12:1–18).

The woman accused of adultery (Nm 5:12–31) must take an oath
of execration, which is then to be written. The writing is then
washed off into water and the woman must drink the water. Unless

the virtue in her is strong enough to repel the curse, the curse will destroy her power to bear.

These examples illustrate the Israelite conception of the word as a dynamic reality. I think they also illustrate the fact that the dynamism is rooted in the dynamism of the personal will of the person who utters the word. They show also that the word possesses an enduring reality which may outlive the person who utters it.

Otto Procksch calls attention to the dynamic and the dianoetic elements in the Israelite concept of the word.[6] Here we notice that Hebrew uses "word" in contexts where in English we use "thing." The word is the reality, and it is the reality as intelligible. In this element the word is thought of as *name*. As we noticed above, the name is the intelligibility of the thing; if we do not know what to call it, we do not know what it is. But in addition, the thing does not become a reality until it gets a name, until it becomes intelligible. The Babylonian epic of creation *Enuma Elish* begins:

When on high the heaven had not been named,
Firm ground below had not been called by name . . .
When no gods whatever had been brought into being,
Uncalled by name, their destinies undetermined —[7]

When man gives a name, he posits the reality of the word. To know the name, and still more to confer the name, gives one power of a kind over the thing named.[8] The Old Testament contains instances of the change of the name of a conquered king by the conqueror; this indicated his power over the satellite, as a father's power over his child is exhibited in the conferring of the name: Eliakim to Jehoiakim (2 Kgs 23:35) and Mattaniah to Zedekiah (2 Kgs 24:17). Hence we may say that the conferring of a name is an exercise of the dynamism of the person communicating itself to the thing named and thus giving it reality. The knowledge of the name is an exercise of the dynamism of the person in the reverse direction, by which the person includes the thing (the "word") within the scope of his own person. Even in a more metaphysical view of understanding, one of the words to describe the process was *apprehendere*. But Thorleif Boman is no doubt largely correct in the contrast he draws between the Hebrew word *dābār* and the Greek *logos*. The root *dbr* is understood by most philologists to signify radically "to drive, to get behind and push." Thus the personality puts itself behind the word and drives it into the external world; but it comes with that which it drives. The Greek *legein*, on the other hand, means radically "to gather, to put in order." This mental process is expressed in the word; but the Hebrew word issues in the deed, the Greek word in understanding.[9] I would myself prefer to substitute *thing* for *deed* in this analysis.

One should not attempt to synthesize a voluntaristic or a pragmatic system of Hebrew thought upon these conceptions. Israelite thought stoutly resists synthesis at every point; the Israelites ignored the paradoxes and contradictions which a speculative synthesis must eliminate. We find certain basic patterns, somewhat loosely organized and not well correlated with each other; these are the background against which the conception of the divine word must be seen, as I trust the following exposition will make clearer.

THE PROPHETIC WORD OF YAHWEH

Oskar Grether collected the statistics on the use of the phrases "word of Yahweh," "words of Yahweh," and "word" in other contexts when it means the divine word.[10] He found that the phrase "word of Yahweh" in 225 of 241 occurrences, about 93 percent, designates the word of Yahweh received or declared by a prophet, and concludes rightly that it is a technical term for the prophetic experience. When the plural, "words of Yahweh," is used, over half of the occurrences designate the prophetic word. When the word is used outside of the genitive relationship with Yahweh, about 300 occurrences, over three fourths of these designate the prophetic word.

Jer 18:18 reads: "Instruction (*tôrāh*) shall not pass from the priest, nor counsel from the wise, nor word from the prophet." We have here three classes of men whose mission it was to speak with a certain authority. *Tôrāh* was traditional instruction, particularly in the cult, but also in moral and religious matters, and there is no doubt that Malachi, the last of the prophets, expresses the ancient

attitude of Israel toward the priest and his instruction (Mal 2:7):
"The lips of the priest shall guard knowledge, and they shall look
for *tôrāh* from his mouth; for he is the messenger of Yahweh of
hosts."[11] The sage gave counsel in virtue of his wisdom, which was
a gift of Yahweh; when he possessed wisdom in an excellent degree,
like Ahithophel, his counsel was as if one consulted an oracle of God
(2 Sm 16:23).[12]

These three had in common that they spoke with a certain
authority; they differed in the type of charism which gave them
authority. The priest was a vessel of tradition, a priestly tradition
which ultimately went back to the foundations of Israel; he was its
custodian and interpreter in his own generation. The sage spoke in
virtue of a gift which enabled him to form wise sayings; but the
sayings, like those of the priest, were his own. The word of the
prophet differed from *tôrāh* and wisdom and excelled them. The
most frequent phrase to describe the prophetic experience is "the
word of Yahweh came to X." This is somewhat nuanced from what
appears to be the synonymous expression, "Yahweh said to X."
When the word of Yahweh comes, the background of the word as
a dynamic entity with its own distinct reality comes into view. The
word is a *something* which the prophet receives. As a something it
is an expansion of a living personality, who in this case
is Yahweh Himself; and it has the power which only that uniquely
powerful personality can give it. Its first effect is upon the prophet
himself. When Yahweh puts His hand to the mouth of Jeremiah,
He puts His word in the mouth of the prophet (Jer 1:9). It is the
conscious possession of the word which distinguishes the true
prophet from the false, and revelation from human invention:

Thus says the Lord of hosts:
"Listen not to the words of the prophets
Who prophesy to you!
They fill you with vain hopes;
They speak a vision from their own minds,
Not from the mouth of the Lord,
Saying continually to those who despise the word of the Lord,
'All shall be well with you,'
While to every one who follows the stubborn promptings of his
    own mind they say,

'No harm shall come upon you.'
For which of them has stood in the council of the Lord,
To see and hear His word? . . .
I sent not the prophets, yet they ran;
I spoke not to them, yet they prophesied.
But if only they had stood in my council,
And had listened to my words,
They would have turned my people from their evil course,
And from their evil doings. . . .
I have heard what the prophets say,
Who prophesy lies in my name, saying,
'I have dreamed, I have dreamed, I have dreamed.'
Will the mind of the prophets ever turn,
Who prophesy lies, who prophesy the delusion of
   their own minds,
Thinking to make my people forget my name —
Through their dreams which they tell one another —
As their fathers forgot my name for the Baal?
The prophet who has a dream,
Let him tell his dream!
And he who has my word,
Let him speak my word in sincerity!
What has the straw to do with the wheat?"
It is the oracle of the Lord (Jer 23:16–18, 21–22, 25–28).[13]

The word is not the only prophetic experience, but it is the distinctive prophetic experience, the possession of which makes a man
a prophet. Both Grether and Procksch call our attention to instances
in which the vision is rendered intelligible by the word.[14] Micaiah
ben Imlah first describes his vision (1 Kgs 22:17) and then explains
with the preface, "Hear the word of Yahweh" (1 Kgs 22: 19–23).
Isaiah's temple vision is followed by the word of Yahweh (Is
6:1 ff.); Ezekiel's vision of the chariot is followed by the word
(Ez 1:1 – 2:8), as is Amos' vision of the plumb line (Am 7:7–9)
and the basket of fruit (Am 8:1–3), and Jeremiah's vision of the
boiling pot (Jer 1:13–19). Amos' vision of the basket of fruit and
Jeremiah's vision of the almond-tree twig (Jer 1:11–12) both exhibit a peculiar conception of the power of the word. The word
qayiṣ, "basket," suggests the word qēṣ, "end"; the word šāqēd,
"almond," suggests the word šôqēd, "watching." It would be a mistake to consider these mere plays on words. Here again the power-

laden word posits the reality which it signifies, and by doing so it makes the vision intelligible. Baskets and almonds are commonplace articles; no one else who sees them thinks of them as heavy with portent of disaster. But to the prophet the names of these articles are the word of Yahweh, which is not spoken idly nor without meaning. Why would Yahweh show the prophet a *qayiṣ* or a *šāqēd?* The word itself tells why. And the mind of the prophet, apprehending the *qayiṣ* or the *šāqēd,* transforms the reality, the thing (Hebrew "word"), into the reality, the word-thing, of *qēṣ* or *šôqēd.* The dianoetic becomes the dynamic.

The word of Yahweh received is a dynamic agent upon the prophet himself. It is put most simply in Amos 3:8:

The lion roars — who does not fear?
The Lord Yahweh speaks — who does not prophesy?

Jeremiah spoke of the assimilation of the word as a putting of the words in his mouth; Ezekiel, with a more detailed imagery, ate the scroll on which the words were written. Although it was a scroll full of threats and curses, he found it sweet to his taste (Ez 2:9 – 3:3). We do not suppose that Ezekiel literally performed this symbolic action; he meant to convey his conviction that the word of Yahweh passed into the prophet, and furthermore that he entirely accepted the word. It was disaster for his nation, but the word of Yahweh was sweet whatever it conveyed. Jeremiah too found the word of Yahweh his joy and delight (Jer 15:16). But he did not always find it a joy. To proclaim the threatening word of Yahweh to an incredulous people made him a laughingstock, a reproach, and a derision. For this reason he tried to withhold it and to keep silence. But he found it impossible to contain; the word of Yahweh was like a burning fire shut up in his bones (Jer 20:7-9). The word which the prophet received was an irrepressible power imposed upon him by a stronger personality; and the strength of that other personality bore down any attempt to suppress the word. Micah described the prophetic experience in similar terms (Mi 3:8):

But I am full of power, the spirit of Yahweh, justice, and strength,
To announce to Jacob his iniquity, and to Israel his sin.

To Jeremiah the word of Yahweh is "fury," which he is weary of attempting to contain; therefore he is to pour it out on all his people (Jer 6:11). With such passages before us, it is not enough to represent the biblical conception of the prophetic experience of the word as a simple hearing. It is the experience of a distinct and compelling reality. The word of Yahweh, like the word of man, is a release of the power of the personality which utters it. He who receives the word is invaded by the personality of the speaker; when the speaker is Yahweh, the transforming influence of the word exceeds the influence of any human speech.

It is a commonplace among interpreters that the spirit of Yahweh plays little or no part as an inspiring agent in the classical prophets of the eighth and seventh centuries; it does not become prominent until the Exile. Yet the difference between word and spirit is not as great as might appear. For the spirit is the breath of Yahweh, and the word is produced with the breath; he who hears the word of Yahweh, also feels His spirit.[15] It is emphasis on word rather than spirit which gives classical prophecy its distinctive character. The spirit is an inspiring agent to action rather than to speech, especially in Judges and Samuel. It falls upon Othniel (Jgs 3:10), Gideon (Jgs 6:34), Jephthah (Jgs 11:29), and Samson (Jgs 14:6, 19; 15:14) and moves them to extraordinary feats of strength or heroism. It falls upon Saul and moves him to ecstatic prophecy (1 Sm 10:10) and to the campaign in defense of Jabesh-gilead (1 Sm 11:16). It falls upon David when he is anointed king (1 Sm 16:13). The spirit also is a creative force (Gn 1:2) and a principle of life (Gn 2.7; Ps 104:30). But the spirit, like the wind with which it is identified, is violent and unpredictable and mysterious. The word, on the contrary, is the principle of intelligibility; it defines what it signifies and identifies the speaker. Unless the word comes with the spirit, there is no revelation and response, no personal encounter.

The Dynamism of the Prophetic Word

This is the effect of the word upon the prophet; but the effect of the word of Yahweh declared by the prophet is even more profound and exhibits the true dynamism of the word in its distinct reality. Frequently the word of Yahweh is said "to be fulfilled" (as in 1 Kgs 2:27, the word which predicted the downfall of the priestly house of Eli) or "to be established" (as in Jer 29:10, the promise of restoration from exile). In these phrases is described the coming into existence of the thing signified by the word, the "fullness" of the reality of word-thing. When man speaks, his word may not be established (Is 8:10); when this happens his word is not true.

The word of Yahweh may be called sacramental in the sense that it effects what it signifies. When Yahweh posits the word-thing, nothing can prevent its emergence; and it is through the word which identifies the object that He brings it into being. Events occur according to the prophetic word of Yahweh, such as the annihilation of the house of Jeroboam proclaimed by Ahijah (1 Kgs 15:29) and of the house of Baasha proclaimed by Jehu (1 Kgs 16:12), and the foundation of Jericho by Hiel in the lives of his firstborn and his youngest proclaimed by Joshua (1 Kgs 16:34). So Ahaziah died according to the word of Elijah (2 Kgs 1:17); the famine of the siege of Samaria was ended according to the word of Yahweh (2 Kgs 7:16); and the deaths of Ahab and Jezebel (2 Kgs 9:26, 36) and Jehu's extermination of the house of Ahab occur according to the word of Yahweh proclaimed by Elijah (2 Kgs 10:17). That we meet in such passages more than the idea of prediction-fulfillment is shown by other passages which more explicitly affirm the power inherent in the word as agent. When Yahweh puts His word in the mouth of Jeremiah, the prophet receives power over peoples and kingdoms to uproot and to tear down, to destroy and to ruin, to build and to plant (Jer 1:9–10). The power of the prophet lies simply in his charism to utter the prophetic word; through his utterance he effects the destruction and the building which he proclaims. The word of Yahweh is like fire, like a hammer that shatters rocks (Jer 23:29). Yahweh hews with the prophets and kills with the words of his mouth (Hos 6:5). Probably the same belief is reflected obscurely in a more popular form when the elders of Bethlehem come trembling to meet Samuel and ask whether his coming is "peace" (1 Sm 16:4); for a prophet's utterance is power-laden and fearful. It appears also in the popular anecdote of Elisha and the irreverent small boys, who were immediately

devoured by bears when the prophet cursed them in the name of
Yahweh (2 Kgs 2:24). The curse of anyone was fearful, but the
curse of the prophet was sure to effect what it signified.

The word which goes out of the mouth of Yahweh is righteousness and it does not return (Is 45:23). For a word to "return"
would be to lose its reality, to fail of its destiny to become a word-
thing. This is more explicit in Isaiah 55:10–11.

> For as the rain comes down, and the snow from heaven,
> And does not return thither until it has watered the earth,
> And makes it give birth and sprout, and gives seed to the sower
>   and bread to the eater,
> So it shall be, the word which proceeds from my mouth, it shall
>   not return to me empty,
> Unless it accomplishes what I will, and does that for which I
>   sent it.

The rain and the snow do not "return"; neither does the word
uttered by Yahweh. It is as infallible in its mission as the forces
of nature. Like the forces of nature, it is endowed with a distinct
active reality. As it does not return to Yahweh, so Yahweh does
not take it back (Is 31:2). In a sense, the word of Yahweh partakes
of the eternity of Yahweh Himself (Is 40:6–8):

> All flesh is grass, and its beauty like the blossom of the field;
> The grass withers, the flower fades when the wind of Yahweh
>   blows upon it; so the people is grass;
> The grass withers, the flower fades; but the word of Yahweh
>   stands forever.

This does not mean, obviously, that the word-thing posited by the
reality of Yahweh is as eternal as Yahweh; the word is here considered as an externalization of the personality of Yahweh, as an
expression of His will. It endures, therefore, as long as the will
which it expresses. There is no agent which can destroy it, corrupt
it, or frustrate it.

We may notice the dynamic reality of the word in Isaiah 9:8:
"The Lord has sent a word on Jacob, and it will fall upon Israel."
What gives this verse its peculiar force is the succeeding context,
which describes a series of coming disasters. Procksch has aptly
spoken of the "explosive force" of the word in this passage, and

the line does seem in a strange way to anticipate the modern delayed-action bomb, which falls quietly to lie upon the ground until it is fused.[16] The word of Yahweh does not always realize itself instantly, and this makes it more terrifying; once uttered, it falls upon its object, and no one knows when it will fulfill itself. But it will infallibly fulfill itself, and the full reality will be that designated by the word.[17]

Grether and Procksch have drawn our attention to the word of Yahweh as the nerve or the hinge of biblical history.[18] When we recall the fact that the history of the Old Testament is compiled from more sources than we can count, composed orally or in writing over a period of several centuries, it is indeed remarkable that the compilers, without planning it so, forged a chain of history whose links are the word of Yahweh. The first event recorded in the Old Testament as we have it is the utterance of God which initiates the creative process (Gn 1:3). In the subsequent history the word of Yahweh occurs frequently; we notice that it comes at Israel's crises of history, declaring that which it brings to pass. Yahweh Himself announces that He will destroy man by a deluge (Gn 6:7). The history of salvation is initiated by Yahweh's call to Abraham to go out from his country to a land which Yahweh will show him (Gn 12:1). The first step in the deliverance of Israel from Egypt and their formation into the people of the covenant is the word of Yahweh to Moses (Ex 3). In the review of the history of the Exodus and the wandering which is found in the historical prologue to Deuteronomy (1–3), the word of Yahweh moves the Israelites at each step from Horeb to Canaan (Dt 1:6; 2:2; 2:18; 2:31; 3:1; 3:27–28). The word of Yahweh occurs even more frequently in the book of Joshua. The call of Samuel ends the period of the Judges and opens the period of transition to the monarchy (1 Sm 3). The word of Yahweh authenticates the desire of the Israelites for a king (1 Sm 8:7) and designates Saul as the king (1 Sm 9:17; 10:17–24). It is the word of Yahweh which rejects Saul (1 Sm 15:10) and selects David as his successor (1 Sm 16:12). At the high point of David's reign the word of Yahweh given to Nathan establishes the eternity of the dynasty of David (2 Sm 7). But it is the word of Yahweh to the same Nathan which sets in motion the disasters which follow David's sins of adultery and murder (2 Sm 12). It is the word of Yahweh declared by Shemaiah to Jeroboam which divides the kingdom of Israel in two (1 Kgs 11:31 ff.). The word of Elijah declares and consummates the fall of the house of Ahab (1 Kgs 19:1–9; 21:17–24), and a prophetic messenger declares the word of Yahweh which makes Jehu the king who executes the word of the prophet (2 Kgs 9:6–10). In the great crisis of the invasion of Judah by Sennacherib, the word of Yahweh to Isaiah declares and accomplishes the deliverance of Jerusalem (2 Kgs 19:20–24).

While certain questions are and ought to be raised about the historical character of some of these episodes and about the sincerity of some of these prophets, these questions have no relevance to our present study, which is the biblical belief in the word of Yahweh. There can be no doubt that the character of the compilation itself as outlined in these passages shows the Israelite conception of history as a process governed by Yahweh and moved to a term intended by Him. History also is "the word of Yahweh," a reality which fulfills the utterance of Yahweh. The word of history is dynamic and dianoetic: dynamic in that it accomplishes what it signifies, dianoetic in that it makes the historical process intelligible. History is then revelation of the purpose of Yahweh, but it is more; as the word is a release of the psychic energy of the personality, so history is a revelation of the character and personality of Him whose word it is. The word affirms not only the thing signified but also the person who utters it.

We may conclude our survey of the dynamic and dianoetic word of the prophet by noticing that there is nothing in ancient Near Eastern religion and literature which suggests this Israelite conception of the word. One may adduce the "determination of the fates" mentioned above; but there is no true parallel. The determination of the fates is a vague and undefined conception compared to the Israelite divine word in history and prophecy. The difference, it seems, lies in the Israelite conception of the word as an extension of the personality; the divine word in Mesopotamia was also a power-laden entity, but we observed that it lapses into magic.

Israelite belief transformed an idea which was common and made of it what it is not in Mesopotamia or Egypt: the self-revelation of Yahweh the speaker. The word is communication, a personal encounter between the speaker and the listener, and it demands a response.

THE CREATIVE WORD OF YAHWEH

When we turn to the word of Yahweh as a creative agent, we reach a point of contact with the literature of Mesopotamia and Egypt quoted above; for it is in this capacity that the divine word appears most frequently.[19] The creative word of Yahweh, according to modern critical dating of the books of the Old Testament, is a comparatively late phenomenon in Israelite literature, appearing first, in all probability, in Second Isaiah about 550 B.C. As we have seen, "to call the hosts of heaven by name" (Is 40:26) is to bring them into being; so also to call the heavens so that they stand up (Is 48:13). But, as Grether points out, Second Isaiah combines two concepts of creation: by word and by work.[20] The hand of the workman appears in 40:12, 22; 48:13. This is without doubt the older Israelite conception and is found in Genesis 2.

The same combination appears in Genesis 1, which is most probably to be dated after Second Isaiah; here Elohim is said to "make" various parts of creation. But the "making" has been sharply reduced in concreteness from the making described, for example, in Genesis 2:7, and is in the final form of the text scarcely more than a restatement of the accomplishment of the creative word. If Genesis 1 is to some extent consciously a response to the Mesopotamian creation myth, as it probably is, it is interesting to note that the creation of Marduk (which is only imperfectly preserved) is creation by work and not by word.[21] The emphasis in Genesis 1 evidently falls on the creative word, and it must have been the deliberate purpose of the writer to propose a more subtle and less anthropomorphic idea of creation by substituting the word. Therefore it is vital to his scheme that Yahweh pronounces the name of the things He creates, thus giving them reality and intel-

ligibility. The creation by word is still more explicit in Psalm
33:6, 9:

> By the word of Yahweh the heavens were made,
> And by the breath of His mouth all their hosts. . . .
> He spoke, and it came to be;
> He commanded, and it arose.

And in Psalm 147:15–18:

> He counts the number of the stars,
> To all of them He gives names. . . .
> He sends His utterance to the earth,
> His word runs very swiftly.
> He gives snow like wool,
> He scatters frost like ashes.
> He casts His ice like crumbs,
> Who can withstand His cold?
> He sends His word and melts them,
> When He blows with His wind the waters flow.

Here the word appears again as an agent with a distinct reality;
it accomplishes the will of Yahweh in nature as it does in history.
It may be said that in this conception of the word nature, like
history, is the word of Yahweh; like history, it is a revelation of
Himself. Another Psalm tells how the word-thing which Yahweh
utters in His creative act is heard (Ps 19:2–5):

> The heavens tell the glory of El,
> And the sky declares the work of His hands.
> Day pours forth speech to day,
> And night declares knowledge to night.
> There is no utterance and no words,
> Their voice is not heard,
> But their voice goes forth in all the earth,
> And their words to the end of the world.

Heaven and sky, day and night, and all the course of nature do
not themselves speak, but they are nevertheless heard because they
are a word, the word-thing emitted by their creator. What they
speak is the personality of Him who utters the word. Man experiences Yahweh in what Yahweh has created.

The Law as Word

Modern critics attach great importance to the "Deuteronomic" movement in Israelite religion and literature. The opinions of scholars on this movement are too varied and numerous to admit of simple classification, and a full examination of these opinions would be out of place here.[22] For our present purpose it is sufficient to notice that the Deuteronomic movement produced the book of Deuteronomy and the Deuteronomic edition of Israelite history — a work which some scholars would call an independent Deuteronomic history extending from the conquest of Canaan to the end of the kingdom of Judah in 587 B.C. The earliest phases of this movement cannot be dated before the seventh century B.C. Hence, with reference to our topic, the Deuteronomic movement presupposes the idea of the prophetic word which we have sketched.

The Deuteronomic movement seeks to catch the fleeting charism of the prophetic word and to fix it in a formula. This formula is law understood in a broad sense as a code of life; and the Deuteronomic revision of Israelite law differs from earlier legal codes in its effort to make this revealed word such a code of life. Israelite law codes contain several words for law, each of which identifies a particular type of law; it is not always easy to determine the type designated, but the words are not mere poetic synonyms introduced for variety of language. These words are *dābār*, "word"; *mišpāṭ*, "judgment"; *miṣwāh*, "commandment"; *ḥuqqāh*, "statute" (following the customary English translations). Albrecht Alt proposed a distinction between casuistic law, which states a judicial precedent and is couched in a conditional form, and apodictic law, which is a direct imperative; this distinction is accepted by all scholars, although the origin of these two formulae is no doubt more complex than Alt thought.[23] The use of "word" to designate an apodictic law is older than the Deuteronomic movement, and indeed older than the use of "word" to indicate the charism of the prophet. Such a law was understood as a direct command of Yahweh. Thus Moses is said to write on tablets the words of the covenant, the ten words (Ex 34:28). The ten words are called the covenant (Dt 4:13); these are the ten words which Yahweh spoke on the mountain in the midst of fire (Dt 10:4). The Decalogue was the "word" of Yahweh in the most basic and fundamental manner. One does not see in this conception of word either the dynamism or the hypostatization of the word which appears in the prophets, but it is the rudimentary phase of the same development.

Deuteronomy extends this conception of word to the entire law given in the book. No one is to add to or subtract from this word (Dt 4:2). Indeed, this word is set against the word of the prophet, which is not to be accepted as true unless it harmonizes with the word of the law (Dt 13:1-5). Yahweh has brought this word near to Israel and put it in the mouth and heart of Israel that they may keep it (Dt 30:14). For this word is the life of Israel (Dt 32:47); man does not live by bread alone, but by every word that proceeds from the mouth of Yahweh (Dt 8:3).[24] It seems most probable here that the Deuteronomic compilers have been affected by the prophetic conception of the word, which they now apply to their compilation of law. In some respects this may be called a weakening of the concept. The written word has not the vitality and the urgency of the spoken word, nor is it so readily perceived as an externalization of the person. The sense of communication is less vivid. It is a step removed from the experience of hearing. The Deuteronomic compilers were not unaware of this, and they conceived Israel as a living reality in which through their compilation each generation experienced anew the revelation of Horeb. So the word is "near" (Dt 30:14); the covenant is made with the present generation, and the compilers insist that the Israelites hear the word "today" (Dt 4:40; 5:3; 11:26-28). The sense of immediacy would be preserved by the tradition of the saving deeds of Yahweh, kept real by their recounting in each generation (Dt 6:20-25; 8:1 ff.; 11:2-8).

Here we are only a step from the last development of the concept of word: the sacred books, and in particular the tôrāh, the Law, as the word of God. It is in this sense that the "word" is mentioned in Psalm 119, the praise of the Law; it has become synonymous with command, statute, ordinance, precept, law, way, decree. Psalm 119 groups these words in each of its strophes and finds a new formula of praise for each. The Law has assimilated into itself the word of the prophet, the *tôrāh* of the priest, and the wisdom of the sage; each of these earlier charisms has lost its identity in the Law.

I remarked above that this development was to some extent a weakening of the older concept of word. It should be added that the conception of the written word of God is a revolutionary religious development of incalculable influence. The concept has been weakened, but some of the dynamism and dianoeticism of the prophetic word has passed to the collection of the sacred books. They become the self-revelation of the personality of Yahweh, and in them, as nowhere else, one can experience the mysterious being whom the prophets knew. They acquire the creative and vivifying power which was attributed to the spoken word.

SUMMARY AND CONCLUSION

At the risk of oversimplifying and overschematizing, I think we can say that the developments and refinements of the Israelite idea of word show a certain consistency of pattern. The basis of this consistency lies in the conception of the spoken word as a distinct reality charged with power. It has power because it emerges from a source of power which, in releasing it, must in a way release itself. The basic concept of the word is the word-thing. The power of the word, as we have said so often, posits the reality which it signifies. But in so doing it also posits the reality which speaks the word. No one can speak without revealing himself; and the reality which he posits is identified with himself. Thus the word is dianoetic as well as dynamic. It confers intelligibility upon the thing, and it discloses the character of the person who utters the word.

Most Old Testament scholars, I think, wonder why anyone has ever thought it necessary to appeal to any source beyond the Old Testament to explain John's application of *logos* to Jesus Christ. The scope of this paper does not include the New Testament use of the term; but we may briefly suggest the connection.[25] A survey of Old Testament use such as I present here indicates that Old Testament thought is a sufficient explanation for the appearance of the term. If we place the New Testament *logos* against this background, which I have called rich and complex, I think we shall see how *logos* is one of the great New Testament "fulfillments." And I think we shall see better the meaning of Jesus Christ to the author of the fourth Gospel and the Church for which he spoke. It was scarcely by mere coincidence or by the casual influence of Stoicism or Philo Judaeus that John has begun his prologue with the Word, thus concluding what Edmond Jacob calls "a unique history which begins with the word of God pronounced in creation and ends with the word made flesh."[26] In Jesus Christ is fulfilled the word as a distinct being; as a dynamic creative entity; as that which gives form and intelligibility to the reality which it signifies; as the self-revelation of God; as a point of personal encounter between God and man.

.4.

The Social Character of Inspiration

R. A. F. MacKenzie said a few years ago that really little progress had been made in the theory of inspiration in the past forty years.[1] After Lagrange's theory of instrumental causality was proposed over sixty years ago, theologians and exegetes settled tranquilly into two camps: one ranged about the *verba et sententiae* (words and ideas) of Franzelin, the other about the instrumentality and verbal inspiration of Lagrange, and practically nothing was added to the discussion. The authors of manuals of theology and of general introduction to the Bible were content with the conventional statements of their thesis and the conventional responses to objections which represented the other thesis. It may be revealing to recall that theologians generally adopted Franzelin's view, and exegetes generally adopted Lagrange's view; but many theologians and exegetes were ill at ease with the theory which they adopted. It is unfair to criticize earlier scholars for producing no creative work on the problem; if the present generation of scholars is correct in the approach it is taking to the problem of inspiration, then scholars of the preceding generation lacked the materials for creative work. We may be wrong in our confidence, but it appears that biblical criticism has now reached a point of maturity where the concept of inspiration can be presented with greater intelligibility.

I attribute this progress to biblical criticism.[2] One of the features of the older view which caused discomfort in exegetes was that it contained no picture of the composition of the inspired book. To say that God is the author of His inspired word, and that the human writer is moved by Him as the instrumental by the principal cause, says a great deal; but it left a vacuum in the only aspect of inspiration which is open to historical and critical investigation, and that is the literary activity of the inspired writers. As criticism made more extensive and more secure progress, it became apparent that the theory of inspiration, even when proposed by such a master of criticism in his day as Lagrange, labored under a defect which could be serious; it was too bookish. The terms which were used in theological writing to describe inspiration were all used with the presupposition that the inspired writer was a responsible and distinct individual like a modern author, who could be identified with his book. Criticism has made it generally impossible to find such responsible individuals who can be identified. Most books of the Bible can be associated with no single name; they cannot be associated even with a single anonymous individual. A theory of inspiration which fits very neatly into the composition of the Pentateuch by Moses — or, to show that the theory is not entirely without roots in reality, into the composition of the epistles of Paul — arouses questions when it is applied to the compilation of the Pentateuch from scattered sources or to the "school" of St. Matthew.

Even more serious is a question which arises from the idea of "book." The received theory, when it spoke of books, meant the books of the canon; and these in turn were distinct books which could be identified by name. Genesis, Samuel, Job, Matthew, Mark were books as *David Copperfield* and *The Origin of Species* are books, even if criticism compels us to attribute them to several anonymous authors rather than to a single individual. After all, the *Encyclopaedia Britannica* is not a book as *David Copperfield* is; it is the work of several authors, and it can be conceived to differ from the biblical books only in the fact that the editors have been careful to identify the several authors and their contributions. Were the *Britannica* to lose its subtitles and names of authors, the critical problem, it seems would not differ from the critical problem of the Bible. The critic would have to recover something which was there and had been lost. Modern criticism, however, tends more and more to show that a search for authors conducted on this assumption is a search for something which was never there and consequently cannot be found; it can only be created by the critic.

The books which appear in our Bible are mostly, as the critics call them, compilations; but even compilation is an inexact term for the complex process of growth and development of which these books are the product. A number of modern scholars speak of "rereading," the reinterpretation of earlier material by later writers. Others speak of the biblical books as the "lived" experience of Israel and similar terms. Where is one to draw the line which defines a book in any sense? The sources of the Pentateuch have been so broken up by the compilers that a complete reconstruction of any single source is impossible. Martin Noth thinks that the Pentateuch itself was created by breaking off two earlier histories. The court history of David was broken by someone between two books, Samuel and Kings. Such editorial work as this is more than a slicing of material into pieces of different size; often enough it involves a new conception. What would be our interpretation of the history of the monarchy if we had Chronicles but not Kings? The obscurity we find in searching for an inspired author is matched by our uncertainty in searching for an inspired book; unless we can answer such simple questions as who did what under the inspiring influence, there is much we do not know about inspiration.

Lest anyone suspect that I am oversimplifying, I wish to recall yet another complicating factor: oral tradition. If one accepted the view of many of the Scandinavian school that the books of the Old Testament were preserved only in oral tradition until the fourth century, the problem of inspiration in the usual sense would be solved; here we would have authors, and here we would have books. But the importance of oral tradition must be conceded under some restraints; if one accepts critical hypotheses to any degree — and most of us do — we can scarcely think that any substantial portion of the Old Testament was written even in its preliminary form before the monarchy. We postulate the survival of the traditions of the patriarchs, the exodus, the settlement, and premonarchic Israel by word of mouth. We postulate further that most of these traditions acquired not one but several variant oral forms; that they were grouped in cycles about personal and local names.

Similar postulates are made for the material from which the Gospels are written, except that a shorter time intervenes between the creation of the tradition and its writing. One must also postulate oral tradition for many of the songs and laws of the Old Testament, for many later pieces of narrative such as the prophetic cycles of Elijah and Elisha, and to an undetermined extent for the oracles of the literary prophets.

Here, it seems, the bookish character of the received theories of inspiration becomes most obvious and most distressing. In the beginning, as linguists love to say, was the word. Man spoke before he wrote. Writing in the ancient world, as Albright has said,[3] was merely a record of speech, an aid to the memory. It was the speaker who composed. I dare say it seems picayunish to urge that inspiration to *write* is not entirely relevant to oral composition; the intellectual processes involved are not that far apart in the two modes of composition. But there is a substantial difference between the transmission of oral tradition and the transmission of writings which, it seems, is relevant. We know, or we think we know, that in the ancient world the manuscript was treated with great freedom; it was subject to the revision and expansion of each successive owner, and it is this constant process which has created our critical problems. In oral tradition the material is flexible to the extreme, and it can be said without exaggeration that each successive bard or balladist was the creator of the story anew. The material was "composed" each time it was told.

Who, then, is the inspired author, and what does the inspired author produce? We find it difficult to believe that the final redactors of the Pentateuch, for instance, were the inspired authors who compiled quite uninspired material, and no one thinks that the final and terminal editor is the only inspired author, whoever he may have been. Therefore we feel the need of distributing the charisma, so to speak, among the various men who contributed to the book — meaning the book we have. To me, at least, this has always seemed somewhat mechanical and contrived. Let us suppose that the Yahwist is the first great literary creator of ancient Israel, and let us suppose that he has transformed a mass of independent scattered traditions into a *Heilsgeschichte;* this much critics give him, and it is enough to establish him as an author. Therefore, just because he is an author, we confer upon him the charisma of inspiration. But we cannot define either his preexisting materials or their balladist authors as clearly, and because we have neither book nor author, we feel we need not distribute the charisma among them. Yet their creative part in Israelite traditions, while less than the part of the Yahwist, is considerably more than nothing. Similarly, critics think they detect oral and literary sources of our Gospels; we may or may not call them Q, but they existed. If Q or the Logia or sources by any name contributed as much to the Gospels as we think they did, were they not also creative sources? I emphasize perhaps too much the term *creative*, but here the experience of composition affects one's thinking about inspiration. One is never more an author than when one engages in creative original composition, which a certain Red Smith (neither a theologian nor an exegete, but a wise man) described as written in little drops of blood. Anyone who has contributed any of this to the Bible, it seems, deserves the charisma of inspiration more than editors, glossators, and redactors. The Yahwist and the authors of the Gospels were the heirs of a faith and a tradition, not its creators.

Yet, as I have remarked above, a simple mechanical distribution of the charisma of inspiration as far as it seems necessary leaves me with the feeling that this explanation is contrived to meet a difficulty. When we do this, we are merely multiplying and fragmentating authors and books in the classical and modern conception of the word; we are not presenting a theory of inspiration which really fits the production of the literature in question. These authors remain anonymous, and the "books" we attribute to them remain vague and undefined. We must ask ourselves, if the identity of the authors and their productions is unknown and apparently unimportant, whether we must not redefine this instrumental cause, this author; whether we should not seek another principle of unity in the literature which will make the charisma more intelligible; for we cannot have intelligibility without unity.

Here we take up a lead which has been given us by Benoit and Rahner; it is a pleasure to acknowledge my indebtedness to these distinguished scholars for what is in my opinion the most constructive addition to the theory of inspiration in the past fifty to sixty years. Both these men have directed our attention to the social character of inspiration. Rahner has proposed that the charisma of inspiration in the New Testament is best understood as a charisma possessed by the Church herself and not by individual writers. Like the apostolic office, the charisma of inspiration is given the Church only in her infancy, and yields to other charismata and functions in the more fully organized and established Church. Those who write the inspired books of the New Testament write them as officers and representatives of the Church, which is the real author of the New Testament.[4]

Such a theory does not immediately appear as applicable to the Old Testament, the book of Israel, the people of Yahweh. Israel cannot be called a church except in the widest and most improper sense of the word. But it is a society. Benoit has recently expanded his own treatment of the social character of inspiration. He has pointed out that inspiration is but one of the charismata by which the hierarchically structured religious community is guided. None of these charismata are properly understood if they are considered as communicated to the individual; they are primarily communicated to the Church within which they are exercised, and for which they are given.[5]

We have noticed above that most of the literature of the ancient Near East, and not only the Bible, is anonymous. Does this peculiar fact, so alien to our own conceptions of literature, signify merely the modesty or the indifference of the composers of ancient literature? Can we not specify more precisely the difference between ancient and modern concepts of book and author? I suggest that the ancient author was anonymous because he did not think of himself as an individual speaker, as the modern author does. He was anonymous because in writing he fulfilled a social function; through him the society of which he was a member wrote its thoughts. He was its spokesman, and the society was the real author of the literature. What he wrote were the traditions of his people, or the record of the deeds of his people, or the beliefs and cult of his people. And so likewise the oral reciter was the spokesman of the group he addressed; he fostered their solidarity as a group in peace and in war by reciting the deeds and singing the songs of their common heritage. The men who wrote the recitals of the deeds of the kings of Assyria and of Egypt are as anonymous as the artists who illustrated these deeds in sculpture. How could they be anything else? The king was the speaker of the recital of these victories, as he was the agent of the victories; and the king was the people, the visible incorporation of the society.

To us such a conception seems to be merely a figure of speech which is more accurately expressed in nonmetaphorical, or less metaphorical, language. Permit me to recall how difficult we find it to express in our own terms any of the basic social concepts of the ancient Near East. Much of ancient history, law, and religion involves relations of the individual with the group which we know we fail to grasp adequately and can translate only into metaphor. Realization of the difference between ancient and modern ideas in this area has been one of the most illuminating contributions of modern scholarship. The concept of the corporate personality, for example, is an important and operative idea in our conception of messianism and of the Church. In attributing the literature of the Bible to Israel and to the Church, we recur to an idea which seems merely metaphorical to us because we no longer have it in our society.

Pursuing this idea a little further, we can ask what the identifying and unifying trait of biblical literature is; and modern scholarship has suggested the answer to this question also. It has been called a recital of the saving deeds of God, a profession of the faith of Israel and of the primitive Church. The modern author is an artist who feels a compulsion to express his individuality through his art; the ancient writer, if we can judge from what he wrote, was more interested in concealing his individuality. He wished to be the voice of Israel and of the Church, to produce in writing utterances which were not the expressions of his own mind but of his society. The Bible is the story of the encounter of God and man, but not of God and the individual man; it is the encounter of God and Israel which issues in the incarnation of Jesus, the new Israel, and His continued life in the new Israel, the Church. The recital and the profession are the work of no individual writer; the writer writes what his society has communicated to him. We should not personify the collection; neither on the other hand should we so disintegrate it into individual atoms that the society ceases to be a reality. The actions of a society and its words are not the actions and words of an individual, nor are they merely the collections of individual words and acts; the speech and the actions of a society have power and meaning which are more than the collection of individuals can exhibit. Israel expressed her faith and recited her traditions through her priests, prophets, kings, poets, sages, and even through her bards and balladists who created and transmitted oral traditions. In the society of Israel these had the mission to speak for Israel.

Assuming that the above considerations have some value — perhaps a rash assumption — one wonders whether they may not lead to a more precise identification of the charisma of inspiration. It is comforting, when one attacks this question, to realize that the danger of reifying the metaphor is no greater now than it has always been. The technical language of theology is full of metaphorical terms. If we consider how Israel described its experience of God, I believe that the two most common terms are the word of God issuing in the knowledge of God, *da'at Yahweh*. Israel knew Yahweh because Yahweh had spoken to Israel. And because Israel had heard the word of Yahweh, Israel could through her charismatic spokesmen enunciate the word of Yahweh. Whether the word was spoken or written is a matter of minor importance in a culture where the spoken word is primary, as it was in Israel and in the primitive Church. Here Benoit's observation is very much to the point; we misunderstand inspiration, or at least we make it more difficult to understand, if we isolate it from the other works of the spirit in the people of God.[6] When Paul enumerated the charismatic officers of the Church as apostles, prophets, teachers, thaumaturges, healers, helpers, administrators, and speakers of foreign tongues, by an almost inexcusable oversight he omitted inspired scribes (1 Cor 12:28); or perhaps they are already mentioned.

No doubt this statement of inspiration suggests some horrid consequences. One may suspect that I am returning to the antiquated and untenable view of verbal dictation. I have no intention of doing this, and I hope my understanding of the word of Yahweh is more sophisticated than the ancient and venerable understanding of revelation as a voice from the cloud. There was nothing wrong with this except that it presumed the word of God must be like the word of man. The word of God, the speech of God, signifies a direct mystical insight and awareness of the divine reality; I conceive it neither as an inner utterance nor as infused species but precisely as an experience of the divine reality. When the prophet utters the word of God, he articulates this experience, he responds to it. Such an experience, I conceive, whatever else one may call it, as an effective movement to speak the word of God, or to write it. But I would insist once more that the spokesman of God speaks for his society; when he speaks, he speaks not only in virtue of his own personal experience and knowledge of God, but in virtue of the faith and traditions in which his experience occurs and without which his experience would not have meaning.

Further questions can arise. Is this not a restatement of the explanation of St. Thomas which identifies the charisma of inspiration with the prophetic and apostolic office? I think it is not, because St. Thomas did not introduce into his discussion the social character of these offices. Nor do I suppose that no one but apostles and prophets produced the inspired books; in fact, criticism suggests that most of the books of the Bible were written by men who were neither prophets nor apostles. It makes no difference; these men were the instruments of God who moved them through the Church.

More serious is the question whether this statement does not identify inspiration and revelation; their distinction is now classic in theological textbooks. To this charge I fear I must plead guilty, but with a petition for mercy; the inspiration and the revelation which I identify are not the inspiration and revelation of conventional terminology. I depart from accepted terminology not only with apologies, but also with fears, and only from the conviction that a better understanding of both is impossible without such a departure. Should the venture prove fruitless, it will have no effect on theological language. It seems to me that the distinction between inspiration and revelation is based on an inadequate conception of both, and I specify. Inspiration has been too closely identified with the individual author and with the written word; revelation has been too simply understood as a revealed proposition, and not as the word of God and the knowledge of God in the biblical sense.

This understanding of the terms also distinguishes the statement set forth here from Franzelin's distinction between *res et sententiae* (material and ideas) on the one hand and *verba* (words) on the other. I do not wish to conceive revelation as an inarticulate proposition which can be formulated indifferently one way or another, and I scarcely think that the direct insight and awareness of God is an inarticulate proposition. It is an experience, I would suggest, like pleasure or pain which has no definition except that which the sentient gives it. We know one person from another, certainly, but we rarely feel the necessity of defining our knowledge; and if we attempt to tell one person what another is like, we often find that we cannot describe with satisfaction a person we have known for many years. Nor would I say that the experience of the word of God has no effect on the formulation of the word by man. No one who has sat at his desk and writhed in pain searching for the one word which will release the pressure of his thought within him will say that the choice of words is an unimportant and accessory feature of authorship; he is more likely to say that authorship is best defined as the selection of words.

Another question may be asked. If inspiration is in the concrete the experience of the word of God and the knowledge issuing from the experience, then, since this knowledge varies from one individual to another, must we not admit degrees of revelation? And has not tradition consistently rejected any conception of more or less inspiration? It has indeed, but it has rejected it in the forms in which it was proposed; and I think it has not been proposed in this form. The vehicle of inspiration, I have insisted, is the community of the people of God, Israel and the Church; once again, I believe, the difficulty arises from isolating inspiration as the charisma of the individual author. We do not deny that the revelation of God to Israel was less than the revelation of the incarnate Word, although we affirm that the term revelation belongs to both. Does it affect the nature of the experience of revelation and inspiration to admit that the Church expresses herself more clearly, more forcefully, more fully through one than through another? In the New Testament Jude and 2 and 3 John have never been as valuable and significant as the Gospels and the great Pauline epistles; and in the Old Testament Chronicles, Ezra-Nehemiah, and 1 and 2 Maccabees are not as significant theologically as Genesis, Isaiah, or some of the Psalms. Many of us, possibly, have often wondered whether the term "inspiration" is not almost evacuated of meaning when we feel we must insist that all these books are equally inspired and equally the word of God. If they are, we must be missing something very important. Is it not more accurate to say that they are indeed the word of God, but less inspired in the sense that the clarity of insight and the vigor of personal response is less in some men than in others?

Finally, we can attempt to set the charisma of inspiration in a larger framework. We notice that the charisma of inspiration, like the apostolic office, ceased with the death of the apostles; and this is not merely coincidental. The charisma of the apostolate and of inspiration endured as long as the Church possessed a living memory of the experience of the incarnate Word, Jesus Christ. And Jesus Christ, in turn, comes as the incarnation of that word which previously God had in sundry times and divers manners spoken through His prophets. The word, more or less clearly heard and clearly spoken, as I have noted above, finally was revealed as a person who perfectly articulates the utterance of God.

Where, then, is the word of God now? And why has the charisma of inspiration passed away? We can ask this question only if we do not realize what the Church is. The Church is Jesus Christ, the Word incarnate. In the Church the word of God is spoken with a volume and clarity not attained in Israel nor the primitive Church. The Spirit which seized the prophets has come to dwell in the Church. The Church does not write the inspired word of God because she is the word of God; the charisma of her infancy has grown into her adult maturity. She does not write the word of God because she is the living word which needs no written record. I quoted above the text which linguists love to accommodate: in the beginning was the Word. Is it not true also that in the end is the Word, the living Word of God which is Christ, who is His Church?

.5.

Pastoral Apologetics and Modern Exegesis

A WELL-KNOWN and highly respected biblical scholar recently delivered an address on messianism at a panel on biblical questions attended by priests. His discourse aroused a number of questions and objections, one of which was: "You cannot present this material to converts from Protestantism." When the speaker answered, "I am a convert from Protestantism myself," the meeting dissolved in laughter, to the embarrassment of the objector, who was unable to pursue his question further. It is my intention to pursue the question here. For the question arose from a genuine and sincere doubt.

THE OLD AND THE NEW

Scarcely any of the clergy can now be unaware that modern exegesis is not universally accepted. I do not refer to the kind of defamation which was repudiated by the Catholic Biblical Association at its meeting in August, 1961, although this defamation has had an undetermined effect. The hesitation arises from some obvious facts which I set forth with no intention of patronizing. Most of our clergy have been trained in an exegesis which they believe differs sharply from "modern" exegesis. That they were trained in an older form of the discipline is neither their fault nor the fault of their instructors — admitting that the word *fault* is perhaps not in place here. Nor is it the fault of the clergy that they are not familiar with newer methods and conclusions of exegesis. No one who knows anything of the life of the parish priest expects him to have the time for the extensive serious reading which is necessary before one can feel at ease with modern exegesis. I ask no more than a sympathetic hearing of the case which I am about to present.

Key Positions

Pastoral apologetics differs notably from theoretical apologetics. The seminary course deals with general arguments; pastoral apologetics faces concrete individuals with an unlimited variety of intelligence, education, and background. Pastoral apologetics must meet the needs and answer the questions of the individual person. The priest who instructs has always drawn principally upon the resources of his theoretical apologetics for the excellent reason that he had no other major source. His formal presentation usually does not differ too much in outline and emphasis from the seminary course; and when he adapts it to the questions and the objections of particular persons, he never withdraws from certain key positions of the theoretical apologetics. A number of such key positions, based on the New Testament, are the genuinity and historical character of the Gospels, the messianic claims of Jesus Christ, and the miracles of Jesus as evidences of His claims. If these key positions are shaken, the priest feels not only that his practical use of apologetics is rendered nugatory, but also that his own belief is being undermined. Two factors combine to make him think that modern exegesis is attacking his key positions: one is the type of defamation which I mentioned above, and the other is his own lack of detailed information about the principles and methods of modern exegesis.

Modern interpreters are convinced that their work is intended to help and not to hinder apologetics, and that it does effectively help; evidently a meeting of minds is imperative if modern interpreters are to live peacefully with their brother priests. Of those topics mentioned I choose the genuinity and historical character of the Gospels as an occasion to set forth some of the reasons why we believe our work contributes, as it ought, to the priestly work of preaching and instruction. I state with all the convictions I have that I can do no more than introduce the question and suggest the answers; material is now available for the person who wishes to find a full answer.

Eyewitnesses and History

The theoretical apologetic treatment of the genuinity and the historical character of the Gospels is based on a conception of history which took form in the nineteenth century and ruled several generations of historical scholarship. This conception of history founded historical knowledge on the documentary account of the eyewitness. Without such documents there was no history. When critics proposed that the Gospels were not eyewitness documents and therefore not historical, apologetics affirmed that they are eyewitness documents and therefore historical. It was not in biblical studies that this concept of the historical witness was first abandoned, but in profane history. The critics and the apologetes agreed in an implicit definition of the historical witness; it now appears that in this point of agreement both were in error. Consequently, the historical character of the Gospels is not assured by a demonstration that they are written by Matthew, Mark, Luke, and John, just as it is not weakened if they are not the work of these four men. The question of "genuinity" in the classic sense of the word is irrelevant to the historical character of the Gospels. Modern interpreters, therefore, look now not to the individual authors (of whom Mark and Luke have withstood criticism), but to the source on which the authors of the Gospels depended whoever they were: the proclamation of Jesus by the first generation of the Church, the living memory of Jesus. The historical value of the Gospels turns not upon whether the individual authors were "informed and veracious," but on whether the primitive Church was informed and veracious.

The historical value of the Gospels demands definition. Traditional apologetics arose from a univocal conception of history as the eyewitness document. If history is not formally and exclusively identified with the witness of such documents, with what is it identified? To broaden the concept of history seems to many to admit the danger of historical skepticism, not only in the Bible but also in profane history. Here one must recall that historical skepticism arises from demanding of history more than it can do, as much as from anything else. The ideal of history as proposed by Leopold von Ranke was to narrate events exactly as they happened; and if this is the attainable aim of history, then surely one will find such a narrative in the Gospels if anywhere. Recent historical method does not believe that a narrative of events "exactly as they happened" is within the reach of history. If this be true, is one to deny that the Gospels also can attain such a narrative? And if they cannot, is their credibility thereby weakened to the point where they no longer are reliable sources?

FOLKLORE AND HISTORY

The import of such questions has led biblical scholars to assess much more thoroughly the historical value of what is called popular narrative or folklore. In older apologetics the very names were enough to cause a shudder, and this is not surprising; the apotheosis of the eyewitness document was enough to reduce folklore to worthlessness. But folklore is not worthless; on the contrary, it is a primary historical source which is for the greater part of mankind the only source of their knowledge of the past. The criticism of popular tradition differs from the criticism of documents, and the limitations of folklore must be recognized. So also must its possibilities be recognized, and these possibilities include a substantial preservation of the memory of the past. If one objects that "substantial" is not enough, he must remember that substance is reality, and that it is enough in almost every department of life. No one but the professional historian seeks accuracy in every detail and he knows that usually he cannot have it. Folklore presents the past imperfectly remembered and imperfectly narrated, but it is the past; it is not something else.

The past in popular tradition is never the bare facts narrated without feeling or conviction. Folklore is the work not of individual narrators but of a community, a society; and it is of the highest importance to recognize the social character and purpose of folklore. A community, whether it be as small as the family or as large as the political society, remembers and tells its past because in its traditions it affirms its identity and its distinction from other communities. What it is in the present is determined by what it has done and experienced in its past. The character of a community, like the character of the individual person, is at any given moment a complex of its natural endowments and its adventures in life. Its traditions are precious, because its traditions are the community itself. Every community idealizes its past, of course; but idealization is not of necessity a distortion of the past so that it is no longer a truthful account. Traditions affirm what a community believes itself to be and desires to become as well as what it has been and is; but the identity of a community or person must include its ideals and ambitions as well as its achievements, for these are a vital part of the existent self. The student of traditions recognizes this and must learn, when he seeks the history of the community, to distinguish between the narrative of events and the affirmation of ideals. When he does this, he makes an explicit distinction which uncritical popular tradition does not make and does not need.

VALUE AND LIMITATIONS OF FOLKLORE

We grant without disturbance the limitations of folklore: its imperfect retention of details, the freedom of narrative with which it creates the event anew in each retelling, its inability to produce a unified and sustained account, its transfiguration of events and persons, its simplification of issues. These limitations do not destroy its capacity to reveal the character of the community in the story of its past. But they do authorize the modern historian, who attempts a work which folklore never attempted, to exercise the methods of literary and historical criticism. The danger of the critical historian is that he will destroy the vital reality of popular tradition. In the study of popular tradition every detail is meaningful, even details which are not historical in the modern sense of the word. The creative details of folklore not only disclose the minds of the creators, but also the nature of the persons and events which are transfigured in the narrative. A false historical perspective easily leads the student of folklore to dismiss as irrelevant certain unhistorical details; in the larger sense no detail is unhistorical.

GENUINITY OF THE GOSPELS

What has been said hitherto is said generally, with no regard to the Bible or to any particular body of traditions; it is said with the intention of showing that the values of tradition are found in any tradition, granting that some traditions have a higher degree of historical value than others. Such a general review of the nature of tradition is necessary before we can put the Gospels against this background; and it is to the Gospels that we now turn.

The social character and function of tradition show why the classical idea of the genuinity of the Gospels as the work of the four men whose names they bear is not important. Whether these four or some other four or many men wrote them, they come from the community of the early Christian Church, which alone can authenticate them. Our modern ideas of individual authorship must be revised when we deal with biblical literature. The biblical authors almost entirely are not consciously individual artists. There are, of course, exceptions; the epistles of Paul are as sharply individual as any writings in any literature. The prefaces of Luke and Acts are written in the style of Hellenistic historians, who signed their names. It is evident that once Luke gets beyond his prefaces he conceals himself behind his material and writes in what can be identified as "evangelical" style, which does not exclude differences in style and composition. Nevertheless, the three Synoptic Gospels, when set against other ancient literatures, exhibit distinctive common traits; and these traits come from no individual writer. It is the merit of Form Criticism that it has identified the source of evangelical style as the preaching and teaching of the early Church. This Church is in a true and proper sense the author of the Gospel.

THE GOSPEL AND THE CHURCH

And it is here that we must notice that we speak of the Gospel before we speak of the Gospels. It is the Gospel that is our primary witness; the Gospels as literary productions depend upon the Gospel. This was recognized in the early designations of the literary productions as the Gospel according to Matthew, Mark, Luke, and John. There is one Gospel for the very good reason that there is only one Jesus and only one Church. The question of the genuinity of the Gospels is whether the Church is the author of the Gospels; and the question so posed contains its own answer. But in order to avoid the ambiguity implicit in the question so posed and answered, we must identify this Church more precisely.

Here the New Testament itself identifies the Church. It is by no means an anonymous crowd retailing bits of gossip at random; it is the eyewitnesses and ministers of the word (Lk 1:2), the witnesses of the Resurrection who were with the company from the baptism of John to the day when the Lord was taken up (Acts 1:21–22). The Gospel is the work of the men who knew Jesus personally and had heard His entire preaching; and the early Church was perfectly aware that its testimony of Jesus could rest upon no other source. In the apostolic witness it had the only link between Jesus and those who believed in Him because of this witness. The security of faith did not repose upon individual persons, however unimpeachable their information and veracity, but upon the entire apostolic witness, the group which had no other principle of unity besides Jesus Himself. The existence of the Church was the supreme witness to the reality of Jesus.

How did the Church present her witness of Jesus? I said above that we now see that it is necessary to redefine the historical character of the Gospels. It is to be observed that redefinition implies no lowering of the historical value of the Gospels; we hope that it will afford a deeper understanding of their historical value, and thus a more profound insight into the persons and events of the Gospels, particularly of the one person who is in fact the Gospel, Jesus Christ. We must notice first of all that it is the Gospel, that unique form of literature which arose spontaneously from the unique person and life which it presents. The Gospel is not a record of events in the classical and usual sense of the term. The Gospel is not a biography of Jesus and makes no pretense of being a sustained connected narrative of events exactly as they happened. The Gospel did not come into being as the fruit of research and the critical evaluation of its materials. The Gospel was spoken before it was written, and the earliest forms of the oral Gospel can be seen in the speeches of Acts. The Gospel was proclaimed or preached; it is an announcement of the good news, of the supreme saving event which is the climax of the history of salvation in the Old Testament.

Faith, a Total Surrender

That which is proclaimed is Jesus Christ, His person, His life, death, and resurrection. The proclamation demands more than a simple historical assent to the narrative; it demands faith in Jesus which is a surrender to Him, a total acceptance of Him and through Him of the salvation which God makes possible only through Him. The Gospel does not argue; it simply proclaims Jesus Christ and presents those who hear it with an unavoidable choice. The Gospel comes to the first generation of the Church as Jesus Himself came during His public life. Once one sees Him, no other motive is required for surrender to Him. The purpose of the proclamation is to make Him live for those who hear it. It is therefore vital that the Gospel present the real Jesus.

But it must be noticed that the Gospel presents the total Jesus, if I may use the expression: Jesus Lord, Jesus the Christ or Messiah, Jesus who died, rose, and ascended. To many of us this aspect of modern interpretation appears to introduce an undesirable element of obscurity. Because modern apologetics has attempted a "purely historical" approach to the historical career of Jesus of Nazareth, many students of apologetics believe that the Gospel must take the same approach to the historical career of Jesus of Nazareth, unless it wishes to run the risk of begging the question. So let us face the fact that the Gospel is a product of faith and a proclamation of faith and ask ourselves whether it could have been anything else, and whether a proclamation of faith is *ipso facto* unhistorical; for if I understood my contemporaries correctly, this principle is implicit in their unwillingness to hear the Gospel called a proclamation of faith.

That faith is based on history and rises from history is a commonplace in modern apologetics, as it is basic in the Church's understanding of herself since her origins. But what does this mean? Modern historians distinguish history as event and history as record; and the use of the word in common speech is often ambiguous. The Catholic Christian faith is based on history as event, not on history as record. From the proclamation history as record can be written, but it was not written by the early Church. This is a question of literary form and definition, not of the reality of the event; but it is not an accessary question. If we are to understand the Gospels, it is vital that we understand what the Church which produced the Gospels thought it was doing. Nothing which we know of the Church and of ancient literature contemporary with the Gospels suggests that the Church thought it was writing history as record. It seems to follow from this that any apologetic which is based upon identifying the Gospel with history as record is not securely founded.

VALUE OF POPULAR TRADITION

We return, then, to where we were before: to the question of the value of popular tradition, its capacity to remember and relate the past in its reality. Nineteenth-century investigation of the life of Jesus created an unfortunate distinction between the Jesus of history and the Christ of faith. The Gospels, historians asserted, presented the Christ of faith; we must go behind the witness of faith to find the real Jesus, concealed beneath the transfiguration of faith. Several generations of scholarship have now proved that this approach is bankrupt. Some, like Bultmann, believe the real Jesus is simply unknown and unknowable. The majority of critics recognize that the Jesus of history is the Christ of faith, that the faith of the Church was directed to a historical person known personally to the leaders of its first generation. The question of the reality of the event does not turn about the details of the narrative; a superficial study of the parallel passages of the Synoptic Gospels will show at once that the Gospel placed little importance in whether an event occurred now or then, here or there. The witnesses of the Gospel were not thought unfaithful to the event if they adapted and altered the traditional material to meet the needs and the condition of particular groups of Christians; they were aware that the same Jesus could not be presented in entirely the same way to Palestinian Jews, Hellenized Syrians, and Greeks, and they did not hesitate to expand or omit. This is popular tradition. The question of the reality of the event turns upon whether they present the real Jesus or some other person, and very few doubt this among modern critics of the Gospel. The tremendously vital and compelling personality which emerges from the four Gospels, as compelling in the Gospel, we think, as He was in His Incarnation, imposes His reality and genuinity upon all who read them with attention.

No doubt this approach, the original approach which the Church herself took, may raise the question which the modern candidate for instruction could propose: Is all this real? The Church would answer, I think, that no one who has once seen the real Jesus, the Jesus of history and the Christ of faith presented in the Gospels, can doubt His reality. That faith can be refused to Him is evident; but whenever faith is given, it is given ultimately not because of apologetic demonstration but because He commands faith by what He is. It scarcely seems possible for apologetics to meet all the subterfuges and evasions which men employ to explain their refusal of faith; is faith not refused ultimately because men do not wish to surrender themselves totally to Him?

Nevertheless, apologetics wisely attempts to close at least the major loopholes; and modern theoretical apologetics as a theological discipline seems actually to have evolved less as a positive synthetic exposition than as a response to positions which were thought to weaken the credibility of the Gospels. I have already indicated that theoretical apologetics is sometimes in danger of rehearsing opinions which are no longer important; and I add that it also faces the danger of concentrating too much on the loopholes. In some instances we are so intent upon solving objections that we never establish a positive position. It is here that the proclamation of the Gospel keeps our mind upon what is our ultimate purpose; it should also disclose to us the means which we have for achieving that purpose.

PASTORAL APOLOGETICS AND THE GOSPELS

For the purpose of pastoral apologetics surely is not to answer objections nor to confute adversaries, but to bring men to a profession of faith. The space available does not permit me to speak of the further step in apologetics, the profession of faith in Jesus Christ and the Church which is one with Him, and this can be set aside as another and a large topic; but the profession of faith is surely a surrender to Jesus Christ primarily, and this is involved in our discussion of the genuinity and historical value of the Gospels. Ultimately the Gospel is its own vindication, because it is the revelation of the reality of Jesus Christ.

I hesitate to draw practical conclusions for pastoral apologetics, because my state of life and my experience do not recommend me as a practical adviser. But this article can scarcely stop without some expression of opinion on the use of this material; I have already remarked that biblical interpreters are deeply aware of their responsibility to the Church and to their brother priests. Practically, then, I am persuaded that the treatment of genuinity and the historical value of the Gospels which one finds in theoretical apologetics has little or no use in pastoral apologetics. It is evident from what I have said that this treatment does not seem to me to describe the Gospels as they are. If we take the Gospels as they are, we shall present them as the proclamation of Jesus Christ, the witness of the primitive Church to Him in whom the Church believed.

Nor shall we attempt a formal demonstration of their historical value, particularly since this demonstration as expounded in most books implies a conception of history which is no longer that of historians. Whether we shall attempt to explain the nature of popular tradition depends, it seems to me, on the education of the persons under instruction. I have at times asked people how much they knew of the history of their family or their city or their country, and they have usually been surprised to find that almost all they know of the past is folklore; and since folklore is sufficient for its purpose, they can see that it is sufficient in the Gospels also. Folklore is so native to humanity that it seems a distraction to involve people in questions of historical criticism which they are unable to grasp. But there is scarcely any reason for concealing from them the unique literary form of the Gospels, which reflects the unique event which they witness.

If the priest possesses sufficient erudition, he may, if he wishes, show his pupils that the gospel traditions beyond doubt reflect Palestine of the first half of the first century A.D. I have not memtioned this because few even among scholars possess this erudition, and I do not know how well it would be appreciated. I suspect that in pastoral apologetics such material would be generally irrelevant. From what I have said it is evident that I think the most compelling argument for the historical reality of the events is the events themselves. Here, possibly, we priests may ask ourselves whether the use of theoretical apologetic arguments is not a substitute for something which we know we ought to do, but perhaps feel that we are unable to do.

JESUS CHRIST, THE GREATEST ARGUMENT

What we ought to do is what the proclamation is intended to do: to make Jesus Christ so real and so living to those whom we instruct that it is difficult to resist Him. Do we not share the conviction of the early Church that the personal reality of Jesus Christ compels surrender as no argument can? Is it possible that we hesitate to rely upon this, our greatest apologetic demonstration, because we are not sure that we know Him well enough to present Him with conviction? The early Church knew Him in its apostolic witness; if our own vision of Him is obscure, we shall scarcely think that the vision will move others. These are delicate personal questions which I apologize for raising; but every priest knows that the priest is personally identified with his work.

So we return where we began, to the Gospels. They are the proclamation of Jesus Christ, and to know them is to know Him as well as He can be known. Candidly, we shall in our apologetics dispense no more of the wealth of the Gospels than we ourselves have acquired. I do not wish to imply that the priest should be disappointed because he cannot communicate the fullness of the Gospels in his own work, whether with Catholics or with candidates for instruction; this is impossible, and he can do no more than lay the foundation of fuller knowledge. But this much he can do, and this much he ought to do. The one thing which is within the reach of anyone who seeks instruction is the apprehension of the historical person of Jesus Christ, or at least the beginning of apprehension. At some point the candidate will feel the attraction, and then he must either yield to it or give up further instruction. What the priest says at this point can be terribly important.

PART III

MYTH AND THE OLD TESTAMENT

.6.

God and Nature
in the Old Testament

THE word "nature," in modern speech, is used in an amazing variety of senses and applications. In approaching the question of God and nature in the Old Testament, I use the word "nature" as signifying the material universe. The *Oxford English Dictionary* gives two definitions in which this sense is found: "the material world, or its collective objects and phenomena"; "the creative and regulative physical power which is conceived of as operating in the material world and as the immediate cause of all phenomena." The reality underlying these two definitions is one and the same, and the same view of the material world appears in both. This is the conception of the material world as a closed and unified system. In the second definition, this system is hypostatized as "a creative and regulative force." "Nature," in this sense, is often used as a circumlocution for God. The modern Christian view of nature does not differ from the agnostic view as far as the intrinsic constitution of nature is concerned; the Christian theologian regards God as the First and Ultimate Cause, and considers natural agents as immediately operative in phenomena. This closed and unified system is governed by "laws," which, to the scientist, are really inductive formulations of the constant behavior of natural agents.

The origins of this modern idea appear in the natural philosophy of the Greeks, who were the first to find a single word for nature:

kosmos. This word, which signifies the beauty of order, was applied in Greek philosophy to the universe as a single whole; and the first efforts of Greek natural philosophy were devoted to the discovery of a single principle which would explain this single reality. This idea has persisted through medieval and modern thought, through the great days of the natural sciences in the past three centuries; and a belief in the ordered regularity of nature and the constancy of its laws is fundamental to the modern natural sciences, and to the practical application of science to the control and use of natural forces.

Here, as in so many departments of knowledge, popular thinking and habits of speech are behind the most advanced specialist views. In classical physics and chemistry, nature was a precision machine which man could but imperfectly imitate. A recent theological writer has noticed the change in the scientific climate of opinion:

> Science is no longer as certain of itself as it once was. Natural laws . . . "are only probably true, though the probability in favor of some of them may be so great as to approach, though never reach, certainty. A few years ago we all should have been willing to bet heavy odds that Newton's laws of gravity and the constancy of the chemical elements were accurately true, yet Einstein and Rutherford have proved us wrong" (Dampier). . . . We no longer conceive of nature as a closed and rigid system. . . . For the principle of the uniformity of nature, it appears, governs, not the objective world, but our thinking about it. . . . The current use of such terms as "creative evolution" and "emergent evolution" shows how far we have departed from the strictly mechanical view of the world. We have to recognize that in nature freedom and creativity are primary, uniformity and rigidity only secondary.[1]

One professional scientist states the case even more frankly:

> We have now seen that six important consequences follow from the mere fact of the atomicity of radiation, coupled with those well-established facts of the undulatory theory of light that have been mentioned. These are:
> (1) So far as the phenomena are concerned, the uniformity of nature disappears.

(2) Precise knowledge of the outer world becomes impossible for us.

(3) The processes of nature cannot be adequately represented within a framework of space and time.

(4) The division between subject and object is no longer definite or precise; complete precision can only be regained by uniting subject and object into a single whole.

(5) So far as our knowledge is concerned, causality becomes meaningless.

(6) If we still wish to think of the happenings in the phenomenal world as governed by a causal law, we must suppose that these happenings are determined in some substratum of the world which lies beyond the world of phenomena, and so also beyond our access.[2]

NATURE IN ANCIENT NEAR EASTERN RELIGIONS

At every turn, the historian finds himself forced to adjust his habitual ideas and modes of thought to those of an ancient culture which lacked many of the concepts which are almost instinctive for the modern man; and one of the ideas which most needs adjustment is that of "nature." The idea of nature, as defined in the *Oxford Dictionary*, did not exist in the cultures of the ancient Near East. The difference may be most simply and sharply stated by saying that the material world, in all these cultures, was in some way identified with the deity; but here there is danger of oversimplification. One should not assert that all the deities of these cultures were nature-gods; the origins of the idea of the divine are too mixed to permit such a simple explanation. But one may say that the deity, in the religions of the ancient Near East as they are known to us, was primarily a force operative in natural phenomena; and herein these religions are closer to primitive culture than to modern civilization.[3]

John A. Wilson finds that the Egyptian idea of nature was dominated by what he calls "consubstantiality." "There was . . . a continuing substance across the phenomena of the universe, whether organic, inorganic, or abstract. . . . To the ancient Egyptian the elements of the universe were consubstantial. If that be true, the terms which he knew best — human behavior — would be the frame of reference for non-human phenomena."⁴ This means that the elements of the universe, like human beings, were viewed as friendly, hostile, or indifferent: a personalization which is far removed from the *kosmos* of the Greeks, or the "nature" of the modern scientists, governed by "physical laws." Among the Mesopotamian peoples, according to Thorkild Jacobsen, the cosmos was viewed as a state. "The Mesopotamian . . . saw the cosmos as order, not as anarchy. But to him that order was not nearly so safe and reassuring as it was to the Egyptian. Through and under it he sensed a multitude of powerful individual wills, potentially divergent, potentially conflicting, fraught with a possibility of anarchy. . . . To the Mesopotamian . . . cosmic *order* did not appear as something given; rather it became something achieved — achieved through a continual integration of the many individual cosmic wills, each so powerful, so frightening."⁵ In each of these religions, there is no idea of nature as a closed and unified system; the unity of the material world is political, not mechanical. Jacobsen has pointed out that the relative regularity of natural phenomena in Egypt, with its equable climate, permitted the Egyptian a greater reliance upon the order of nature; the Mesopotamian, who lived in a wilder and more unpredictable natural milieu, saw the integration of cosmic forces as an unstable equilibrium, which could and did break down into catastrophe.

In these religions, then, natural forces were personalized; and the great gods of these religions were nature-gods. As far as the history of religions can trace the idea of the divine, the simplest and most primitive apprehension of the existence of powers which are uncontrollable by man is formed from the perception of natural forces. The civilizations of the ancient Near East did not, in this respect, advance very far beyond the ideas of primitive man. As long as the concept of "nature" is lacking, the evident conflicts of natural forces make it impossible for man to attribute these uncontrollable powers to any single subject. So each of them which he apprehends as distinct is identified in some way with a superior being, endowed with human characteristics of intelligence and passion, differing from man only in the possession of greater power. The deities thus elaborated are not transcendent, but immanent;

they are circumscribed by the "nature" from which they are educed. There is no similarity between this primitive concept and the personification of nature in modern poetry and popular speech. To explain reality, we refer to our philosophy of nature; to the ancient man, personalization was his philosophy of nature, by which he explained reality.

The deities of nature-religion are utterly dependent upon the concept of "nature" which exists in the culture where these religions arise; and a study of this concept is a prerequisite for the understanding of these religions. Since the concept of nature itself is fluid, the idea of the divine also remains without exact definition. The identification of nature and deity is not perfect. In the religions of Mesopotamia, there were many areas of nature which were not controlled by the "gods." Instead, these areas were the province of demons, beneficent or maleficent.[6] The distinction appears to be based on the cosmic scope of the forces involved, and not on the ability of man to control the forces. The cosmic force which is observed in the storm is not so readily imagined as present in a toothache or sour milk; yet, in each case, man meets forces which he cannot control with the means at his disposal. Here religion touches upon magic. The cosmic forces can be approached only by propitiation; the lesser natural forces were thought to be subject to the control of occult means. But, whether we deal with religion or with magic, the place of "nature" in religion is determined, in the first place, by man's ability to control natural forces; when he learns to control them, the resident divinity is evicted. Control, in turn, is based upon observation of the "course of nature," of the fixity of natural properties and patterns of behavior. Such observation is in itself a kind of control. The modern astronomer is no more able to "control" the object of his science than was the Babylonian astrologer; but his observation of the celestial bodies makes it clear to him that they neither influence nor foreshadow the course of human events.

If this line of thought were pursued to its extreme, it would lead to atheism — or materialism, if the word be preferred; "Nature" replaces God. At this point theistic philosophy diverges from the

path which leads to monism. The philosopher is not theistic because he does not share the modern concept of nature as a closed
and unified system; for he does share it. But he realizes that he is
still in the presence of a force which he cannot control. He cannot
locate this force within the limits of observed natural forces, and so
must go beyond them, beyond the limits of the material universe;
he must conceive a deity which is transcendent, and find a rational
solution of the antinomy of a closed system, observed by the
natural sciences, and a transcendent agent, postulated by the
primary principles of reason. So Aristotle describes his Prime
Mover, and so St. Thomas describes God in his Five Ways. In
modern philosophy, as in the religion of the ancients, man still
goes to God through "nature."

The ancient conception is designated by Millar Burrows as
mythological, i.e., prescientific. "It involves the personal, even
anthropomorphic element, treating as the acts of a personal being
or beings what a scientific world-view sees as the operations of
impersonal forces or laws." For the modern man, Burrows notes,
this is a false, or, at best, a poetic figurative expression of truth.
Burrows prefers an understanding of myth which has become
current: myth is "a symbolic, approximate expression of truth which
the human mind cannot perceive sharply and completely but can
only glimpse vaguely, and therefore cannot adequately or accurately express. . . . It implies, not falsehood, but truth . . . an
insight more profound than scientific description and logical analysis
can ever achieve."[7] This sense of myth would be disputed by some;
but, without quarreling about the word, the point is worth our
notice that, for the ancients, the "operations of impersonal forces
or laws" were unknown; they did not formulate general laws
describing the constancy of phenomena, nor did they exhibit the
curiosity which leads the scientist to search for the identity of the
natural forces which produce the phenomena. Their attribution of
the works of nature to personal beings, therefore, is scientifically inadequate; it is totally false only on the assumption that there is no
personal being above and beyond the material universe, however
"vaguely glimpsed" and "inadequately expressed" the affirmation of
such a personal being may have been.

THE HEBREW CONCEPTION OF NATURE

It is against this background of ancient categories of thought that we must approach the Hebrew conception of nature. A study of the Hebrew idea of nature was undertaken by the late Wheeler Robinson, who treats the subject at some length; it has been relatively neglected by the biblical theologians.[8] Robinson begins by remarking that Hebrew has no word for nature. "The only way to render this idea into Hebrew would be to say simply 'God.' "[9] The Hebrew found in God what was abiding in the flux of things. But this identification is sharply distinguished from the ancient Semitic personification of natural forces as nature-deities. The Hebrew showed, in contrast to modern man, very little aesthetic and romantic appreciation of nature.[10] But the Hebrew had a profound appreciation of the mysteriousness of nature; "nature is full of mysteries which are beyond man's achievement, mysteries which point to a divine activity that is beyond man's comprehension."[11] Order, which the Hebrew recognized in nature, is viewed either as a covenant of Yahweh with creatures or as "wisdom." "Wisdom was the first product of God's creative activity, for it is the condition and instrument for the creation of all things."[12] The Hebrews attributed psychic life to inanimate objects and to separate parts of the human body. "There is a realistic extension of anthropomorphism to Nature as well as to God."[13]

The animism which Robinson attributes to the Hebrews corresponds to the modern personification of "Nature" as a whole, and at the same time suggests the "consubstantiality" and the principle of substitution which Wilson has pointed out as characteristic of Egyptian thought. Egyptian ideas cannot be schematized; but, if they could, they would be classified as monism. Hebrew thought cannot be so classified. Hebrew personification is applied to distinct objects. It can be questioned whether Robinson's examples really show a prelogical animism. The Hebrews possessed that peculiar awareness of nature and sensitivity to what we moderns call its "moods" which is common to all those who live close to nature, and whose lives are much more affected by the action of its forces than is the life of modern civilized man, living in an artificially controlled climate, and securing his food and clothing by purchase. To such men, nature appears as friendly or hostile. They will easily speak of it as capricious, bounteous, spiteful; its good will is to be placated, its attacks repelled. In addition, the Hebrews sensed a community of nature with the moral life of man, with his good fortune and ill fortune. But in none of these do I find an attitude which can accurately be likened to prelogical animism.[14] The question is not thereby settled, and may deserve more searching investigation; or it may be merely a question of terminology. At best, the terminology of Robinson seems misleading. The Frankforts have rejected this terminology, which has long been accepted in the history of religions, and have proposed another designation: "The fundamental difference between the attitudes of modern and ancient man as regards the surrounding world is this: for modern, scientific man the phenomenal world is primarily an 'It'; for ancient — and also for primitive — man it is a 'Thou.' "[15] The Frankforts' opinion may be thus summarized: for ancient man, nature had no meaning except in terms of human experience. They did not distinguish the animate and the inanimate. Again, there seems to be an oversimplification. A more highly personalized view of nature, which undoubtedly appears among the Hebrews and all the other ancient Semitic peoples, is not the same thing as a lack of distinction between the animate and the inanimate. Nature is personalized especially when it manifests itself as unpredictable and uncontrollable, characteristics which we associate with persons; modern scientific man, who has reduced both of these elements to smaller dimensions, is less inclined to personalize the objects and the phenomena of nature.

We ask ourselves, then, what was the position of Yahweh in this scheme of nature. It is no longer necessary to discuss the proposition that Yahweh was a nature-deity; this opinion now has few defenders.[16] Hence the general position of Yahweh in relation to nature may be described as intermediate between the nature-religion of the ancients and the Aristotelian-Thomistic scheme of modern Catholic theology. The Hebrews had, in common with the one, a transcendent deity; like the other, they had no philosophy of nature.

YAHWEH AS CREATOR

Logically, Yahweh first appears as the creator of nature; but a number of writers have denied that this logically prior idea was chronologically early. Ludwig Köhler, for example, asserts that the idea of creation was late in appearing; it was a conclusion, not a principle, in Hebrew thought.[17] Many older writers thought that the idea of creation first appeared in Second Isaiah. Wheeler Robinson seems to lean in this direction:

> It is by the conflict of ideas that truth chiefly develops, and we may be sure that the conception of Yahweh owed no little of its enlargement to the clash with that of the star-gods of Babylon. The primary conception of Yahweh which made such progress possible cannot have been itself a development from natural phenomena. Its inspiration was derived from the very different realm of human history. Yahweh's ultimate relation to things is a derivative from His primary relation to men.[18]

Irwin, on the other hand, says: "The basic fact for Israel's faith was the physical world."[19] The truth must lie somewhere in the middle. The physical world is a less prominent motif in the conception of Yahweh than the world of history, in the sense that it is mentioned less frequently; this does not, of course, imply that it is less important. Much depends on what we mean here by creation; it is not a univocal idea in the biblical texts. Lack of precision makes it impossible to identify the Hebrew idea of creation with the technical idea of creation in modern theology. It is scarcely possible to find this technical idea even in the first chapter of Genesis. On the other hand, this chapter contains a world-view with elements which are essentially Babylonian, and which are older than anything in the Old Testament. In both Babylonian and Egyptian religion the creation story appears in several variations. The story is universal in scope; the question is the origin of the material world, as far as this world was known. The Hebrews had sufficient contact with their neighbors to raise the problem of cosmic origins; and, whatever may have been the earliest form of the Hebrew cosmogony, the Old Testament has left no evidence that the Hebrew ever attributed the origin of the world to any other cause than Yahweh.

But it is true that we cannot say how early this belief appeared, nor what form it took in its first appearance. The physical world is not the basic fact in the accounts of the patriarchs and Moses; there the basic fact of Israel's faith is rather the revelation of Yahweh by which the covenant was formulated. This has been pointed out by Phythian-Adams: ". . . the complete reversal [in Ps. 104] of what we should call the normal order is both startling and unambiguous. The devout Jew is not called to worship the Redeemer of Israel because He is the Maker of all men; he is called to worship Him as Creator *because* He is Jahweh, the Rock of Israel's salvation in the wilderness, and because He then and there made Israel His own peculiar people."[20] If we add to this the consideration of the prophets, we should say that in the prophetic literature the character of Yahweh is more and more intimately revealed, not as the lord of nature, but as the lord of human life, who imposes moral obligations. Precisely here, it would seem, the Hebrew belief in Yahweh shows its distinctive character; He is known primarily not by His manifestations in the physical world, but by communication through the prophetic word.

Two Creation Accounts

There are two accounts of creation in the first two chapters of Genesis. Of these two accounts, the second (2:4b–25) is generally regarded as the earlier, the first (1:1–2:4a) as the later. Even a casual reading discloses that the second is not really a creation account, in the sense of cosmogony; its emphasis and interest is on the origin of man, and, in particular, on the origin of man as bisexual. The creation of the lower animals is mentioned explicitly, but only to heighten the contrast between man and the lower animals. Other objects of the material world are taken for granted; of the earth and the heavens it is said, parenthetically, that Yahweh "made" them, and vegetation arises when Yahweh "rains." Yahweh is the only operative cause in the whole account. Animal life He creates by "forming"; the word suggests the work of the potter, and this is the image the author wishes to convey. The action is described explicitly in 2:7; a human corpus is molded, and life is breathed into it. The same word, "formed," is used of the lower animals (2:19), but the inspiration of life is omitted. This omission may be deliberate, to signify the excellence of man.[21] If so, the idea was not shared by the author of Ps. 104:30: "When you send forth your breath (*ruah*), they are created." The woman is not "formed," but "built"; the image is not exactly the same, but no real divergence can be intended. In all of these processes Yahweh is the "Maker"; the anthropomorphism is obvious. The author does not intend to limit the power of Yahweh; but his choice of images shows that he has not formed a conception of the divine activity which is essentially different from his conception of human activity.

When we move from the second creation account to the first, we find ourselves in a different context of ideas. No longer is man the focus of interest, to the exclusion of other beings; the scope of the first account is cosmic. There is a careful division and enumeration of the works of creation which is intended to be complete, according to the ancient idea of the visible world:

The Heavens and the Earth	And Their Hosts
1. Light	5. Celestial Bodies
2. Sky	6. Birds and Fish
3. Land and Sea	7. Terrestrial Animals
4. Vegetation	8. Man

Except man and the terrestrial animals, none of these works is mentioned explicitly in the second account. The position of man, and the unusual solemnity of the formulae of 1:26–27, show that the author intended this work as the climax; like the author of the second account, he regarded man as the chief of the works of God. But his world-view is more spacious.

The process of creation differs in the two accounts. In the first account God (*Elohim*) is not the "Maker," although the word "make" is used a number of times; He produces His works by word, by *fiat*. Creation by word is no less anthropomorphic than creation by work; but the author certainly desires to reach a higher level of representation. God is compared not to a craftsman, but to the highest of human beings, the king, who commands the works which others accomplish. But the word of God is His worker; He has and needs no assistants nor servitors. As in the second account, God is the sole operative cause; there is no question of His absolute supremacy over nature in either account.

At the same time, the idea of creation is imprecise. Creation by word and creation by work are irreconcilable; and neither is an adequate expression of reality. The word *bara'*, as it is explained in lexica and commentaries, is used only of the divine productive activity;[22] this, however, tells us nothing of the difference between divine and human activity as it was conceived by the Hebrews. There is no suggestion in either creation account that the Hebrews asked themselves whether God made from nothing. For them it was enough to say that the heavens and the earth and all that are in them came from Yahweh alone. On the other hand, a comparison of Genesis with the Babylonian *Enuma Elish* shows that the Genesis creation account rejects explicitly the idea of a primeval uncreated principle as it is exhibited in the *Enuma Elish;* for their view of the structure of the material universe was identical with that of the Babylonians.[23] Had they asked themselves whether the productive activity of Yahweh presupposed any material cause, they would, by the logic of their idea of the divine supremacy, have denied it; but to ask such a question belongs to a philosophy of nature. The Hebrews did not ask it, because they had no such philosophy. The demands of Hebrew belief were met if they excluded from their cosmogony the theogony which was characteristic of Egyptian and Babylonian myths.

CREATION AND CHAOS

In rejecting the primeval uncreated principle, the Hebrews did not abandon it altogether. There are a number of allusions in the Old Testament to creation imagined as a victory of the creative deity over a chaotic monster.[24] This myth of a combat between the creative deity and the chaotic monster appears in several forms in both Babylonian and Canaanite literature. In the *Enuma Elish* "mother Tiamat, who gave birth to them all," is the spouse of Apsu; this is the primeval pair from whom all the gods are generated. The combat arises when Apsu is slain by Ea, and Tiamat resolves in revenge to kill all her offspring. Marduk is chosen as champion of the gods, defeats and kills Tiamat, and from her gigantic carcass makes the earth and the sky. In the Ugaritic tablets, Aleyan Baal engages in combat with an adversary Mot, and with a draconic adversary called Sea-River.[25] The verbal parallels between the Ugaritic tablets and several Old Testament passages make it impossible to suppose anything but direct dependence.[26] But it should be noticed that these allusions occur only in poetry, and that no consistent form of the myth can be reconstructed from the Hebrew allusions. Consequently, it is not accurate to speak of the Hebrew "myth" of creation. But the Hebrew idea of creation, precisely because it was vague and undefined, did not forbid the employment of certain mythological traits as poetic embellishments. For the myth, as it was adapted by the Hebrews, was another expression of the divine supremacy and independence; philosophical reflection would not admit such an expression, but the Hebrews were innocent of philosophical reflection. Köhler asserts that the idea of Yahweh as a warrior-hero (Ps 89:14; Is 51:9; cf. also Ex 15:3) is derived from His victory over chaos in creation, and not from His deeds on behalf of Israel.[27] This is, perhaps, too simply stated; in the mighty deeds of Yahweh for His people, Yahweh appears as the lord of nature. But Köhler's point is well made; the title of warrior-hero does imply that Yahweh is lord of nature.

CREATION AS A CONTINUOUS ACTIVITY

The myth, besides, permitted the Hebrew poet to voice an idea which is characteristic of the Old Testament: that creation is a continuous activity.[28] The "rest" of God after His creative work (Gen 2:2) is a theological invention, intended to adapt the works of creation to the week and the Sabbath.[29] In the myth, the monster of chaos is identified with the sea or the primeval abyss, which is sometimes said to be slain (Ps 73:13–14; 89:11; Is 51:9–10; 27:1), sometimes said to be bound (Ps 89:10; 104:6–8; Job 26:12; 38:8–11). In the latter conception, the monster is kept under constant restraint; were Yahweh to relax its bonds, the world would relapse into chaos. In this employment of mythological allusion there is a poetic expression of a profound truth.

The same truth is expressed elsewhere. Each manifestation of the dominion of Yahweh over nature may be conceived as a reenactment of the drama of creation. The forces of nature were not apprehended by the Hebrews as static, nor, again, as mechanical; in each of their operations they are moved by the power of Yahweh. Yahweh brings forth the host of heaven, by number, and calls them by name (Is 40:26). He does this not only in their first creation, but in their daily appearance; for He marshals the host of heaven (Is 45:12), and when He calls to them, they arise together (Is 48:13). It is He who makes dawn and darkness; He turns dense darkness into dawn, and darkens day into night (Am 4:13; 5:8). He measures the waters in the hollow of His hand (Is 40:12); He set the sand as a boundary for the sea, as an everlasting barrier (Jer 5:22). The life which He gave He sustains; He gives breath to the people upon the earth, and spirit to those who walk in it (Is 42:5). It is He who brings forth fountains in the valleys for the beasts of the field to drink. "He makes grass grow for the cattle, and herbage for the working animals of man, to produce bread from the earth, and wine to gladden man's heart." The animals wait upon Him for their food in due season. When He gives, they gather; when He opens His hand, they are filled with good things. When He takes away His breath, they die and return to dust. But when He sends forth His breath, they are created; and thus He renews the face of the earth (Ps 104:10, 14–15, 28–30). Thus the Hebrew was not blind to order and regularity and purpose in nature; but for him these were identified with the present activity of the divine creative will. Schultz has said: "Between the order of nature and the will of the living God there is no antagonism; the two are the same."[30]

ORDER AND WISDOM IN CREATION

But the creative will is not arbitrary or capricious; its order and regularity the Hebrews saw as wisdom. Wisdom was the first of the works of God, before all creation; and when He established the heavens and the earth, wisdom was with Him (Prv 8:22 ff.).[31]

"Yahweh by wisdom founded the earth, and by insight established the heavens; by his knowledge the depths are cleft open, and the clouds drip dew" (Prv 3:19–20). The author of Psalm 104 admires the wisdom by which God provides food and shelter for man and for so many species of animals: wild and domestic, birds and beasts, on the earth and in the water. "How many are your works, Yahweh! In wisdom have you made them all" (Ps 104:24). The cycle of birth and death (Ps 104:28–30), by which the life of the world is constantly renewed, is a work of divine wisdom.[32] There is a magnificent hymn of the divine creative wisdom in Job 38–39, where similar works are enumerated: the foundation of the earth, imagined as a vast edifice; the enclosure of the sea; the succession of dawn and dusk, light and darkness; the storehouses of snow and hail; the direction of the wind, the rain, the lightning; the courses of the constellations; the provision of food for wild beasts, and the mystery of their birth; the creation of wild animals such as the wild ass, the wild ox, and the ostrich, which man cannot subdue or domesticate. Wisdom is here more than cleverness; it is a directive intelligence, which maintains order and harmony among so many conflicting and divergent agents. The wisdom of the peasant, who brings forth grain from the ground, is taught him by Yahweh: "This also comes from Yahweh of hosts, whose counsel is marvelous, whose wisdom is great" (Is 28:23–29). Wheeler Robinson has remarked that wisdom is the nearest approach in the Old Testament to a philosophical unification of nature: "It is subjective, in the sense that it is God's, and proceeds from Him, yet it is also objective, in the sense that He employs it in the creation and conservation of both Nature and human life."[33] He also points out that the idea of order in nature is expressed by the Hebrews as a "covenant" (cf. Hos 2:18; Jb 5:23); but this image is less common and characteristic than the idea of wisdom. Wisdom is not purely the order of nature, and certainly not a mechanical order; but nature, in its regularity, its unity amid diversity, constantly demonstrates a superhuman intelligence and the constant and effective direction of a superhuman will. Here is manifest the highly personalized conception of nature which is characteristic of the Old Testament.[34]

CREATION IN ANCIENT RELIGIOUS MYTHS

Creation by word and creation by work both appear in Egyptian and Babylonian literature. In the older and simpler cosmogonies, the creative deity was a "Progenitor" and a "Maker." But there is, in the Memphite theology, a far more reflective conception of Ptah as the deity who created by word. John A. Wilson says:

> [The earlier creation texts] have been more strictly in physical terms: the god separating earth from sky or giving birth to air and moisture. This new text turns as far as the Egyptian could turn toward a creation in philosophical terms: the thought which came into the heart of a god and the commanding utterance which brought that thought into reality. This creation by thought conception and speech delivery has its experiential background in human life: the authority of a ruler to create by command.[35]

The creation by word in Genesis 1 lacks the involved idea of "thought conception and speech delivery" of the Memphite theology; yet, like it, it has its "experiential background" in "the authority of a ruler to create by command." Marduk, the creative deity of the *Enuma Elish,* is a "Maker," as are other creative deities in Mesopotamian sources. It is true that Marduk, in Tablet IV, demonstrates his creative power by annihilating and restoring a garment "by the command of his mouth."[36] As Gunkel remarks, this is a conjurer's word;[37] Marduk's display is the disappearing act of the stage magician. There is no similarity between this and the formula of Genesis: "And God said: Let there be light; and light came into being." Hence, while the idea of creation by word and that of creation by work are found elsewhere, they assume a distinctive form in the Hebrew creation accounts.

The difference between the creative deity of the Hebrews and the creative deities of other ancient peoples lies, as has often been pointed out, in the supreme independence and transcendence of Yahweh, and in His unicity. I have remarked above that the divine independence is implied in the more homely account of Genesis 2 as well as in the more refined account of Genesis 1. The divine transcendence is not so obviously implied; but Genesis 2 is in accord with Old Testament ideas. Here, as elsewhere, Yahweh is not a nature-deity. He is likewise the only agent. In polytheism, the idea of the creative deity becomes hopelessly confused as the positions of different deities, each of whom has a title to creation, are reconciled. Thus, in older Mesopotamian cosmogonies, Anu, Enlil, and Ea were creative deities; in the *Enuma Elish* creation is attributed to Marduk.[38] In Egypt also several deities are called creators.[39] Furthermore, in these religions a cosmogony is, in its initial stage, a theogony. The utter absence of such features in the Hebrew accounts must be deliberate; and few pages of the Old Testament are better calculated to show the loftiness of the Hebrew idea of God than the creation accounts.

YAHWEH, LORD OF THE STORM

As the creator, sustainer, and lord of nature, Yahweh manifests Himself in natural phenomena. And while no area of natural forces is excluded from His domain, it is true that the Hebrews saw Him by preference in some phenomena and ignored His presence in others. A page of A. C. Welch, which bears on some other points besides the one under discussion, deserves to be quoted in full:

> Jahveh [in the JE patriarchal stories] is also spiritual, in the sense that His relation to nature is that of a free personality. One prefers to say His relation to nature rather than to the universe, because the book does not bring Jehovah into a close connection with creation, and does not conceive Him as holding a definite relation to the world as a whole. Possibly the idea of the world as a whole has not risen before the thought of the writers; certainly, if it has, it does not bulk largely in their minds, for Jahveh's relation to the world is not conceived as a relation to the world-whole, but rather as a relation to the individual nature-phenomena and especially to the terrible aspects of nature which have always attracted men's awe. Now, when Jahveh brings earthquake and storm, He always stands behind the nature-phenomenon, and is never contained in it. The very variety of events with which He can be brought into connection is the sufficient proof that He is identical with none. He sends

pestilence and causes drought; He rains down fire, and is attended by earthquake. If Jahveh were conceived as the god of the storm, it would be difficult to account for His association with pestilence. The fact that He is associated with all these natural events shows that He is contained in none, but is conceived as able to use each in order to fulfil His will. . . . These phenomena of nature which have always roused men's interest, especially at a certain stage of their mental and religious development, claimed the attention of the Hebrews also as subjects for religious thought, were referred by them to the one God of the people, and could not be conceived by them as escaping, any more than aught else, from His control. The significant matter is that they are always believed to be under His control. Jahveh's relation to the Cosmos, and especially to the nature-phenomena, has not been a subject of reflection; but Jahveh's nature is so conceived and so thoroughly held aloft from being contained in nature that the people are sure, when the period of reflection comes, to follow the higher line of theological thought.[40]

With the caution indicated by Welch in mind, we may notice that Yahweh is often associated with the storm. So many and so striking are the biblical allusions to this that some have thought that Yahweh was originally a storm-god.[41] The thunder is the voice of Yahweh (Ps 29:3-9). It is in a storm that Yahweh rescues His people from Egypt (Ps 77:16-20). He speaks and raises the storm-wind; He stills the storm to a whisper (Ps 107:25-29). He comes from afar in blazing anger, amid heavily rising banks of clouds; He makes His glorious voice heard, and the descent of His arm seen, in furious anger, and flame of devouring fire, amid cloudburst, and rainstorm, and hail (Is 30:27, 30). In the storm and tempest is His way, and clouds are the dust of His feet (Na 1:3). He is also lord of the earthquake; the epithet which the Greeks applied to Poseidon, "Earth-Shaker," is apt for Yahweh as He appears in Hebrew poetry. The mountains quake before Him, and the hills melt (Na 1:5). He stretches out His hand, and the mountains quake (Is 5:25). He makes the cedars of Lebanon skip like a calf, Lebanon and Hermon like a wild ox (Ps 29:6). It is He who sends forth wind and rain from their storehouses. He cleaves a channel for the torrent, and a way for the thunderbolt; He sends forth the lightning, and tilts the clouds (Jb 38:25, 35, 37).

THE STORM THEOPHANY

It is in the great theophanies that Yahweh appears most clearly as the Lord of the storm (Jdt 4:4–5; Ps 18:8–16; 68:7–9; Hb 3:3–15). The theophany of Sinai, in which the covenant was established between Yahweh and His people, came as a storm theophany. "There were thunderclaps and flashes of lightning and a dense cloud and the sound of a trumpet, very loud. . . . Mount Sinai was all smoke when Yahweh came down upon it in fire, and its smoke ascended like the smoke of a kiln" (Ex 19:16, 19). This historic event has left its traces upon the poetic theophanies. Even in the theophany of Ezekiel 1 Yahweh approaches in a storm cloud, although the prophet forgets it when he begins to describe the chariot. The theophany of Psalm 18:8–16 may be taken as typical:

> The earth quivered and rocked,
> And the foundations of the mountains trembled,
> And rocked when He was angry.
> Smoke arose from His nostrils,
> And fire devoured from His mouth;
> Coals were set ablaze from it.
> He bowed the heavens, and came down;
> Thick darkness was beneath His feet.
> He rode upon a cherub, and flew;
> He sped on the wings of the wind.
> He made darkness His lair;
> His pavilion about Him was the darkness of the heavens.
> Before Him moved dense clouds,
> Hailstones, and coals of fire.
> Yahweh thundered from the heavens,
> The Most High uttered His voice.
> He shot forth His arrows, and scattered them;
> His thunderbolts, and He routed them;
> The depths of the sea were laid bare,
> And the foundations of the earth were uncovered,
> By your wrath, Yahweh,
> By the fierce blast of your anger.

It is as the helper of His people that Yahweh most frequently appears in the storm; He is most terrible when He scatters the enemies of Israel. Against the Canaanites, He appears from Edom when the earth quaked and the clouds dripped water, when the stars from their courses fought against Sisera (Jdg 4:4, 20). He cast great hailstones from heaven upon the Amorites, and slew more of them than Israel slew by the sword (Jos 10:11). The clouds are His chariot, the winds His messengers, the lightning His minister (Ps 103:4). He is the "Rider of the Clouds" (Ps 68:4), an epithet applied also to the Canaanite Aleyan Baal.[42]

It seems impossible to reach any decision to the question whether the phenomena of the theophany are those of the storm or the volcanic eruption. A. C. Welch, who insists that it is a volcanic eruption, remarks with some acidity that hills are not in the habit of melting like wax before a thunderstorm.[43] Those who interpret the theophany in terms of the storm urge, with some plausibility, that the allusions to volcanic phenomena are obscure, nor do they appear in all the theophanies; it is difficult, besides, to discover the volcanic area where the Hebrews would have become acquainted with volcanic phenomena. One might account for both by supposing that the theophany combines phenomena of storm and earthquake. The theophany is a literary creation of the poet's imagination, not a description of an actual event. For the poet, the essential idea is the presence and activity of Yahweh in nature, not the precise identification of the phenomena. Thus Calès remarks of Psalm 18:8–16:

> One should not look for a symmetrically and logically constructed allegory, as a western imagination would conceive it. The psalm draws its traits from various sources: the theophany of Sinai; great cosmic disturbances; hurricanes and fearful storms, such as arise in the rocky deserts of Sinai and Palestine; perhaps, more or less indirectly, the great cosmogonic poems of Babylon, etc.[44]

The classical model of the theophany appears to be the theophany of Sinai, as it was related in Hebrew tradition. It is certainly the oldest form of the theophany, and no other reason suggests itself why Yahweh should by preference be seen as present and active in the storm except the traditional association of the storm theophany and the covenant. It would be only natural for the Hebrew to think of Yahweh manifesting Himself in the form and circumstances of the event which was of such historic significance for His people.

On the other hand, the details of the theophanies are expanded beyond the details of the Sinai narratives. It is possible that they are affected also by the account of the passage of the Red Sea, although these are more difficult to trace. Some details are borrowed from foreign sources; but there is no pattern in extrabiblical literature after which the biblical theophany is formed. In the Gilgamesh Epic, ". . . a black cloud came up from out of the horizon. Adad thunders within it. . . . The raging of Adad reached unto heaven, turned into darkness all that was light . . . the land he broke like a pot."[45] In a hymn to Adad, Adad rides upon the storm and the hurricane; his glory covers the world; his light appears afar, and his voice is heard at a distance; the hailstones are in his hand, and he sends forth the lightning as his messenger.[46] Thus the idea of riding upon the clouds (the cherubim are so identified in these passages), and of sending forth the wind and the thunderbolt as messengers, are common to the biblical theophany and the hymns to the storm-god. The darkness and the earthquake are features which are mentioned in the Sinai narratives.

The theophany, then, is not a simple thunderstorm, nor yet an earthquake nor a volcanic eruption, but a manifestation of Yahweh in a convulsion of nature. As a literary device, it is an expression of the Hebrew idea of the divine power in nature. The power there manifested is not blind; the theophany is an appearance of the divine wrath, especially of the wrath of Yahweh against the enemies of Israel. This idea is, of its very nature, primitive; it is difficult to see how Duhm could have treated it as a late literary conceit.[47] In theophanies where Yahweh does not appear in His wrath, one may suspect that the theophany is composed purely for its imaginative values after the manner of earlier theophanies; such, for instance, is the theophany of Ps 104:2–4. But in the earliest forms of the theophany, the deity of the theophany was in a special way the God of Israel, and, in particular, the helper of Israel. It is difficult to find any reason for this except the theophany of Sinai, which associated Yahweh once and for all with the phenomena of this solemn occasion.

THE THEOPHANY OF ELIJAH

It is surprising, therefore, to find one theophany in which it is denied that Yahweh is in the storm (1 Kgs 19:11–13):

> There was Yahweh passing by; and there was a great and mighty wind which rent the mountain and shattered the rocks before Yahweh; but Yahweh was not in the wind. And after the wind came an earthquake; but Yahweh was not in the earthquake. After the earthquake came lightning; but Yahweh was not in the lightning. After the lightning, there was the sound of a gentle whisper. Now when Elijah heard it, he wrapped his face in his mantle and went out and stood at the entrance of the cave. Then a voice came to him.

When we recall the traditional concept of Yahweh in the theophany, the denial that Yahweh is in the storm or the earthquake here appears altogether deliberate. But what is the meaning of the denial?[48] It may be parabolic: the overthrow of the Baal cult is not to be accomplished by violent means, or by a great display of power. For the Baal also was a nature-deity; and Yahweh would not be distinguishable from the Baal by a mere display of power in nature. Such a display is narrated in 1 Kings 18; in the competition between Elijah and the prophets of the Baal on Mount Carmel, it is Yahweh who sends the lightning to consume the victim. Our narrator represents this display as failing to accomplish its purpose. This, we say, may be the meaning of the passage; but one feels the danger that it reads too much into the text. But the passage certainly does not mean that Yahweh is not present in such phenomena; such a denial would run counter to the whole traditional conception of Yahweh, and would be out of accord with the context of the passage. For the contest between Yahweh and the Baal was waged precisely on the ground of dominion over the forces of nature. When Elijah demands that the people choose between Yahweh and the Baal, he means that there can be only one lord of nature; it is proper to divinity to possess this prerogative. If Yahweh is *elohim* (which no Hebrew would deny), then there is no room for a Baal who has the power of granting fertility. Hence it appears more probable that the denial that Yahweh is in the wind or the earthquake is a denial that He is identified with these forces as a nature-deity. Baal, or any nature-deity, was not a truly cosmic deity. Yahweh, on the contrary, was the lord of all the forces of nature, but in none, in the sense that no particular force was His proper domain. He is equally powerful and active when there is no such display of powers; and His will is accomplished by hidden means, as well as by the spectacular. The theophany of Elijah is a refinement upon the theophany of Sinai.

FERTILITY CULTS

Man's sense of his dependence upon the divine is nowhere more apparent than in his quest for food. In ancient agricultural societies this sense developed into the fertility cult. For the tiller of the soil success is conditioned upon the cooperation of a large number of natural factors, such as the fertility of the soil, moisture, sun, and wind, and the overcoming of such hostile elements as insects and disease. Though the modern farmer is able to exercise some control over several of these factors, he still regards his work as more or less of a gamble. The ancient peasant had much less control. In Mesopotamia and Egypt moisture was controlled by irrigation and the peasant had learned to increase the fertility of his soil. In Palestine the peasant was at the mercy of an annual marginal rainfall and he was helpless against disease and insects. For him the succession of the seasons was not an effect of "physical laws," but of the determination of a superior will which could, for reasons unknown to man, alter its decision. Hence the importance of the fertility cults in the ancient Semitic world. The forces of fertility in human and animal life also were subject to the same arbitrary will.

The study of the fertility cults of the Canaanites was much advanced by the discovery of the Ugaritic tablets at Ras Shamra in 1929. These tablets were the first literary remains discovered of the religion of the pre-Israelite inhabitants of Palestine, which is alluded to so frequently in the Old Testament.[49] There are two characteristic features of the Semitic fertility cults: the prominence of the goddesses of fertility, and the dramatic representation of the death and resurrection of the god of vegetation. Albright points out that the extraordinarily fluid character of the Canaanite deities makes it difficult to fix the functions and interrelations of the gods.[50] In addition, the great epic of Aleyan Baal is not completely preserved. In general, the myth of the death and resurrection of the god runs as follows: the god of vegetation or fertility is slain by enemies, who represent the natural forces which annually destroy vegetation. The god is buried, as seed is planted. He is brought back to life to enjoy the sexual union of his consort — Anath at Ugarit, Ishtar in Mesopotamia. There is a combat between the god (or the goddess, or both) and the enemies, from which the god emerges victorious as a creative deity. This myth was dramatized in the temple liturgy. The most important liturgical function of the king was his part in this festival; but we do not know the rite in details. In Mesopotamia, the king, who was identified with the god of fertility, received his royal power anew each year at the New Year festival. In more ancient times, the death of the god was very probably enacted on a human victim; but there is no evidence that this was a regular practice in the period from which the literary remains have come. Human sacrifice, however, remained in practice, at least as an occasional rite in times of crisis, in the Semitic world during the period of the Hebrew monarchy. The sacred marriage of the god and the goddess was represented by the king (or a priest) and a priestess.

The myth and ritual were, in essence, mimetic. The annual cycle of life from death was seen as a truly divine force at work; but the alternation of life and death was a combat between opposing forces on the divine level. At the heart of this cycle was the mysterious force of sex; and sex was deified in the fertility goddess. The liturgical enactment of the myth assured the victory of the god over his enemies and the renewal of life. The king, as representative of his people, entered into the divine mysteries and communicated in the divine force of life. But such a communication was due to each of the worshipers also; and this was accomplished by sacred prostitution, in which the worshiper and a priestess reenacted the sacred marriage of the god and the goddess.

It is clear from the Old Testament that the Hebrews rejected, vigorously and definitely, this cult and the belief upon which it was based; it is also clear that it was not rejected without a bitter struggle. It has often been said by many of the older writers on the history of Hebrew religion that Yahweh was originally a mountain-god, or a storm-god, with no fertility function; that the Hebrews, a nomadic people, had no place in their life for an agricultural deity. It is no longer possible to make such sweeping assertions. We should base our assumptions primarily upon Hebrew traditions. The spring and fall festivals are certainly old, older than the impingement of the Canaanite cults upon Hebrew religious practices. It would be better to say that the Hebrews, in earliest times, attributed fertility to Yahweh simply and without reflection; and that it was only after they had become acquainted with the Canaanite mysteries that they began to think of Yahweh as a god of fertility.

YAHWEH, THE DISPENSER OF FERTILITY

That Yahweh is the dispenser of fertility is an idea that runs through all strata of the Old Testament. He blesses fields, gives of heaven's dew and earth's fatness (Gn 27:28). The God of Jacob blesses Joseph with the blessings of heaven above, of the abyss beneath, of breast and womb, of fatherhood, of man and child (Gn 49:24–26). He blesses the offspring of man and the produce of the soil, grain, wine, and oil, the progeny of the flock (Dt 7:13; Jer 31:12; Jl 2:19). He visits and enriches the land, prepares grain, saturates the furrows, softens the soil with showers, blesses the young growth; His paths drip fatness, the pastures are covered with flocks, and the valleys with grain (Ps 65:10–14). Yahweh gives prosperity, and the land yields its produce (Ps 85:13). He gives rain for the seed, and wheat as the produce of the soil (Is 30:23). God gave the increase to the flocks of Jacob (Gn 31:7–9). Yahweh gives children (Gn 21:2; 28:31; 30:2; 33:5); children are an inheritance from Yahweh (Ps 127:3). Rain is a gift of Yahweh (Lv 26:4; Dt 11:13–15; Jer 5:24), which He sends at the behest of a prophet (1 Sm 12:17–18; 1 Kgs 19:41–45). Johannes Pedersen has well pointed out that the place of fertility and the fertility deities is occupied in Hebrew belief by the idea of blessing.[51] "The blessing comprises everything in life . . . it is the positive strength of life." It gives the power to multiply: fertility in the family, the field, and the herd. It is a vital power, communicated from God to men; an act of the gracious will which diffuses its own goodness.[52] Thus, to the Hebrews also, fertility was the manifestation of a divine power at work; but the nature of the power was conceived in a totally different way from that of the fertility cults. Yahweh, the dispenser of fertility, is not Himself a part of the process of fertility. He has no female consort; the Hebrew language does not even form a feminine of the noun for deity. He possesses none of the traits of the fertility gods. The Hebrews, who were not unwilling to draw upon Semitic mythology for poetic embellishments,[53] have left no allusion in the Old Testament to the myth of the dying and rising god in connection with Yahweh. Such a rejection cannot be merely coincidental.

COLLISION OF HEBREW AND CANAANITE BELIEFS

Was it always so? Was there, as many historians of Hebrew religion have thought, a "transfer" of the functions of the fertility god to Yahweh? There was a development; Yahweh was certainly more of a patron of fertility after the collision of Hebrew and Canaanite beliefs than He was before. But, as we have noticed above, we cannot trace a stage in Hebrew religion when Yahweh was not a cosmic deity; hence the forces of fertility also must be under His control. But reflections on the implications of Yahweh's cosmic rule, and, in particular, on the manner in which He dispenses fertility, appear to have come only during the early period of the monarchy; and the struggle between Yahweh and the fertility gods appears to have continued down to the fall of the kingdom of Judah. Even after the fall of Jerusalem, the women of the group which fled to Egypt still practiced the rites of the "queen of heaven," Ishtar (Jer 44:15–30). The allusions to the adoption of the fertility cults by the Hebrews are too numerous for citation. It is more probable that this adoption was syncretistic; it was not a question of the rejection of Yahweh, the national god, but of adopting the cult of Baal in addition to that of Yahweh, or, what was worse, of attributing to Yahweh the character of the Baal.[54] The combat may be illustrated from the writings of Hosea and the Elijah narratives of 1 Kings 17–19.

The image of marriage, which Hosea employs as a parable of the relations between Yahweh and Israel, is probably chosen as a polemic against the sacred marriage of the fertility cults. Yahweh has a spouse; but it is the people of Israel. Their union is not the licentious union of the cult, but a union of love and fidelity. It is the people of Israel who have debased the union by their cult of the Baal. Hosea makes it clear that the Israelites attributed fertility to the Baal:

> She said: "I will go after my lovers,
> Who gave me my bread and my water,
> My wool and my flax, my oil and my drink . . ."
> But she did not know
> That it was I who gave her
> The grain and the wine and the oil (2:7, 10).

It does not seem that the Israelites abandoned the worship of Yahweh for the worship of the Baal; rather they attributed to the Baal the gift of fertility. But there is something more fundamental in the words of the prophet. The Israelites had given Yahweh Himself the title of Baal; although they did not realize it, this was to destroy Him. The character of the Baal was altogether alien to that of Yahweh. If Yahweh is made a fertility deity, this is really a renunciation of Him. The application of the title is evident from Hosea 2:16–25. Yahweh must once more lead the people into the desert, as He did at the time when He first chose it for Himself; there it will learn that He is Yahweh.

> Therefore I am going to persuade her,
> And I will lead her into the wilderness,
> And I will speak to her heart. . . .
> And she will answer there as in the days of her youth,
> As in the day when she came up from the land of Egypt.
> It will come to pass on that day — the oracle of Yahweh —
> She will call me, "My husband";
> She will no longer call me, "My Baal."
> I will take the names of the Baals out of her mouth;
> They will no longer be invoked by their names.

When this happens, Yahweh will once more manifest His good will by bestowing fertility:

> It will come to pass on that day — the oracle of Yahweh —
> It will speak to the heavens,
> And they will speak to the earth;
> And the earth will speak to the grain and the wine and the oil.

The error of the worship of the Baal is to be corrected in the only effective way: by a demonstration that Yahweh alone has the power to bless. That which they ask of the fertility god, they shall not receive; Yahweh will withhold it, until they learn to ask it from Him, as they did before.

The narrative of 1 Kings 18–19 is to the same purpose. Under Ahab and his Canaanite queen Jezebel the worship of the Baal of Tyre was promoted under royal patronage. That this was syncretism has often been pointed out; Ahab gave his sons names with the theophorous component — *yah,* and sought out prophets of Yahweh before he went out to battle against the Arameans (1 Kgs 22). Yet Elijah insists that a choice must be made; to lean upon two deities is to limp; "if Yahweh is *elohim,* follow him; but if the Baal, follow him" (1 Kgs 18:21). The power of Yahweh, again, is to be demonstrated by His control of rain; the three years' drought is interpreted by the prophet as an effective proof that it is Yahweh who is the lord of fertility, and the drought is ended at the prophet's intercession on Mount Carmel (1 Kgs 18:41–45). Once again, it is clear that, in the prophet's mind, to limit the cosmic domain of Yahweh, or to make of Him a natural force, is to destroy Him.

It seems, however, quite inaccurate to say, with Irwin, that "the belief in Yahweh as the giver and guardian of the increase of flock and field was hard won only through the struggle of a succession of prophets," and that "from the time of the entry into the land, the people had accepted somewhat fully the Canaanite theology which credited Baal with this bounty."[55] In this view — a more refined statement of an opinion which is a commonplace in the classical histories of Hebrew religion — there was, under the influence of the prophetic doctrine, a "transfer" of the functions of the Baal to Yahweh. We are justified in asking for more evidence that Yahweh never was the dispenser of fertility. There must have been some-thing in the inner principles of the traditional worship of Yahweh which made it possible for the prophets to assert His supremacy over the forces of fertility, and to bring about a total rejection of the fertility cult with all its works and pomps.[56] This can be nothing but the character of Yahweh as a cosmic deity, above and master of all natural forces, identical with none. This is the picture of Yahweh which appears at all levels of Hebrew tradition. Albright notices:

> It is very significant that no Astarte plaques or figurines have hitherto been discovered in any early Israelite levels in central Palestine. This is true of the four phases of Iron I which the writer excavated at Bethel; it is equally true of the excavations at Gibeah, Tell-en-Nasbeh, and Shiloh. To be sure, such figurines may be found at any time, since it would be very rash indeed to say that they were never used in Israel proper. However, their absence so far from these levels is in striking contrast to their frequency in corresponding deposits of the Late Bronze and Iron II (from the ninth century onward), and requires an explanation.[57]

Albright himself connects the absence of these figures with the aniconic (imageless) character of Yahwism. We may add that it is most easily explained on the assumption that the Astarte cult was not practiced in the early days of the settlement; and the absence of these figures is difficult to square with the assertion that the Canaanite theology had been accepted somewhat fully from the time of the entry into the land.

Thus it is clear that the Hebrews shared a fundamental idea of the ancient Semitic peoples; but they formulated it in their own way. This fundamental idea is the belief that the bounty of nature is not the result of a concatenation of natural forces operating according to fixed laws, but of the communication of a divine attribute. The peculiar Hebrew character of the belief appears in their attribution of the bounty of nature exclusively to the will of the deity. The regular course of the seasons was not the drama of a dying and rising god; it was the result of the covenant of Yahweh with an ancient patriarch, a promise that He would not, as the story of the Deluge told of Him, again annihilate the human race by permitting the regular course of nature to lapse:

> I will never again curse the soil on account of man; for the designs of man's heart are evil from his youth. I will never again smite every living being, as I have done.
> All the days of the earth,
> Seed and harvest, cold and heat,
> Summer and autumn, day and night:
> They shall not cease. (Gn 8:21–22).

The Hebrew sought fertility by petition and sacrifice, not by myth and ritual. It is perhaps worth notice that the agricultural feasts of the Hebrews were harvest festivals: Mazzoth, Weeks, Ingathering. If there was a New Year's festival similar to that of Babylon and Canaan, it has vanished without a trace in the Old Testament. The Hebrew thanks Yahweh for fertility, and offers Him His portion of its fruits in sacrifice. The feasts are, in Pedersen's well-chosen words, "a direct sanctification of nature." This should not be understood to mean that nature is not already a part of Yahweh's domain; it is rather man's recognition of the sanctity of nature as blessed by Yahweh.

FERTILITY AND DIVINE KINGSHIP

The affirmation that there is no trace of a New Year's festival of the Hebrews similar to that of Babylonia and Canaan may appear too sweeping, if we recall the theory of Mowinckel and others that the feast of Tabernacles was identified with a New Year's feast of the enthronement of Yahweh.[58] It seems to me, in view of the great reserve with which exegetes have received this thesis, that it is unnecessary to enter into a detailed discussion of the question here; and this is especially true because the New Year's festival proposed by Mowinckel is not a cyclic cultic renewal of fertility. The theory, however, has called attention to an exegetical fact which has been little noticed: that the kingship of Yahweh is associated with his reign over nature. Oesterley notes that the title of king is applied to Yahweh in ten Psalm passages, three prophetic passages, and implied in one Psalm passage. The throne of Yahweh is mentioned in eight Psalm passages (of which one is identical with the passage which implies the title of king, Ps 9:7); it occurs eleven times outside the Psalms (of which there are two in Isaiah, two in Jeremiah, three in Ezekiel; the distribution is not great). The phrase, "Yahweh is become king," occurs in five Psalm passages (of which two are identical with those mentioned above), once outside the Psalms.[59] From this it is clear that the kingship of Yahweh is characteristic of the Psalms; it is easy to see why Mowinckel concluded that it is a ritual motif. Now, of these Psalm passages, the idea of throne or kingship occurs in a context of Yahweh's dominion over nature in seven. In Psalm 29:10, "Yahweh sits over the flood; Yahweh sits as king forever," the idea is expressed as the conclusion of a psalm which glorifies the power of Yahweh in the storm. In Psalm 74:12, "Elohim is my king from of old, who wrought victory in the midst of the earth," the context is that of the creative victory of Yahweh over the monster of chaos.[60] In Psalm 89:14, "Righteousness and justice are the foundation of your throne," there is no obvious reference to the rule of Yahweh over nature; but the verses follow immediately upon a context (vv. 9–12) which alludes to the victory of Yahweh over the chaotic monster, and His creative work. In the royal psalms, 93, 95–100, the allusions to Yahweh's dominion over nature are clear in Psalm 93, where the might of Yahweh is contrasted to the roaring of the sea; some commentators have seen in this another allusion to Yahweh's imprisonment of the sea.[61] Psalm 95:3 associates the title of king with creation, as does Psalm 96:5. In Psalm 97 the kingship of Yahweh is associated with a storm theophany; cf. Psalm 29. These passages make it clear beyond doubt that the basis of the kingship of Yahweh is not merely His covenant with Israel and His redemption of Israel from bondage, but also His cosmic rule over nature, which rests, in turn, upon His prerogatives as creator. In a word, Yahweh is king of the world before He is king of Israel. This is not the only motif of the kingship of Yahweh; in other passages His kingship means that He is the warrior who fights the battles of Israel, or the judge who punishes the wicked and vindicates the righteous. We may observe in the kingship of Yahweh three concentric circles: the narrow circle in which He appears as the warrior-king; the wider circle in which

He appears as the cosmic lord; and the extreme in which He appears as the king of justice. One need not suppose that these three circles represent a chronological evolution of the idea. Rather the kingship of Yahweh merges several conceptions which we meet in our consideration of God and nature. Yahweh's kingship is based upon His creative dominion; as the lord of nature, He directs nature to His purpose, whether it be to fight the battles of His people, or to punish them for their rebellion, or to vindicate the righteous. His final dominion is eschatological. This should not be questioned, although the eschatological motif is by no means as clear in the royal psalms as Mowinckel has made it out to be; but it does appear in the eschatological consummation of nature, which I discuss below.

NATURE AND DIVINE WRATH

The Hebrew was aware that, while the order of nature was firmly established by the "covenant" of Yahweh, nature was not perfectly in harmony with the desires of man. He knew the hostility of nature. It was by no means an uncommon idea in ancient Semitic religion to attribute such hostility to the anger of a god; if nature's blessing was a gift of divine beneficence, then its hostility must be a sign of divine anger. Jacobsen quotes the following Babylonian poem:

> Enlil called the storm.
>   The people mourn.
> Exhilarating winds he took from the land.
>   The people mourn.
> Good winds he took away from Shumer.
>   The people mourn.
> He summoned evil winds.
>   The people mourn.
> He called the storm that will annihilate the land.
>   The people mourn.
> He called disastrous winds.
>   The people mourn.
> Enlil . . . called the great hurricane of heaven.
>   The people mourn.
> The hurricane howling across the skies,

> The people mourn.
> The shattering storm roaring across the land,
>   The people mourn.
> The tempest which, relentless as a flood wave,
> Beat down upon, devours the city's ships,
> All these he gathered at the base of heaven.
>   The people mourn.[62]

The storm of this poem was, in reality, an invading Elamite army; but the poet conceives it as the storm by which Enlil executes the divine decree. The human catastrophe was conceived as a catastrophe in nature, which was the instrument of divine anger. The forces which bring forth nature's bounty may turn destructive. In polytheism, this meant that fertility was assured not only by securing the goodwill of beneficent deities, but also by propitiating those who were apt to be ill-disposed.

The anger of the god was not, in Babylonian religion, divorced from ethical motives. In a penitential psalm, the singer confesses his guilt; if his sin is removed, the anger of the god will be appeased.[63] But we should not, it seems, read too much into this. The psalm in question is a mechanical formula which may be addressed to any god; and the singer does not know what he may have done to anger the god. The same vagueness appears in other penitential psalms. If the gods are angry, it is because of some sin; but sin does not always anger them. So the worshiper does not know what it is that angers the god. Sin here has a broad meaning; it includes indeliberate fault and error, and ritual imperfection. The singer asks: "How long, O my goddess, until your hostile heart be quieted? Man is dumb, he knows nothing. Mankind, everyone that exists, what does he know? Whether he is committing sin or doing good, he does not even know." Jastrow has written of the penitential psalms:

> The misfortunes of life, more especially those which could not be so readily ascribed to the presence of evil spirits, filled the individual with his sense of guilt. In some way, known or unknown to him, he must have offended the deity. The thought whether the deity was justified in exercising his wrath did not trouble him any more than the investigation of the question whether the punishment was meted out in accordance with the extent of the

wrong committed. It was not necessary for the deity to be just; it was sufficient that some god felt himself to be offended, whether through the omission of certain rites or through an error in the performance of rites or what not. The two facts which presented themselves with overpowering force to the penitent were the anger of the deity and the necessity of appeasing that anger. Beyond that conclusion the Babylonians and Assyrians did not go, but this reasoning also sufficed to bring the conviction home to him that his misfortunes were the result of some offence. The man afflicted was a sinner, and the corollary to this position was that misfortunes come in consequence of sin. Through the evils alone which overtook one, it became clear to an individual that he had sinned against the deity.[64]

This passage summarizes well both the ethical quality of the penitential psalms and their ethical inadequacy. To the Mesopotamian, the anger of the gods was capricious.

The "Sacramental" Character of Nature

Between this and the Hebrew conception of the anger of Yahweh as manifested in nature there is an evident difference. Basic to the Hebrew conception of the anger of Yahweh is the covenant; it is infidelity to the covenant which angers Yahweh and moves Him to punish sin by the agency of natural forces. Yahweh withholds rain, or sends it upon one city and not upon another, upon one field and not upon another. He smites with blight and mildew, and sends the locust to devour trees and vineyards; and in spite of this, the Israelites do not return to Him (Am 4:7–8). Yahweh thunders at the head of His army of locusts, and the prophet calls to His people to return to Yahweh with their whole heart (Jl 2:11–12).[65] Jeremiah says of his people:

They do not say to themselves,
"Let us reverence Yahweh our God,
Who gives winter rain and spring rain in due season,
And keeps for us the weeks appointed for the harvest."
It is your crimes that have disturbed this,
Your sins that have withheld the blessing from you (5:24–25).

Hosea curses the Israelites with infertility:

> Give them — Yahweh, what can you give?
> Give them a miscarrying womb and dry breasts (9:14).

He threatens them with starvation:

> They have sown the wind,
> They shall reap the whirlwind.
> The standing grain which has not yet sprouted
> No meal shall it yield;
> Even if it should yield,
> Strangers shall devour it (8:7).

It was because the returned exiles have failed to finish the Temple that they reap scanty harvests (Ag 2:15–19). Disease is a "stroke" of Yahweh; it is Yahweh who sends it, and Yahweh who cures (Gn 12:17; 20:17–18; 1 Sm 5:6 ff.; 6:19). This is in contrast to the Babylonian belief that disease was the work of demons. Medicine was primitive among the Hebrews; in most instances the cure of disease, like its rise, could be traced to no definite cause. Pestilence, which destroys on a large scale, was attributed to Yahweh in a special way (Lv 26:25; 2 Sm 24:15; Ez 14:9; Am 4:10). In the great blessings and curses of Leviticus 26 and Deuteronomy 28 prosperity is made to depend entirely on the fidelity of the Hebrews to the covenant of Yahweh; and these discourses appear to be a summary statement of the teaching of the prophets. A. C. Welch has written:

> God uses the outward world, its catastrophes and its blessings, to enforce the purpose which He is bringing to light in man; and in particular God moulded the outward world that He might manifest His purpose in the world through Israel. The position implies that nature is sacramental, and involves great consequences. . . .[66]

For the Hebrew, the order of nature is integrated into the moral and religious order. Its regularity is due to the will of a benevolent deity; but peaceful and orderly relations between God and man are conditioned upon man's submission to the divine regulation of human conduct. A disturbance in the moral order has an inevitable effect in the physical order; God employs the order of nature to chastise.

To the modern man, such an idea may seem childish and inadequate. He has been taught to interpret the course of nature as a regular succession of regular phenomena produced by causes acting according to their fixed natural properties. To him, there is really no such thing as irregularity or disorder in nature; what the Hebrew regarded as the sign of God's anger is equally the result of causes acting according to their properties. The Hebrew sees nature only as it has meaning for man; the scientific observer interprets nature in itself — forgetting, perhaps, the saying of Isaiah that "God formed the earth and established it; he did not make it a chaos, but formed it to be inhabited" (45:18). The modern man will object to the Hebrew conception of the course of nature as too crass and mechanical; and, while he admits that it rises to a higher ethical and theological level than the superstition of the Babylonian, he finds that it fails to interpret nature as it is; it is a "myth."

The idea of nature as sacramental, as Welch calls it, is found not only in the passages quoted above, but elsewhere in the Old Testament. It is implicit in the narrative of Genesis 3. The Old Testament sees a correlation between physical and moral evil, the one proceeding from the other. It bases this view on the unity of God, who is lord both of nature and of man, who has created nature "not a chaos, but to be inhabited"; who must, if He is to be consistent with Himself, manifest the same attributes in all His providence. The Hebrew sees sin not merely as moral, but as a cosmic disorder; and the very real personality which he saw in Yahweh responds personally to cosmic disorder. It is possible, of course, to take a mechanical view of this quality of Yahweh; but it was impossible for the Hebrew not to accept it as basic. As a *total* interpretation of reality, it is unscientific; in the same way, the scientific view, as a *total* interpretation of reality, is irreligious.

EXTRAORDINARY PHENOMENA OF NATURE

Hitherto we have considered what we would call the ordinary or regular phenomena of nature. Nature also exhibits herself in ways which we regard as in some way extraordinary or unusual. It is true, of course, that the modern man who has even a tincture of scientific information regards most "extraordinary" events as "regular." An eclipse, or the apparition of a comet, are "extraordinary," if we consider them in relation to a single lifetime; but they are "regular," in the sense that they follow known laws of nature. The Grand Canyon is "wonderful" only in the sense that it is singular, not in the sense that it is mysterious. In serious discussion, we reserve the words "wonderful" or "marvelous" for phenomena which are mysterious: of which we have no explanation in the laws of natural agents.

Modern Catholic theology distinguishes the "miraculous" from the "marvelous." The marvelous and the miraculous have this in common, that they excite wonder: and wonder arises ". . . because the events are rare, unexpected, from unknown causes, with a stupendous effect, or also because they surpass the power of natural causes."[67] The name "miracle" is applied to those effects which transcend the power of natural causes; otherwise, extraordinary phenomena are called "marvelous." The miraculous is a clear sign of divine intervention: "the ordinary event cannot be a sign leading to the recognition of the activity of an extraordinary agent. But the miracle is a sign of the special intervention of God."[68]

This conception of modern theology presupposes a philosophy of nature as a closed and unified system which is identical with that of classical science. It presupposes a knowledge of natural causes, and an analysis of their powers. It distinguishes clearly between effects which are within the competence of natural agents, and effects which surpass it; only the latter are attributed directly to the action of God. Natural phenomena which are rare, extraordinary, or which can be assigned to no definite cause, are called marvelous, providential, coincidental.

It should be noticed that this philosophy of nature and of natural causes is not, and does not pretend to be, a total and an adequate explanation of reality. For, taken by itself, it does not reckon with the divine action in ordinary phenomena; it tends to regard nature as a machine which, once it is set in motion, has within itself all its operative principles. In Catholic theology, of course, this notion is not taken by itself; the regular and ordinary course of nature is attributed to what theologians call the divine *concursus*. Neither is this concept an adequate explanation of reality; for it leads, if followed to its logical extreme, to an imagined distinction in the divine operation itself, which would be altogether unreal; the distinction exists in the kind of works produced, and not in the divine operation, which is one simple reality. Now the distinction in the kind of works produced is a distinction of the human mind, which distinguishes the miraculous from the marvelous; and this distinction is founded upon a concept of nature as a unity and a philosophy of nature which are the products of Greek thought and the modern natural sciences.

THE "MARVELOUS" IN THE BIBLE

Can such a distinction be attributed to the Hebrews? What did the marvelous mean to them? Wheeler Robinson has attempted to answer this question by going to the concordance.[69] I have checked his findings, and the results are interesting for the present discussion. Hebrew employs three words to signify the marvelous: *'ôt*, *môpēt*, and *pālā'*. The first meaning of these words seems to be: *'ôt*, a *sign*, something which attracts attention; *môpēt*, a *wonder* — in usage, it often signifies *portent*, a sign of a future event; *pālā'*, to *surpass* the ordinary or the expected. A study of the incidence of these words shows that they are applied with no distinction which corresponds to the modern *miraculous* and *marvelous*: *ôt* is applied to such things as Gideon's fleece (Jgs 6:17), the regression of the shadow on the sundial (Is 38:3–9; 2 Kgs 20:8–9), the proofs of Moses' commission (Ex 4:9, 28, 30), the plagues of Egypt and the events of the Exodus (twenty-five times out of seventy-nine, more frequently than to any other single item). On the other hand, the rainbow is an *'ôt* of the covenant (Gn 9:13), Isaiah and his sons are *'ôt* and *môpēt* to the Israelites (Is 8:18), and the strange conduct of Isaiah in walking barefoot and unclad is also an *'ôt* and a *môpēt* (Is 20:3). In these last two instances the words signify the remarkable and the portentous. The names of the sons of Isaiah, and his strange conduct, excite wonder and portend the future.

Môpēt is used once of the feats of a false prophet (Dt 13:2–3); this can scarcely be the work of Yahweh, but it excites wonder. The Psalmist in his afflictions is a *môpēt* (Ps 71:7) — again, an object of wonder. The idea that there is something awful and mysterious in great suffering appears elsewhere without the word (Jb 2:11–13; 6:21; Is 52:14–15). Ezekiel's grief for his wife is a *môpēt* (Ez 24:24, 27); it excites wonder and portends the future. The word is used thirty-six times, nineteen times of the plagues of Egypt.

The verb *pālā* appears most commonly in the Niphal plural participle, *niplā'ôt*. For this word Robinson suggests *wonders*. The verb is used of the crossing of the Jordan (Jos 3:5), and a number of times of the plagues of Egypt. It is used of a riddle which surpasses human understanding (Prv 30:18), of the mysteries of God (Ps 131:1), and of the mysteries of divine providence (Jb 42:3). Jonathan's love of David surpassed the love of women (2 Sm 1:26). The word is used of God's mysterious providence over Israel (Is 29:14); the element of mystery lies in the fact that it is Yahweh who is responsible for the woes of His own chosen people. The works of God which are called *niplā'ôt* are, most frequently, His works of judgment and redemption (Pss 9:2; 26:7; 40:6; 71:17; 75:2; 98:1; 105:2, 5; 106:22; 107:8, 15, 21, 31; 111:4; 145:5; Jer 21:2), sometimes for the people of Israel, sometimes for the individual; otherwise they are the works of creation (Jb 5:9; 9:10; 37:14; Pss 107:24; 136:4), or they are the works of God without specification (Pss 72:18; 86:10; 96:3; 119:18, 27). In later Hebrew, the word appears of human agents in an enfeebled sense (Dn 8:24; 11:26).

The use of these three words shows that none of them has the specialized theological sense of *miracle*. The common element in all the instances of these words is the wonderful, the marvelous; there is no analysis of the basis of the wonder, nor of the degrees in which *wonderful* may be predicated. The basis of wonder in the works of judgment and redemption is not the rare or the extraordinary, but the saving will of Yahweh toward His people; Yahweh is never more wonderful than when He appears as the helper and savior of Israel. Nor does the use of these words show that the

Hebrews had the idea of *miracle,* without a special word for it. The element of wonder in the works of creation is nowhere more emphatically proposed in the Old Testament than in the book of Job (4:8–10; 9:5–10; 26:5–14; 36:26–37:18). This wonder reaches its climax in the great speeches of Yahweh (38:1–41:26). The "wonders" here enumerated are the earth, the sea, light and darkness, rain, wind, snow and hail, the constellations, the lightning and the clouds, wild beasts and birds, the hippopotamus and the crocodile; they are all instances of the creative wisdom which surpasses human understanding. Throughout the book the wonderful and mysterious government by God of human events is illustrated by His wonders in nature; but these wonders are of the sort enumerated in the speeches of Yahweh. The author of the book here exhibits ways of thinking which are characteristic of the Old Testament. For him, every work of God, when examined, is wonderful. The whole creation speaks to him of the mysterious and overwhelming supremacy of God. It is less than just to say that this conception is founded merely on ignorance of physical agents and physical laws, on a simple and unscientific observation of nature. It is rather derived from a profound insight into the reality of God in nature, and the removal of any limitation of His power over nature. "Is anything too wonderful (*pālā'*) for Yahweh?" (Gn 18:14). St. Augustine has written a paragraph which is, in one respect, of a genuine "Hebrew" cast:

> The miracles which our Lord Jesus Christ accomplished are truly divine works, and they warn the human mind to perceive God in the visible world. For God is not the kind of substance which can be seen with the eyes, and the miracles by which he at once rules the whole world and administers the entire creation have grown ordinary by custom, so that almost no one takes the trouble to notice the wonderful and stupendous works of God in any one grain of seed; so according to his mercy he has preserved for himself certain things which he can do at the opportune time beyond the usual course and order of nature, so that those to whom his daily actions have grown ordinary may be stupefied at the sight not of what is greater, but of what is unusual. For the government of the entire universe is a greater

miracle than the feeding of five thousand men with five loaves; but no one wonders at the government; they marvel at the feeding of the five thousand not because it is greater, but because it is rare. For who is it that now feeds the whole world, if not he who creates the harvests from a few grains? So this is the way God acts.[70]

THAUMATURGY

It is marvelous also when Yahweh's power over nature is communicated to men. The most striking examples of this are Moses, Elisha, and Elijah. The prophetic narratives attribute much more thaumaturgic power to Elisha than to Elijah. The thaumaturgic power is treated as part of the prophetic power in Dt 13:2–3; there it is supposed to be possible even in a false prophet. But it is a remarkable fact that thaumaturgy plays no part in the mission of the Old Testament prophets, except for Elijah and Elisha. The thaumaturgy of Moses and Aaron is matched by the Egyptian magicians, up to a point at which the magicians are forced to admit that the finger of *Elohim* is at work (Ex 7:20–8:19); the idiom is that of the Hebrew narrator. It is not the intention of the author to imply that the finger of *Elohim* was not at work before this point, and still less that the Egyptian magicians have received from Yahweh occult powers over nature. The existence of magic and sorcery was taken for granted; the Hebrews made no effort to rationalize them. But the Hebrews were certain that the power of Yahweh was superior to any occult forces. Hebrew law prohibited the practice of the occult arts as contrary to the religion of Yahweh; no other ancient Semitic religion was so intolerant. Magic is a pretended control over natural forces and phenomena. The concept of Yahweh as creator and lord of nature left no room for such practices. Whatever might be the skills of the practitioners of these arts, the Hebrews knew that their pretensions were essentially false, although we find no effort to explain their feats as the work of fraud. If Yahweh chose to accomplish the same results through His own representatives, this was not due to any occult skill, but purely and simply to His own supreme will.

THE EVENTS OF THE EXODUS

The difference between the Hebrew and the modern attitude toward the wonderful is well illustrated in the events of the exodus. Of all the extraordinary events in Hebrew history, the most *wonderful* was the deliverance from Egypt: the classical interposition of Yahweh on behalf of His people. Here Yahweh had directed the cosmic forces to liberate His people from the land of bondage and bring them into the land which He had promised their fathers. The series of events, as it is related in Exodus, Numbers, and Joshua, comprises the following: the "plagues," a series of disasters which afflicted the Egyptians; the passage of the Red Sea (rather the northern extremity of the Gulf of Suez, wherever this is to be located in the thirteenth or twelfth century B.C.); the pillars of cloud and of fire; the marvelous provision of food and water in the desert; the passage of the Jordan; the fall of Jericho. The events of this series have one common feature: they are all phenomena for which the Hebrews had no explanation in the operations of natural forces.

This series of events made such a profound impression upon Hebrew tradition that modern historians, unlike those of earlier generations, are unwilling to treat them as purely imaginative. And the acceptance of the historical character of these events has educed a number of efforts to do what the Hebrews could not do: to discover what natural agents may have been at work. Alfred Guillaume has examined most of the miracles narrated in the Old Testament.[71] He thinks that modern science has in several cases provided the explanation: suggestion, as in cures; the magic arts, as for Moses, Elijah, and Elisha; the creation of legend, as in some of the Elijah stories; poetic imagery, as in the passage of the Red Sea and the story of Joshua and the sun; hypnotism, as in the story of Isaiah and the sundial, or that of Elisha and the Aramaean horsemen; coincidence in nature, as in the exodus narrative. In the exodus ". . . there was no miracle save the miracle of the revelation of God's purposes in history. The Hebrews themselves accepted these remarkable coincidences as indications that Yahweh had called them forth from Egypt because of His love for them and His desire to reveal Himself to them. To the Hebrews, they were examples of Yahweh's intervention in nature."[72]

W. J. Phythian-Adams has proposed a more elaborate analysis of the events of the exodus. At the center of all the phenomena he supposes volcanic activity at Mount Sinai (which must, therefore, be located in the volcanic plateau of northern Arabia) which had effects in Egypt and the rift of the Jordan valley, hundreds of miles away; and all the extraordinary phenomena of the exodus narrative are explained as volcanic, or as the effects of volcanic disturbances. Phythian-Adams does not on this account believe that the term *miracle* should not be applied to them. He finds in the events a threefold "Miracle of Coincidence"; "the Miracle of Material Coincidence: the impact of purely external phenomena upon the normal human senses of Israel and its enemies"; the Miracle of Spiritual Coincidence: "the presence, at that critical moment in the midst of Israel, of one who may justly be called its master-soul (Moses)"; "the Miracle of Sacramental Coincidence: the fact, namely, that there was in the nature of the phenomena themselves a reservoir of inexhaustible spiritual significance."[73] Spiritual coincidence, as enlarged by Wheeler Robinson, means ". . . the possibility of the continued and ever larger interpretation of the redemptive work of God which the subsequent religion of Israel actually displays." The same writer goes on to remark: "Our modern analysis of Biblical miracles so far as it accepts them as historical events of some kind or other, shows a longer and more complex chain of cause and effect than the Hebrews recognized; yet it still leaves open the equal possibility of faith in a divine Agent. . . . The essential truth for Biblical faith is that Nature, like history, is wholly under God's control; the manner of that control, which means the way in which successive generations formulate it for themselves, is of much interest, but in the long run of secondary importance."[74]

DIVINE ACTIVITY IN NATURE

What is to be said of such attempts to rationalize the events recorded in the Old Testament? They may proceed from a philosophical judgment that the miraculous in the theological sense is impossible. Such a judgment, founded upon a deistic view of nature as a closed and unified system (or expressed as a concession to this view), is irreconcilably opposed to the biblical idea of God and nature. But such efforts to rationalize do not, in themselves, imply such a theological judgment.[75] But they may not only carry the exegete beyond his task of interpretation; they are also likely to lead him to one of two extreme positions: either that the historical truth of the narratives can be preserved only by rationalizing the events; or that the objective veracity of the narrator can be defended only by supposing that the Hebrew's sense of the marvelous was the same as that of modern man. Such attempts at analysis are a purely modern discussion, which can be conducted only in terms of modern philosophy and science; once the discussion has been moved to this ground, we are out of touch with our Hebrew sources. If our study of the Hebrew idea of God and nature shows anything, it shows that the Hebrew sense of the divine activity in nature was much more profound than the modern sense. There can be no question that the Hebrews recognized a divine intervention in the events of the exodus, nor that they called that intervention marvelous; but they made no attempt to analyze the marvel, nor could they understand the question. The narratives are not the work of a dispassionate observer of natural phenomena, writing as the scientist reports a laboratory experiment; they are popular tradition. That which first seizes our attention is what the Hebrew narrator regarded as marvelous; and to him, the *marvelous* fact before all else was that Yahweh delivered His people from oppression and brought them into the land promised to their fathers. To accomplish this end, Yahweh disposed of nature as He disposed of men; for He is the lord of nature and the lord of history. The fundamental question about the narrative of the exodus is the fundamental question of the whole of Hebrew history: whether one accepts the effective divine interposition in human affairs as a fact and a factor in history. The modern view of God and nature which would not recognize an effective divine interposition through natural causes without the miraculous element cannot be reduced to the biblical idea of God and nature. The Hebrew mind, as it viewed God and nature, was not deceived if it recognized Him, without any analysis, in the extraordinary events which accompanied their deliverance, since they recognized His activity in the ordinary and regular succession of phenomena in ways in which modern man does not recognize it; how much more surely, then, is He active when nature contributes to the salvation of His elect. Here, as elsewhere in the Old Testament, nature is not reality considered in itself; it is under the sovereign control of Yahweh, and whatever happens in nature is His work, and has its place in His plan.

The Eschatological Consummation of Nature

Nature has its place also in the last act of human history — "the day of Yahweh." The judgment of Yahweh upon men touches the material universe also. An impressive passage of Jeremiah expresses this idea:

> I saw the earth — it was utter chaos;
> The heavens — their light was gone.
> I saw the mountains — they were quaking;
> All the hills — they were swaying to and fro.
> I looked — there was no man;
> And the birds of the heavens — all had flown away.
> I saw the garden land — it was a desert;
> And all its cities were torn down,
> Before Yahweh — before his fierce anger (4:23–26).

In apocalyptic passages the description is heightened to the utmost of the poet's ability. The earth becomes desolate, and the courses of the heavenly bodies are disturbed (Is 13:10; 24:3, 23; Jl 3:3–4; Am 8:9). The earth languishes and shakes under the vengeance of Yahweh (Is 13:3; 24:4, 19–20; Am 8:8; 9:5). Yahweh smites His draconic adversaries, Leviathan the fleeing serpent, and Leviathan the twisted serpent, and the dragon in the midst of the sea, as He smote them on the day of creation (Is 27:1). For the earth itself is conceived as sharing, in some mysterious way, the guilt of man:

> The earth is polluted under the feet of its inhabitants,
> Because they have violated laws, transgressed statutes,
> Voided the everlasting covenant (Is 24:5).

Therefore a curse devours the earth; as the earth itself was obliter-
ated in the Deluge because of universal sin; so in the day of
Yahweh nature must perish with those who sinned through her.
The author of the Wisdom of Solomon, a much later writer, who
was subject to some degree to the influence of Greek philosophy,
conceives nature as the weapon by which Yahweh punishes the
wicked (Wis 5:17–23; 11:15; 16:15–19:24). This is a schematiza-
tion of the idea which pervades so much of the Old Testament,
that the hostility of nature is the work of the wrath of Yahweh.

But the apocalyptic destruction of nature is a prelude to its messianic renewal. The desert will be transformed into fertile land
(Is 32:15; 35:1–2). Streams will burst forth in arid regions (Is
35:6–7; 41:18–20). Wild beasts will become tame and peaceful (Is
11:6–9). The fertility of the land will be marvelously great (Ez
36:6–12; Jl 4:18; Am 9:13–14). There will no longer be any alternation of seasons, nor even of day and night (Za 14:6–7). It is a
creation of a new heaven and a new earth (Is 65:17).

This aspect of the messianic hope of the Hebrews is derived from
their conception of God and nature. The material world is the scene
of human existence; they had no conception of an immaterial existence. But the material world is imperfect, sometimes destructive of
man's labors. This is due to the imperfect relationship between man
and the Creator. As long as man continues to irritate the anger of
Yahweh, this condition will endure. But in the messianic consummation the wrath of Yahweh will vanish; perfect righteousness will
mean the constant blessing of Yahweh upon nature. This has been
well stated by A. C. Welch:

> When God's kingdom came to pass on earth, it was to put
> right more than a human disorder, it must redress the order of
> nature. . . . Isaiah's expectation that, when God came to dwell
> with men on earth, all the disorder of nature was to cease, is
> the proof of how there had arisen in the mind of one who saw
> the world as governed by one supreme will to one sovereign end,
> and who looked for the divine intervention in the whole world-
> order, the sense that more needed to be set right than the rela-
> tions of men to each other. God, who was to make new condi-
> tions for His faithful people, was to make them not merely by

breaking the rod of the oppressor, but by renewing the earth, the fulness of which was His glory.[76]

Here, again, the Hebrew conception of nature diverges sharply from that of modern man. The conquest of nature and its subjugation to the will of man is both the boast and the ambition of modern science and technology. The removal of natural obstacles to human well-being, the conversion of natural sources of energy to man's uses, the conquest of disease, pests, aridity, inequalities of climate and soil — all these things, and many others, have been attacked, not without success, by modern techniques. If the Hebrew remained true to his idea of God and nature, he would have to regard such enterprises as futile; physical regeneration will come only as a result of moral regeneration. Before man can conquer nature, he must conquer himself. For nature is but an expression of the will of God; and it is the moral life of man which makes him, in biblical language, an object of divine love or of divine hatred.

SUMMARY AND CONCLUSION

In summary, then, a study of the idea of God and nature in the Old Testament seems to show that the Hebrews shared the basic idea of prescientific man that nature was "personalized"; it was not, to them, a unified system governed by "law." Like other ancient peoples, they had the idea of a creative deity; their idea of creation was distinguished by the absolute supremacy, independence, and unicity of this creative deity, less by any difference in the mode of creation, which they conceived as accomplished by word or by work. Creation they saw as a continuing process, exhibited anew in any single phenomenon. A common and characteristic representation of the sovereignty of Yahweh over nature was the literary device of the storm theophany; this showed His activity in the forces of nature. His sovereignty over nature was seen with particular clarity in the causes of natural fertility; this emphasis came as a consequence of the combat between Hebrew and Canaanite religion. They saw nature as integrated into the moral and religious order; it was the expression of the blessing or of the wrath of Yahweh, which came as a response to human behavior. They did not distinguish miraculous effects of the divine causality, since they were without a philosophy of nature; they saw the marvelous rather in Yahweh's works of salvation on behalf of His people. A final establishment of perfect righteousness must mean a destruction of the sinful world and a renewal, or, rather, a re-creation of a world which exhibits perfect harmony.

.7.

The Hebrew Attitude Toward
Mythological Polytheism

STUDENTS of the Old Testament are familiar with certain prophetic passages in which polytheism is attacked.[1] They have noticed that the prophets, in these passages, seem to identify the god with the image, and to scoff at idolatry as folly because it is the worship of wood and stone, the work of men's hands. Aware that ancient polytheism did not simply identify the god and the image, they have been puzzled by what seems to be at best an oversimplification of polytheistic religion. If the student goes to the standard commentaries, he will not find them of much assistance; and so he finds it easier to treat these passages as a literary conceit, an ironical *tour de force*, and go on his way.[2] He has not thought of finding in them a key to the basic pattern of the attitude of the Old Testament toward polytheism.

Yehezkel Kaufmann published an article in the early 1950's in which the common understanding of these passages is completely reversed.[3] His thesis, briefly, is that the Old Testament "shows absolutely no apprehension of the real character of mythological religion." Kaufmann defines three elements of mythological polytheism: the deification of natural phenomena; myth; and the deification of material objects, natural or artificial. Kaufmann asserts that the Old Testament shows no awareness of belief in mythological deities, no knowledge that the heathen worshiped personalized deities. The Old Testament accepts mythology because it is ignorant of the contacts between mythology and religion. The only false

133

god the Old Testament knows is the idol itself, and the only idolatry the Old Testament knows is fetishism. The Old Testament admits the efficacy of sorcery, but it does not admit any divine activity in magic and sorcery. Hebrew law does not proscribe belief in heathen gods or the recounting of heathen myths; it prohibits the worship of idols or the heavenly bodies. It does not forbid images of Yahweh, but "the making of gods." There is no polemic against heathen religion except the contention that it is folly to apotheosize material objects; the Old Testament never advances the basic reason, the denial of the reality of the gods. Consequently, the syncretism which many writers have found in Hosea, the mingling of Yahwism and Baalism, is a product of scholarly romancing.

Where, then, did the Hebrews form their ideas of idolatry? Kaufmann asserts that Israel was as ignorant of heathen religion as the heathens were ignorant of Hebrew religion. The only idolatry the Old Testament knows is the preexilic idolatry of Israel itself; and this idolatry is proved from the texts to have been fetishism. This the Old Testament writers ignorantly attributed to the heathens also. Israel "had no vital, fundamental, psychic experience of polytheism." This has interesting consequences for the history of the development of Hebrew religion. Kaufmann does not admit that the monotheism of the Old Testament arose in any way from a conflict with idolatry; it was the product of an intuitive creation which preceded the conflict. Furthermore, the religion of the Old Testament is not the work of one or a few men of outstanding genius; it is an "intuitive folk-creation," the work of a whole people, and it was formed in the initial period of Israel's existence as a people.

Kaufmann's proposition supposes a view of Israel's religious isolation which is in contradiction to the generally accepted view, and approaches the theories of the early Wellhausen period. Kaufmann does not generalize about Israel's cultural isolation, and so I have not thought it necessary to enter into this question; it is an accepted conclusion of modern scholarship that the thesis of Israel's cultural isolation cannot be seriously sustained. But Kaufmann believes that Israel's religious isolation was as it should be: "every creative sphere is isolated from its surroundings in the same manner."

The question which Kaufmann raises is not whether the Hebrews were opposed to mythological polytheism, but whether they even knew what it was: not whether the religion of the Hebrews was distinctive, but whether its unique character did not prevent them from grasping, even in the most simple and elementary manner, the mind of polytheism. The gods of polytheism are mentioned many times in the Old Testament, often by name, but most commonly as "gods"; if Kaufmann's thesis is correct, in each of these instances is meant not the conception of a personalized higher being, but the image. Baalim and Ashtaroth, Chemosh, Milcom, Dagon, Bel, and others are the material images which appeared in the temples. Kaufmann affirms that there is no allusion to the natural functions of these gods, to their character as deified natural phenomena. This may be conceded; on the other hand, there is no allusion to the identity of god and image, except in the peculiar polemical passages. In general, the Hebrews speak of other gods as we would expect them to.

That there is no allusion to their natural functions, or to their character as deified natural forces, is not altogether true; and not too much should be erected upon the fact that such allusions are rare. A study of the descriptions of the gods in the religious literature of Babylonia and Assyria, for instance, would not betray many such allusions. We do not assume that every deity of polytheism arises from the deification of natural forces; indeed, such an assumption is impossible. In the phase of religion which is represented by the literature of Mesopotamia, the personalization of the deity, or his connection with a particular locality, often has so obscured his "natural functions" that it is difficult, or impossible, to determine his original character. Modern scholars frankly confess that they do not know the original character of Ashur. The uncertainty is only slightly less, if it is less at all, concerning the original character of Marduk.[4] Yet here are two of the greatest of the gods of Mesopotamia. The Hebrews could not have alluded to their natural functions, nor to their character as deified natural forces, because there is no way in which they could have known them. We cannot expect the writers of the Old Testament to refer to the gods of the heathen as a modern historian of religion refers to them.

The attitude of the Old Testament toward mythology is not altogether the same as its attitude toward polytheism. We agree with Kaufmann that there is no trace of any admission of the reality of the gods of polytheism; but the Old Testament is more hospitable toward mythology. There is, as Kaufmann says, no mythology in the Old Testament, and the religion of the Old Testament is nonmythological; but there are mythological allusions, employed as poetic ornament.[5] The Hebrews were not, therefore, ignorant of mythology; but Kaufmann supposes that they never realized its significance, and, consequently, "there is no explicit word of polemic against heathen myth."

Let us examine this question more closely. The two great myths of Semitic polytheism were the myth of creation and the myth of the death and resurrection of the god of fertility. These were combined into one great myth and ritual of the renewal of the cycle of fertility. Not until modern times has anything been known of this mythology, so obscure and scattered are the allusions to it in the Old Testament, so that, at first glance, Kaufmann's thesis may seem extremely probable in this respect. Of the myth of the dying and rising god, I think we may say that this was so abhorrent to Hebrew religious sentiment that the Old Testament writers refused even to mention it, although we are now in a position to know some of the reasons why they spoke of the Baal cultus with such asperity, why it was called "harlotry." But these are references rather to the external features and practice of the cultus, and do not touch precisely the questions raised by Kaufmann. But the Hebrew attitude toward the myth of creation was somewhat different.

Kaufmann's statement that there is "no explicit word of polemic against heathen myth" can be reconciled with the creation account of Genesis 1 only by splitting a hair on the word "explicit." It is no longer possible to assert that the author of this account was ignorant of the myth of creation.[6] The points of contact between Genesis 1 and the *Enuma Elish* have been studied, it appears, exhaustively; but we need not suppose that the writer knew the myth

precisely in this form, since we know that it existed in a number
of variant forms. The myth, however, was one in substance: creation was imagined as the victory of the creative deity over a chaotic
monster. If Genesis 1 is not a polemic against the creation myth,
then I find it impossible to explain why the story was put in this
form at all. And the character of other allusions to the myth of
creation points to the same idea. If creation is imagined as the
victory of the creative deity over chaos, then it is Yahweh to whom
this victory must be attributed. But there was not, and could not
have been, any Hebrew mythology of creation.

The question of Canaanite Baalism demands a particular examination; if the Hebrews knew any form of polytheism, they knew this
form, and, conversely, if they did not know this form, they did
not know any. Kaufmann's position is that the Old Testament knows
no polytheism except the polytheism of preexilic Israel, and that
this was fetishism, without gods and without mythology. The god
was the image, the material object; there was no imagined personalized being which the image represented. This was the only
idolatry which the Old Testament writers knew, and it is against
this that their strange polemic was directed, because they ignorantly
attributed the superstitions of their own people to all other peoples.

Whatever may be said of the texts adduced to prove the existence
of such a peculiarly Hebrew idolatry, it is an uncontested fact that
the superstition which is most vigorously combated in the Old
Testament is the worship of the Canaanite Baal; and this worship
is consistently called "foreign," the worship of "stranger" gods,
something alien to the Hebrew traditions and ethos. This fact has
not escaped Kaufmann; native superstition, he declares, was constantly nourished from foreign sources. Such a conception does not
seem to take the words of the Old Testament seriously. The cult
against which the prophets contended can now be fairly well defined; the Old Testament calls it by its proper name, and alludes to
it in terms which are intelligible against a Canaanite background.
Every feature of the Baal cult which is mentioned in the Old
Testament — the high place, the *massebah*, the *asherah*, ritual
prostitution, human sacrifice — is found in Canaanite religion; and,
in addition, the Old Testament calls it the worship of foreign gods.

If such things do not indicate the adoption of a foreign cult, we may ask how the adoption of a foreign cult could ever be determined.

Scholars have long seen in Hosea evidence of a syncretism of Yahwism and Baalism in this sense, that the traits of the Baal and the rites by which he was worshiped were attached to Yahweh. To Kaufmann, such syncretism is the "product of scholarly romancing"; syncretism was impossible in Israel, because its ideological basis was lacking. The Baal was the image. Without entering into the question of syncretism (I have indulged in such "scholarly romancing" elsewhere), the Baal was to the Israelites, according to Hosea, the god who gave Israel its grain, wine and oil (Hos 2:7); this is certainly not ignorance of the natural functions of the Baal, and scarcely suggests an unawareness of the nature of mythological deities. There is not a word in Hosea to indicate that he identifies the Baal and the image; if he does, it is certainly not uppermost in his mind.

Kaufmann's selection of passages from the historical books to support his contention is, perhaps, too highly selective. What he has done is to adduce some passages in which the image is called the god. This is a point of some importance, which I shall treat at greater length below. At the moment, let us consider his use of the words of the Assyrian commander before Jerusalem as exhibiting the Hebrew attitude as he conceives it (2 Kgs 18:17–19:19). We have, of course, the substance of the Assyrian's words as reported by a Hebrew narrator. Kaufmann asserts that the speaker distinguishes between Yahweh, a living God, and the lifeless gods of the nations which he has conquered. This is not exactly the sense of the words which the Hebrew writer puts in the Assyrian's mouth. He does admit the reality of Yahweh; but he does not deny the reality of the gods of other nations. He admits the reality of Yahweh precisely as a polytheist would admit the reality of the gods of other peoples. But he denies that either Yahweh or the gods of other nations has the power to halt his march of conquest. The blasphemy of his speech, in the mind of the Hebrews, lay exactly in this, that he thinks Yahweh no better than the gods of the peoples he has conquered. Strictly speaking, the speech is not perfectly consistent; the Assyrian claims a commission from Yahweh (18:25), and then denies Yahweh's power to save Jerusalem (18:35). Now for a Hebrew writer to compose such a speech some insight into the mind of polytheism is necessary. To the Assyrian's claim of a commission from Yahweh may be compared Esarhaddon's explanation of the destruction of Babylon by his father Sennacherib: "Anger seized the lord of the gods, Marduk. For the overthrow of the land and the destruction of its people he devised evil plans."[7] Such a statement is unusual in the Assyrian records; the Assyrian kings usually treated their conquests as a demonstration of the superiority of the gods of Assyria over other gods. Babylon was a special case. But the Hebrew narrator could scarcely have shown a finer insight into the mind of polytheism if he had been a polytheist himself.

Two texts from the narrative passages have been briefly dismissed by Kaufmann: "awareness of the mythological nature of the gods is totally absent." The first is the famous text of Judges 11:24, in which Jephthah compares Yahweh's gift of Canaan to Israel with Chemosh's gift of land to the Ammonites. In the tradition Chemosh, god of Moab, has been confused with Milcom, god of Ammon; but this makes no difference. In the idiom of Jephthah, Chemosh does for the Ammonites what Yahweh does for the Israelites, an idiom which the king of Ammon could understand. The text was a classic argument to show that early Israelites admitted the existence of other gods. This it does not show; but it shows even less that Jephthah identified Chemosh with the material image.

The second text which Kaufmann has barely noticed is the story of Elijah on Mount Carmel (1 Kgs 18:20–46). Here, as in the whole Elijah pericope, the struggle is directed against the Canaanite Baal. There is no mention of the image as the center of the cult, and nothing to suggest that Baal, either in the mind of Elijah or in that of the worshipers of the Baal, was identical with the image. The irony with which Elijah taunts the priests of the Baal cannot be reconciled with the denial of a personalized being behind the phenomena. If this is not "polemic against the conception of a mythological Baal," "evidence for belief in a mythological Baal," then we may, once again, wonder what form such evidence and such polemic could take which would identify them beyond all doubt. And it should be noticed that these two passages are not isolated heterogeneous blocks; they employ the common Old Testament idiom and exhibit the common linguistic and ideological background.

The Hebrew codes of law are generally concerned with cultic practices. The rites, ceremonies, and apparatus of polytheistic worship are not to be introduced into the Hebrew community, neither in honor of Yahweh nor of a heathen god. In this sense it is true, as Kaufmann says, that Hebrew law does not proscribe belief in other gods. But, if we are to take words so narrowly, it may equally well be said that it does not prescribe belief in Yahweh. Hebrew law prescribes the worship of Yahweh alone, and strictly forbids the worship of other gods; "belief," in the modern sense, was a concept which does not appear in the ancient Hebrew mind. Where we speak of "belief," "faith," the Hebrew spoke of the "knowledge of Yahweh," "fear of Yahweh"; these are the basic religious words of the Hebrews, and these are presupposed rather than prescribed in Hebrew law, which is directed to external conduct rather than internal sentiments.

There is one sentence in the law codes which does touch upon the idea of belief; it is found in the opening words of the Decalogue (Ex 20:3; Dt 5:7): "You shall have no other gods before me" ('al pānāy, beside me, in my presence, as my equal). If this text were interpreted in Kaufmann's sense, it would make Yahweh Himself an image. Therefore Kaufmann gives the verse special treatment: "[It] may be interpreted as prohibiting the deification of any other spiritual being; it is perhaps directed against a belief in gods. If so, we have preserved in this passage a vestige of the fight against heathenism which took place in Israel with the advent of monotheism." It cannot escape notice that Kaufmann is forced to treat this verse as a fugitive piece. If one is unimpeded by Kaufmann's theory, one sees in the verse a prohibition of the worship of those personalized beings behind the phenomena which the heathen called gods — indeed, against the very belief in such beings. Effectively, it is an affirmation of the exclusive and unique divinity of Yahweh; the Hebrews may not affirm divinity of any other being. Again, the verse falls easily into the common Hebrew idiom, without recourse to any "vestigial" explanation.

The verse can scarcely be understood of images, since it is followed immediately by the prohibition of images. For Kaufmann, this is a prohibition of the "making of gods"; the Hebrews are not to make images "to adore them." Images are prohibited, therefore, because in ancient Hebrew superstition the image was the god. There is no prohibition of images of Yahweh.

Yet the Hebrews did not make images of Yahweh. What we gather from the Old Testament is confirmed by Palestinian archaeology. Albright and others have shown that the calf images of Samaria were not representations of Yahweh, but of the throne upon which He stood invisibly.[8] Here is one of the most striking and distinctive features of Yahwism; there was no other god in the ancient world without his image, and Kaufmann's theory offers no reason for this except that Hebrew law prohibited fetishism, and omitted to prevent the greatest danger of all, that Yahweh Himself should become a fetish. No convincing reason for the absence of images of Yahweh has been adduced except the Hebrew belief that Yahweh could not be represented by image. He was transcendent, "wholly other." The gods of the nations could be represented by image because they did not differ in essence from the elements of the visible universe. To represent Yahweh by image would be to reduce Him to their level.

Kaufmann links magic and divination to mythological religion. Although the question is extremely complex, one may question on general principles whether this connection should be made so simply.[9] The attitude of the Old Testament toward magic and divination is not the same as its attitude toward polytheism. The sorcerer and the diviner exist in actual fact, and their skills are accepted. The Old Testament neither affirms the truth of their claims nor denies it; it simply rejects the practices as foreign to Yahwism, without any analysis of these arts, nor of the causes of any success they may exhibit or claim. Yahweh is not with the practitioners of these arts, and there is no other god who could be with them.

But I believe that Kaufmann has drawn a false contrast between the Hebrew rejection of magic and the heathen acceptance of it. It is true that the Hebrews admitted no divine activity in magic and divination; but the heathens practiced these arts in spite of their religion, not because of it. Magic is opposed to religion, even to a false religion, for the power to which it appeals is not "divine," even in the diluted sense of "divine" which we find in polytheism. It is, precisely, "magical": impersonal, automatic, not the expression of a personal will, and subject to the control of no personal will except through the set formulae of the art. The ancient Semites did not attribute magical results to the divine power any more than the Hebrews did.[10]

The considerations presented so far certainly help, I believe, to define more sharply in our own mind the Hebrew attitude toward mythological polytheism; but they do not touch directly the question with which I introduced this paper, the question of the prophetic polemic against idolatry. There it appears, at first glance, that the writers identify the god and the image, not only in their own minds, but in those of their worshipers. The most original explanation of these passages which I have seen is offered by H. H. Rowley. This polemic he calls an expression of the Hebrew denial of the reality of the gods. The heathens worshiped the god behind the image. To the Hebrews, however, there was no reality behind the image; therefore the worship was actually directed to the image itself.[11] The distinction may appear too subtle; yet it is easier to accept some such explanation than to accept the hypothesis that the Old Testament writers were totally ignorant of the character of polytheistic religion. There are two points, I believe, which may be noticed in this connection.

The first point is the poverty of Hebrew idiom, especially in the expression of abstract concepts. Hebrew has no word for false god, just as it has no word for false prophet. Guillet has pointed out that the Hebrew thought of truth as something substantial; falsehood is unsubstantial, a kind of embodied nothing.[12] But even the words for "god" in Hebrew are not susceptible of refinement and precision of expression. Hebrew had no words for god except 'ēl, 'ᵉlōhīm; to express its own peculiar concept of deity, which was applicable to Yahweh alone, it had no word except the name

Yahweh itself. The words for god had, in Hebrew as in other Semitic idioms, a broader use than the Hebrew concept of deity, strictly speaking, would permit.[13] Their religious ideas ran ahead of their vocabulary. Yahweh alone was *'elōhīm*. But Hebrew idiom knew being concretely at two levels: the world of *'elōhīm* and the terrestrial world. The upper world was the world of Yahweh; the gods of the heathen had no place in the world of *'elōhīm*. But neither did they exist in the terrestrial world; they were simply nowhere. The Hebrew was incapable of describing them as "figments of the imagination," of attributing to them that reality which the scholastics call *esse intentionale;* what had reality, to the Hebrew, was objective and external. What was objective and external was the image, nothing else. But the image was not *'elōhīm*, and did not possess life; Yahweh alone was a living *'elōhīm*. This was the error of polytheism, that it attributed divinity and personality to a subject which did not possess it, which had, indeed, no reality, no substance.

The second point is the significance which the image had in ancient Semitic polytheism. This is somewhat obscure, and perhaps we shall never reconstruct the idea exactly; it is difficult to formulate the irrational. Kaufmann seems to treat the image as purely representational. This is entirely at variance with the findings and the theories of modern comparative religion. Van der Leeuw states that the essential factor in the image is power, power which comes from the actual presence of the divine; Lehmann speaks of the presence of the god in the image, a kind of identification of the god and his image. The most recent and thorough study of the divine image in Israel and the ancient Near East, that of Hubert Schrade, affirms the identity of the god and the image in ancient Near Eastern religions too sharply, if anything; certainly Schrade leaves no room for mere representationalism.[14]

These generalities are borne out by an examination of the place of the image in the temple and the cult. Oppenheim tells us of the consecration which transformed the images into "living" things: "in the cuneiform religious texts . . . the deity actually 'lived.'" The image received all the attentions which the servants of the human king gave to their lord. In the Babylonian cultus, in particular, which centered about a movable image, the treatment of the image as a living being is plainly apparent, and goes beyond any possible comparison with the treatment which is given to such symbols as the flag or the religious image in modern civic or religious ceremonial. No conclusion is possible except that Semitic polytheism believed in some sort of identity between the image and the deity beyond that of representation.[15]

The Old Testament speaks of the image as the god; but in this respect it does not differ from Babylonian and Assyrian idiom. Without going beyond Luckenbill's *Ancient Records,* one may without difficulty collect a considerable number of texts in which the writers speak of the god or the gods where the image is evidently supposed. Assyrian kings carry off, or smash, or cut to pieces the gods of conquered cities. Esarhaddon restored to Babylon its gods, which his father Sennacherib had carried off; Ashurbanipal brought back Nana to her proper residence after she had been kept in Elam for 1635 years.[16] The Hebrew idiom is often in perfect harmony with this. Far from ignorance of polytheistic belief, Hebrew idiom shows an acquaintance with polytheistic belief which is more accurate than we might expect. This should not surprise us; since the discovery of the ancient Semitic world in the nineteenth century we know that the Old Testament shows a keen observation of the world in which the Hebrews lived.

It is extremely difficult, then, to admit the hypothesis of the religious isolation of ancient Israel. The Hebrews were in constant close contact with peoples whose religion was mythological polytheism — Philistines, Canaanites, Moabites, Ammonites, Egyptians, Assyrians, Babylonians, Aramaeans. The excavations of Hebrew sites have revealed a large number of artifacts which belong to mythological polytheism.[17] The very temple of Solomon was modeled after Canaanite temples, and priesthood and sacrifice had certain external elements in common with the priesthood of other Semitic peoples.[18] In addition to this, the idiom of the Old Testament is, with a few exceptions, what we should expect it to be; and these exceptions, I believe, can be made to fit the general pattern. It is true that many of these elements are external; but that familiarity with polytheism, such as these external elements demonstrate, could be accompanied by a total ignorance of the mind of polytheism is a postulate which cannot easily be granted. Hebrew literature mentions foreign religions more frequently, and with more detail, than does any other body of ancient Semitic literature. If this be ignorance, then we can never detect knowledge.

Kaufmann has concluded that the religion of Israel is "an intuitive folk-creation," not the work of one or a few great men. I pass over this conclusion because it does not follow at all from his thesis, even if it were demonstrated, and because it leads us into a field of sociological theory from which I, as an exegete, would prefer to abstain. The school of social thought which is associated with the name of Emile Durkheim has had a notable influence on New Testament criticism and exegesis, less on Old Testament study. It should not be antecedently judged as valueless; the idea of the community in the life of ancient Israel was so different from its idea in modern life that it is fully deserving of closer study. But it should not become a dominant factor, a ready answer to all questions and a universal solution of all problems; history resists ironclad theorizing in any form. I fear that Kaufmann's sociological theories have led him into an untenable position; his conclusion that the religion of Israel is an "intuitive folk-creation" really preceded his argument that the ancient Hebrews were ignorant of the nature of mythological polytheism. The argument has here been examined, I believe, on its own proper grounds, which are historical; on these grounds I find it, at least as it is proposed here, unacceptable.

.8.

The Literary Characteristics of Genesis 2–3

By the literary characteristics of Genesis 2–3, I mean the literary species of the passage as a whole, its relations to extrabiblical literature, and its unity.

A consideration of these questions leads one at once into the enormous mass of literature on the Paradise narrative, which I make no attempt to review. Feldmann's review in 1913 issued in a book of over 600 pages. I must take most previous studies for granted, referring by choice only to those which are more recent or of more permanent influence upon exegesis. I make no pretence of having seen all the literature.

A Review of Opinion

As far back as 1913, Feldmann accepted the judgment of Lagrange and others that the Paradise story is not literal history, nor allegory, nor myth, but "folklore." Lagrange classified Genesis 1–11 as "primitive history." History rests upon chronology and geography; these are not found in Genesis 1–11.[1] Oral tradition "cannot preserve facts and circumstances without the help of some very definite point by which to fix their position in time and place."[2] Tradition hands down certain customs. Tales often told and diffused in different places lose their original proper names and local color. "If memories fail, tradition creates."[3] There is no "real history" in the Bible extending from the first man down to Jesus Christ.[4] The primitive history of the Bible differs from such historical works as the books of Kings. On the other hand, it has drawn nothing from

146

the Babylonian stories.[5] Primitive history is not myth, but it has an external resemblance to myth.[6] These stories relate some events which, like those of mythology, are unreal, and there is no reason to think that the author of the stories believed in the reality of the fact.[7] "Legendary primitive history has its place between the myth, which is the story of things personified and deified, and real history."[8] There are no historical records of the time before Abraham.[9] "When the Bible tells us that the arts developed little by little, that nomadic life gradually assumed its own general characteristics, different from those of town life, that men did not always play the kinnor and flute, nor work brass and iron — it is impossible otherwise to conceive the beginning and progress of civilization. But can that be said to constitute history, duly noted and handed down?"[10] The proper names in these chapters are not historical; often they are etiological, and thus obviously invented — such as Jubal (the musician), the father of all musicians. "It was quite out of the question to write real history. . . . The Bible is taken up with tangible things, with discoveries which are still known; it relates their origin and progress, and leaves them in a hazy light, which has no outward semblance of actual history. . . . Could the author have told us more clearly that there exists no history of these periods?"[11] The Israelites, unlike the Greeks, often merge the ancestor with his descendants.[12] Lagrange sets Genesis 2–3 aside; but when he resumes its consideration, he does not understand it as outside the class of primitive history. "On account of the Church's definition, I believe in original sin according to the Church's definition; but abstracting from this dogmatic point, based upon the unshakeable foundation of revelation, there can be no objection to assigning primitive history its true character."[13]

Lagrange denies the presence of myth, but admits mythological traits. He attributes some subtlety to the author in thinking that the author was aware of the unreality of some elements of his stories; this opinion agrees with the more recent judgment of scholars on ancient authors and their material.

Feldmann also accepted the "historical-folklore" interpretation. He finds that in principle it already existed in Christian antiquity.[14] The historical nucleus of the events narrated is vested in details which do not correspond to reality in the proper sense. Comparison shows not only a close connection between the traditions of different peoples, but elements in the Israelite form which are common to ancient Oriental modes of thought. It is quite probable that the Jahwist was acquainted with the modes. He was free to use ideas which were current among his people, derived either from common ancestors or from exchange with neighboring peoples, to represent truths and events of profound significance. The Paradise of the past, like the biblical Paradise of the world to come, is artistically described. The author of the Paradise narrative was not the man to regard the details of his story as historically real.[15]

The interpretation which Heinisch presents in his commentary is more conservative than that of either Lagrange or Feldmann.[16] He assumes as probable that the story rests on an immediate revelation to Moses. He follows what he himself calls a "historical-allegorical" interpretation. This means that the historicity of the story in essential points is maintained, while freedom in conception and form is admitted. The essential points, according to Heinisch, are those mentioned in the *quaesitum* to which the response of 1909 was given. In discussing these points, Heinisch distinguishes between the formal element and the religious element. Heinisch thinks it impossible to distinguish in every detail where the author represents reality, and where he presents doctrine under the vesture of images. These ideas are not modified in his more recent work, with two rather important exceptions: he withdraws the hypothesis of immediate revelation to Moses, and does not think that the existence of an original tradition can be affirmed with all certainty.[17]

A. Bea, S.J., commenting on the response of 1948, has pointed out that the first task of exegesis is to determine the intention of the sacred writer.[18] The intention of the author is manifested in his manner of speaking, the concrete circumstances in which he writes, and his choice of literary form. Genesis 1–11 appears in the dress of a historical narrative; but the meaning of *history* must be determined. In the literature of the ancient Semitic peoples, history means the transmission of particular facts in the form of annals, a mixed presentation of facts and legends or myths, or popular tradition orally transmitted. It is for the exegete to determine what events and doctrines the sacred author intended to relate, speaking the language of his time, using the literary forms of his contemporaries, speaking to a people of a determined profane, intellectual, and religious culture.[19] To accomplish this, all the scientific, paleontological, historical, epigraphic, and literary material must be collated.[20]

A recent French Catholic commentator on Genesis, the lamented J. Chaine, has followed the lines of Lagrange.[21] After pointing out the resemblances and the dissimilarities between Genesis 2–3 and other ancient Oriental material, he asks how such "special resemblances" and such "profound differences" are to be explained.

He rejects the hypothesis of a primitive tradition: "we must take our stand upon the level of revelation."[22] The religious truths of creation and the fall came to the Hebrews by the revelation of God to their ancestors. In the oral transmission of these truths they were invested with the concepts and images proper to the times and the people; and these were the concepts and images of the ancient Semitic world. "See why it is necessary to distinguish clearly religious truth and its expression; it is this distinction which allows us to explain the differences and the resemblances which exist between the first chapters of Genesis and the Assyro-Babylonian texts."[23]

Hermann Gunkel's treatment of folklore has had such widespread and lasting influence that we must recall at least its main lines; his introduction to Genesis has affected all subsequent commentators, whether they accept his propositions or not. Gunkel begins by observing that historiography in the modern sense does not appear among uncultivated peoples. Before history is written, the events of the past are recounted in popular tradition (*Sage*).[24] Popular tradition is thus defined by Gunkel: "popular and poetic narratives of ancient tradition, which treat of persons or events in the past."[25] He gives six sets of criteria by which folklore is distinguished from history. (1) Folklore originally appears in oral tradition, history as written documents. Folklore arises in cultural levels which do not write; and oral tradition is not of such a character as to maintain itself pure through a prolonged series of transmission. To folklore are due variant forms of one and the same account.[26] (2) Folklore deals with personal and family stories; history is concerned with great events of public interest.[27] (3) History, to be credible, must be traced back to firsthand evidence; folklore is dependent both on tradition and on imagination. Folklore cannot preserve minute details of a narrative; these are supplied by the imagination of the raconteurs, which, again, exhibits itself in variant forms of a single account.[28] (4) The "most significant" criterion of folklore is that it narrates the impossible. Gunkel does not mean here the miraculous element. Here are some of his illustrations: the number of animals in the ark; Ararat, the highest mountain on earth; the reality of the firmament; the origin of the stars after the plants; the derivation of all the streams of the earth from a single source; the chronology of 2666 years from the creation to the Exodus.[29] (5) Comparison of folklore both with certainly historical Hebrew narratives (such as 2 Sm 9–20) and with folklore of other peoples. The differences, in one case, and the similarities, in the other, show us the type.[30] (6) the poetic tone of folklore. History is prose and prosy; folklore is poetic by nature. This is not, says Gunkel, a hostile judgment, but an understanding of the nature of literature. Folklore must delight, elevate, inspire, console; to measure it by the standards of prose is barbarism ("es gibt auch fromme Bar-baren").[31] Bea has well pointed out that the ancients knew only three ways of recounting the past: annals, mixture of myth and legend, and folklore.[32] Whenever an ancient source goes beyond the mere annalistic recording of facts, the elements of folklore begin to appear. This means that it exhibits a poetic and imaginative character, a freely inventive embodying of the event which it recounts.

Gunkel goes on to distinguish two types of folklore in Genesis: (1) the traditions of the origin of the world and the primitive ancestors of man (Gn 1–11); (2) the traditions of the patriarchs. He finds two conceptions of God in these groups. In the early traditions God is viewed more universally; the narratives tell of His fearful judgments and suppose a great cleft between God and man, while God is, at the same time, represented anthropomorphic-ally, and the divine action is, with a few exceptions, the central feature of the story. These Gunkel contrasts with the patriarchal narratives, which have their scene in Canaan; which deal with a single family and its relations with God; in which God manifests His favor rather than His judgments; in which men are the chief actors. Because of these differences, Gunkel calls the first group "faded myths." But the myth is a *Göttergeschichte*. Genesis, he says, contains no myths in the true sense. But these stories show mythological traits which are derived from Semitic myths. Like the etiological myths, they answer certain questions. It is here that the Israelites give their own peculiar interpretation of certain universal human problems, the most profound questions of the whole race.

In considering the artistic form of the folklore of Genesis, Gunkel first asks whether it is prose or poetry; and, with almost all exegetes, he denies any metrical form.[33] A second characteristic is archaism; the stories were already old when they were put in writing. Are they, then, the work of a single author, or the common possession of the people? Certainly a single mind stands at the beginning; but they come to us through many hands, each of which has left its impression, so that they have become a common possession.

A highly important question is the unity of the legend.[34] One may consider the unity of the whole Pentateuch, or of Genesis, or of the "folklore book," of the folklore cycle, of the single tradition; which of these is decisive? Gunkel answers that folklore, of its very nature, consists of single traditions; the single tradition is the unit of which the larger unities are composed. Therefore each individual story is first of all to be interpreted in itself. The "context" of the cycle or the book is of later origin. The story in its earliest form is short; artistic elaboration is a work of later and more cultivated minds. The number of actors is small, two or three. The story unfolds itself in scenes, which are often variations of the same pattern.[35] The principal characters are not delineated; a single episode exhibits one or two traits of their character. Hence the principal actors appear as types rather than as individual personalities. In some cases the types represent peoples or social classes. In a folklore cycle, of course, the character of the hero takes on a more definite form.

Folklore and its oral tradition by their very nature antedate written documents; hence the history of the tradition, as sketched by Gunkel, is of necessity highly speculative.[36] Some of the folklore is of foreign origin; for the primitive history Gunkel accepts the theory of Mesopotamian provenance. But folklore in general is not of a uniform character; the diversity of origin is evident from the diversity of details and background. For the folklore of Genesis, Gunkel indicates a number of such heterogeneous elements. Foreign elements are, as far as their religious character is concerned, brought into harmony with Israelite conceptions; and Gunkel thinks that this assimilation can be traced in other details also. Folklore which was associated with one particular place was often contaminated by the folklore of another place or circle; and a similar contamination occurs when stories of diverse origin are collected into a cycle. The same phenomenon is observed of time; the background of the story is changed by changed conditions. The key to these divergences, according to Gunkel, is the variations which can be observed in different forms of one and the same story. In particular, Gunkel calls attention to the fact that the religious ideas of a narrative may be those contemporary to the recounting of an event, not to the event itself. He qualifies this, however, by quoting with approval the remark of Gressmann that the religion of Genesis is not simply the religion of Israel. The same principle he applies to morality. In consideration of all these possible modifications, he confesses that we are often unable to determine the original form and purpose of a particular story.

This general summary of Gunkel's opinions is not intended to imply an uncritical acceptance of them. But it is evident that in many respects Gunkel's exposition is in harmony with the views of the interpreters quoted above. A comparison of these views with the very brief remarks on literary form and species contained in the *Divino afflante Spiritu* and the letter to Cardinal Suhard of 1948 shows that it is possible to work on principles which are accepted by exegetes of different beliefs and widely different critical and exegetical views.[37]

Now if we consult once more the interpreters of Genesis 2–3, we see that the chapters are not taken as folklore pure and simple. Père Dubarle classifies them as wisdom literature; other writers, similarly, give them a sapiential or prophetic character.[38] By this they mean that the story is intended to propose religious truths and moral principles in narrative form. The narrative, that is, is not esteemed for its own sake, nor did the author think it of primary importance that he should preserve the narrative as he found it. In adapting it to his purpose, which is didactic, the author has allowed himself that liberty of conception and expression which is characteristic of folklore in all its forms. In a word, there is no small similarity, in this respect, between the Paradise story and the "historico-didactic" account of creation in Genesis 1:1–2:4a. I do not wish to commit here the error of assigning *a priori* the literary species of the passage; I wish merely to summarize the more important opinions proposed by respected authors, and to take these opinions as a working hypothesis. We are not obliged to begin our investigations *in vacuo*.

Comparative Material in Ancient Literature

The first step in determining more precisely the literary species of the Paradise story should be to compare it with other narratives and to determine whether it is dependent on any other work. Here there is no need to delay; this work of comparison has been done many times, and its conclusions may be found in all the commentaries cited above. It is an accepted conclusion among modern exegetes that there is no extant piece of literature which is the source of the Paradise story. The attempts which have been made to establish a dependence on Mesopotamian literature have all broken down against the unique character of the story.

But it would be a mistake to conclude from this, as some have done, that there is no connection between the Paradise story and other ancient narratives. The story as a whole is independent, but this does not imply that it is independent in all details. An examination of the relevant texts on the origin of man discloses that any similarity in detail is to be found in the Mesopotamian stories alone. These relevant texts are few and fragmentary. No Mesopotamian account is as anthropocentric as the Paradise story; this is one of its most striking and distinctive traits.

The material out of which man is made is not always the same in these accounts. In a fragmentary creation account man is made of clay, as in Genesis.[39] The same is true of Enkidu in the Gilgamesh epic, who is not, however, the first man.[40] In *Enûma Elish* man is made of the blood of the slain god Kingu, an ally of the chaotic monster Tiamat.[41] In an Egyptian account man is also made of clay by the potter gods Ptah and Khnum.[42] These texts seem to suggest that the idea that man is a creature of clay, molded by the divine hand, was fairly well diffused. But it was not the only idea. One may ask whether there is not a relationship between the blood of the god in the Mesopotamian account and the breath of Yahweh in the Paradise story. To the Hebrew narrator the idea that man was mixed of the blood of Yahweh was inconceivable; yet the traditional idea was that man partook, in some way, of the divine nature. It is altogether possible that the author wished to preserve this idea, and so invented the much nobler image of the breath of God to express it. The Bible more than once exhibits the common Semitic idea that the life was in the blood (e.g., Gn 9:4). It uses a different idea here, and the motive suggested explains it.

Nowhere in the accounts of the origin of man do I find the production of a single pair, except for a badly broken tablet which has lost its context.[43] All the other creation accounts speak of the creation of men, in several cases of men in a city, which obviously supposes a number. This concept appears also in Genesis 1:26–27, which does not at all imply a single pair. These passages would seem to put it beyond the doubt that the ordinary Sumerian and Babylonian conception of the origin of man was that man arose as a group. Indeed, in the close social organization of the Mesopotamian cities the idea of a single pair would have been impossible. The same principle is valid for the nomadic pastoral group, in which the individual or the family had no existence outside the clan.

Besides the fragmentary tablet mentioned above, there is only one place in Mesopotamian literature where we have the description of a single pair living alone. This is Utnapishtim and his wife, the survivors of the Deluge. Oddly enough, they also live in a "Paradise of delight," and they are immortal. They are "like to the gods. In the distance, at the mouth of the rivers, Utnapishtim shall dwell."[44] In the Sumerian flood story, this is Dilmun, "the land of the living." Kramer identifies the two on the basis of the phrase, "the mouth of the rivers"; and he locates Dilmun at the mouth of the Tigris and Euphrates.[45] Eden also is situated where a river branches into four streams; shall we call this "the mouth of the rivers"? The picture of the happy couple in Tablet XI of the Gilgamesh epic has an undeniable, if merely external, resemblance to the picture of Paradise. This by no means demonstrates literary dependence; but we do have here the one passage in ancient Near Eastern literature which resembles a very distinctive feature of the Paradise story.[46] Now the Gilgamesh epic is a compilation of independent stories; and there is no reason to suppose that Dilmun appeared in Sumerian and Babylonian literature alone as the home of primeval man.

Morris Jastrow once proposed a resemblance between the biblical Adam and Enkidu, the companion of Gilgamesh.[47] This parallel has generally been rejected. Jastrow tried to stretch the resemblance farther than it would go by drawing a parallel between the seduction of Enkidu by the harlot and the temptation of Adam by Eve.[48] Enkidu is described as half man, half beast; he is not the first man, but is made of clay by Aruru to do battle with Gilgamesh. He lives with the wild beasts in the open field, but abandons this manner of life after he is seduced by the harlot and becomes a city dweller. In rejecting Jastrow's theory, scholars have perhaps too hastily denied any resemblance between the figure of Enkidu, living alone in the state of nature, and the biblical Adam living, however briefly, alone with the beasts. As far as it goes, the resemblance (again, a merely external resemblance) is obvious; and the author of Genesis could easily have known the story of Enkidu.

The only Hebrew variant of the Paradise story is the episode found in Ezekiel 28:12–15. The popular story to which Ezekiel alludes is thus summed up by Cooke:

Once there lived in the garden of God, with the cherub who kept it, a glorious being, blameless by nature, gifted with wisdom and beauty; and he roamed at will among the flashing stones of Paradise. Then came the tragedy. Elated by these tokens of favor, he grasped profanely at yet higher honors. Punishment followed swiftly; the cherub drove him from the garden on the sacred mountain, and hurled him to the earth.[49]

There are some indisputably common features in the two passages: Eden, the garden of God, primeval perfection and bliss, a fall. But there are some even more remarkable divergences: in Ezekiel the garden is full of precious stones; there are no trees; the being is clothed; he is endowed with marvelous attributes; he does not keep and till the garden, which is located on the mountain of God; there is no serpent; and, most important of all, there is no woman. To say that this passage is an imaginative handling of the Paradise story by Ezekiel is surely to abandon literary criticism; yet this opinion was proposed by Kraetzschmar.[50] Gunkel, on the contrary, called it an older and more mythological recension.[51] This seems to be also the opinion of Cooke, who believes that the mountain of God, the stones of fire, and the gemmed robe are Babylonian — "not that Ezekiel borrowed them directly, but the folklore upon which he drew had been steeped in Babylonian mythology from early times." He also points out that the being in the story is not said to be the first man, although this may be implied. Hölscher regards it as a Babylonian myth.[52] It is scarcely conceivable, if the Paradise story of Genesis was current, that the prophet would weaken his allusion by so altering it. But this introduces an interesting question. The passage is either original with Ezekiel or, in the views of such radical critics as Irwin, much later. In the critical hypothesis the Jahwist account took form in the ninth century. If such a variant account as this were current enough three hundred years later to be used as it is here, then Hebrew oral tradition must have preserved a marvelous flexibility even after it had been written down. But can we be sure, with Gunkel, that this is an older, and more primitive, version of the story? With the evidence available, it is hard to see how we can determine which of the two is older. We must, at the moment, be satisfied with the probability that they were both current.

What conclusions can be drawn from these comparisons? At this point, nothing more definite than something similar to those which have been drawn concerning the creation account of Genesis 1. The simplicity and sublimity of the Hebrew account, when it is compared with the Mesopotamian cosmogony, stand out in bolder relief; yet there can be no doubt that the Hebrew narrative moves in the same circle of ideas as the Babylonian myth. Similarly, in Genesis 2–3 there is no comparison between the Paradise story and any Mesopotamian myth; here also the dignity of the Hebrew narrative, the profound religious truths which it expresses, raise it far above such stories as those of Enkidu and the harlot. Is it not true, at the same time, that the Hebrew narrative moves in the same circle of ideas? We see these common ideas in the Hebrew account and in Mesopotamian mythology: a terrestrial Paradise inhabited by a single happy pair; a man living in solitude apart from civilization; man formed from clay mixed with a divine element. Some other common ideas will appear in the discussion which follows. This does not mean that the Hebrew narrative is derived from Babylonian myths, and I do not imply that it is. It does mean that, when we investigate the ideas of the ancient Semitic peoples, we find that the author of the Paradise story knew them and expressed them. It would be an unfounded assertion to say that he formed these ideas independently.

The Unity of the Narrative

The question of the literary form and characteristics of the narrative reduces itself, sooner or later, to the vexing question of its unity. This does not mean the literary unity of the passage as it stands. With the majority of exegetes I accept the story in its present form as the work of one mind, and that a mind of no small dimensions. The question is the unity of the material which he employed. The first eleven chapters of Genesis are a collection of originally independent and unconnected stories. Have we here also a compilation of two or more stories, or is there only one? Neither is it a question of whether the narrative contains disparate elements; it

certainly does, and, as Coppens has pointed out, nothing but ignorance of Hebrew and a total lack of the critical sense would permit
one to affirm that the Paradise story is perfectly homogenous.[53]
It is important to disengage these disparate elements; but this does
not, of itself, answer the question of the original unity of the story.
Here again the question is large; I do not even pretend to have
seen all the literature, and I can mention only selected works.[54]

There is very general agreement that the pericope of the rivers of
Paradise (2:10–14) is secondary. This is accepted by Feldmann and
Heinisch.[55] In addition, Feldmann believes that 2:4b is corrupted;
2:5 is secondary; 2:6 is misplaced and perhaps should follow 2:9;
2:8b, 15 are duplications; 3:20 is secondary. Scholars of more extreme critical views, basing their conclusions upon more or less the
same verses, have attempted to reconstruct two or even three strands
of narrative which the author has compiled into one. Abraham
Menes distinguished two *Sagenmotiven,* a Paradise motif and an
agricultural motif.[56] The Paradise motif is of Babylonian origin, the
agricultural motif Palestinian. In the Paradise motif man lives alone
among the beasts. Johannes Meinhold has a still more complicated
analysis: J[1] is nomadic, J[2] agricultural.[57] Joachim Begrich finds one
complete narrative supplemented by fragments from another.[58]
Begrich has emphasized the fact that the narrative as it stands is
thoroughly Israelite. Behind it, however, there is a peasant story
and a nomad story; the peasant story forms the main strand. Within
this strand there is a compilation of an originally independent creation story, and a Paradise story in which the only actors were
the woman and the serpent. Simpson has distinguished a garden
saga and an Eden saga; the garden saga is original, the Eden
saga secondary.[59] Coppens regards 2:8b as a gloss, 2:10–14 as
secondary, 2:15, 23 as later additions.[60] A. Lefèvre has recently
distinguished a history of Eve and a history of the garden of
Eden.[61] A review of these articles leaves one with the impression that none of these schemes is quite successful, and the
conviction that Coppens is correct in saying that nothing but
ignorance and a lack of the critical sense will permit one to say that
the narrative is entirely homogeneous. The analysis of parallel narratives is not as successful here as it is, for example, in the Deluge
story; on the other hand, critics have pointed out a number of
faintly discordant elements which it would be unscientific to dismiss
altogether. It will be worthwhile to review them here.

The rivers of Paradise, as we have seen, are almost universally regarded as secondary. This block of verses can be removed from the context with no loss whatever, and the idea does not reappear in the story. But it has been woven into the context. The "duplicate" of 2:8b in 2:15 is a necessary resumption, once the description of the rivers has been introduced. If it is true, as several critics think, that an oasis is described in 2:6, then the rivers are out of harmony with the 'ed of 2:6. But if 'ed represents edu, "flood," this discordance is removed.[62] The idea of an oasis as the scene of the narrative is out of harmony not only with the rivers but with the whole conception of the garden and of Eden. The names Tigris and Euphrates and the picture of a river which is divided to irrigate the ground suggest Mesopotamian cultivation. Eden is a Mesopotamian conception, and it may be an Akkadian word, edinu, "the plain." But in any case, the geography of Eden is altogether unreal; it is a Never-never land, and attempts to locate it, even in the author's mind, are futile. Now Eden cannot be removed from the narrative. The garden reappears throughout the two chapters, and it is the scene of the action of Chapter 3. The position of 2:6 after 8 or 9 can be defended only if 2:10–14 are excised. But what reason could there be for the transfer of 2:6 to its present position, even on the hypothesis that 2:10–14 are secondary? And if the scene, apart from the possibility that 2:6 describes an oasis, is Mesopotamian, why should the rivers of Paradise be treated as secondary? What independent elements there are in the narrative have now been so closely connected that it is impossible to disengage them. We may get some idea of the nature of these independent elements from the description of Eden in Ezekiel 28; but we cannot, on the basis of the passage in Ezekiel, detach them from each other.

The two trees of 2:9 have offered difficulty. Syntactically, the attachment of the two trees to 2:9a is clumsy. Yet they must be introduced somewhere. The title, "tree of knowledge of good and evil," is proleptic here; it has no meaning apart from the subsequent narrative, which it presupposes. Now it is quite true that the two trees never again appear together. Yet the sin in Chapter 3 is certainly the eating of fruit; it is a sin from which man comes to know good and evil, and thus becomes like 'elōhîm; and it suggests another possibility, the eating of the fruit of the tree of life, and a further assimilation to *'elōhîm* by immortality. Further, the two trees are in the midst of the *garden* in *Eden*. Again, if one attempts to disengage elements which may have been originally independent, the narrative falls apart.

The name of *man* is several times involved in a wordplay. *'Ādām* and *'adāmāh* recur throughout, and the assonance is deliberate. It occurs in 2:7, where *'ādām* is made of *'āpār min hā'adāmāh*. Why does it not reappear in the companion piece, 3:17b, although it is found in 3:17a? In their present form, these two verses demand each other; and they cannot be isolated. On the other hand, a different wordplay occurs in 2:23: *'îš* and *'iššāh*. This, again, does not reappear. But it is somewhat remarkable that the pair is called in Chapter 3 *hā' ādām we'ištô*. There is, of course, no complementary word for *'ādām*, as *'iššāh* complements *'îš*; I speak of usage, not of etymology. But the use of this designation in the context suggests both *'ādām-'adāmāh* of 2:7 and *'îš-'iššāh* of 2:23; and they cannot be disengaged unless one follows the radical suggestion of Begrich that *'ādām* did not appear in the original Paradise story at all.

Is there a certain ambivalence toward agricultural life in the narrative? In 2:15 man is set in Eden to guard it and to till it (*le'ōbdāh*); in 3:23 man is expelled from Eden to till (*la'abōd*) the soil (*'adāmāh*). In 3:19 man is to eat bread in the sweat of his brow; in 3:18 he is to eat the grass of the field. These two are not the same. Certainly, it is some explanation to say that the curse consists in this, that the soil will be undocile to man's cultivation; and if one does this, then one must omit 3:18b or, with Meinhold and Begrich, incorporate it into a nomadic story. In either case, one conclusion is inevitable: the story as a whole has an agricultural background (if the nomadic life is mentioned at all, it is mentioned as an accursed mode of existence), and must come from an agricultural society. Chaine has noticed that "guard" shows that the author here forgets that the man is alone.[63]

If no parallel narratives can be successfully isolated, is it possible that the literary seam occurs between the creation account and the story of the fall? We cannot answer this before we isolate the creation account, and in this there are three stages: the man, the beasts, the woman. It is true that these three stages are now separated by the trees of Paradise (2:9), the rivers of Paradise (2:10–14), and the resumption (or duplicate) of 2:15; and all of these are questioned in the hypotheses of parallel narratives, and are treated as secondary by Feldmann and Coppens. The precept of 2:16–17 may seem indispensable for Chapter 3, but it can well be supplied by 3:3, which could be the first mention of the precept as well as a repetition. The difficulty here is that the elements which are heterogeneous cannot be blocked off into a creation narrative and a sin narrative. It is also true that Chapter 3 is intelligible as a unit without presupposing Chapter 2 at all.

These examples will perhaps illustrate the difficulty of analyzing this passage. At first glance it appears that the mechanical methods of analysis employed at times with great success will do their work here also. One isolates distinctive features, and then checks off all the verses in which these features are found. One then adds the results and comes up with two or more documents. This method presupposes a mechanical compilation, and is successful only when the presupposition is correct. Here the analysis must be more subtle, because we are dealing with an author who is, by common consent, one of the most subtle in the Old Testament. If we grant, as it seems we must, that he has used material from diverse sources, we must also grant that he has assimilated this material and fused it into one account which is his own. The material from the sources has lost its distinct identity, and shows traces only where the assimilation, because of the nature of the material, is imperfect. This implies that the Paradise story, in its present form, did not exist before its composition by the author of the account of Genesis; and we do no more than justice to the genius of the author if we accept this implication.

Preexisting Materials

But if we cannot reconstruct the sources of the story, we may by an examination of details arrive at least at some determination of the preexisting material which the writer employed. This is to accept, with most commentators, the substantial unity of the account. By so treating the narrative I do not wish to regard the question of its unity as altogether decided; I mean merely that, with our present knowledge of ancient Near Eastern literature, we have no reason to suppose two or three strands of narrative. But we cannot ignore the possibility that further discoveries may reveal an earlier form of the story.

We may first consider 2:7, in which man is made of "dust from the soil." The play on 'ādām-'ᵃdāmāh is obvious. I have pointed out above, after many writers, that the idea of man from clay is not uncommon in ancient Near Eastern literature, and that it is very probable that the author knew of this and used it. What is original is the union of clay with the divine breath. The whole picture is highly imaginative and indicates the peculiar position of man as the link between the animal creation and the divine. This is by no means too subtle an idea; clay mixed with the divine blood, as in the *Enûma Elish*, expresses substantially the same idea. The kinship of man with the animals is further indicated in 2:19, where almost the same words (*yāṣar, 'ᵃdāmāh*) are employed to describe the creation of the beasts. This is altogether artificial and tends to the author's purpose; man was not in fact nor in the cosmogony of Genesis 1 created before the lower animals. The divergence from Genesis 1 need not be deliberate, but we are certainly in the presence of different conceptions. *'Āpār* is not used in 2:19; this word has a peculiar force when used of man, since it is resumed in the sentence of mortality in 3:19.

The creation of woman is of a different character. In the first place, we have in other ancient sources no indication of a separate creation of the two sexes. The idea found in the *Timaeus* of Plato that the original human beings were asexual does not appear in ancient Near Eastern literature, nor is it a common Greek idea; it may have been Pythagorean.[64] In the *Enûma Elish* the distinction of sex is as primeval as the world, as deity itself. Here, on the other hand, it seems no exaggeration to say that the creation of woman is the climax toward which the whole preceding narrative tends. Compare, for instance, the preliminary utterance of 2:18, the mystic sleep of 2:21, and the introduction of woman to man in 2:22, which elicits the doxology of 2:23, with the terse and comparatively undramatic recital of 2:7. And if the preceding verses show the kinship of man with the brutes, the naming of the animals shows his superiority; he is not one of them, nor can he find a mate among them. To give him a fit companion requires a new creative intervention. More than this, the narrative treats woman as an equal and a partner of man. This feature does not appear in any ancient Near Eastern story. Now if the contrast between man's kinship with the brutes and his superiority to them suggests two different sources — which I am not prepared to concede — it must certainly be granted that they have been marvelously united into a perfectly drawn picture of the paradox that is man. The stages — man, beasts, woman — are not fortuitous; they are the work of the creative imagination of the Hebrew storyteller, who thus expressed profound truths.

Now if the creation account of Chapter 2 leads up to the creation of woman as its climax — and so I have taken it — there are two questions which arise. Is the divergence between the glorification of woman in Chapter 2, and the attribution of the disaster to the woman in Chapter 3, so great that we must suppose that the two accounts were originally independent? Certainly, such a suspicion would not be altogether unfounded; but here again the two ideas have been so well united that we can scarcely hope to trace any sources. In the present narrative a striking contrast is drawn between the primitive condition of woman, the "helper" for the man, his partner and equal, and the condition of woman as it was in the ancient world: the property of man, the most valuable of his domestic animals. We shall perhaps do better if we attribute this contrast to the author of the story, to whom the conception of the Paradise narrative as a whole belongs, than to any source which he employed.

The second question which arises may be put as follows. The creation account of Chapter 2 reaches its climax in the doxology of 2:23 and the *mašal* of 2:24. If one attempts to read this account apart from its usual context, one feels that something is missing. The expected climax is not the meeting of man and woman, but the consummation of sexual union. This is not mentioned until 4:1, which Meinhold actually incorporated into the Paradise story.[65] If this verse was originally a part of this story, its place is at the conclusion of Chapter 2, not between 3:20 and 3:24a, where Meinhold put it. Shall we say that this climax is insinuated in 2:25?

Such delicate insinuation is characteristic of the Victorian novel rather than of the Old Testament, or of ancient Semitic literature. The climactic structure of Chapter 2 suggests very strongly that the original conclusion has been suppressed by the author. If this is true, then the literary seam between the creation account and the story of the fall has been identified; the author of the Paradise narrative has employed a preexisting account of the creation of man and woman which had its climax — and its conclusion — in the consummation of sexual union. He suppressed the conclusion, we may suppose, in order to unite this account with that of the fall, which is of necessity thus detached, in its original form, from the creation account. If the discordant elements of the two chapters are to be explained by a diversity of sources, then the explanation which I propose here affords some motivation for the manner in which the sources were fused.

The creation narrative is interrupted by 2:9–17. Now if some critics are right, these verses are a true interruption, alien in origin. I have pointed out above that the resumption of 2:8b in 2:15 now connects them with the context. Furthermore, it is altogether natural that the narrative of the creation of the man should be followed by a description, or at least a mention, of the place where he is to dwell. It would have to come here or after the creation of the woman, where it would be no more in place. In fact, it would appear anticlimactic after the solemn effatum of 2:24. Is it not better to understand these verses as a part of the introduction to the creation of the woman? The man is created and set in his dwelling; but he lacks a partner to share his life and his dwelling.

On the other hand, the description of Paradise cannot be Israelite. If we concede with Begrich the essentially Hebrew character of the narrative, we must except these verses. This, however, is not a sufficient reason for thinking them secondary. We can do this only if we are certain that the author has used no non-Israelite material. It is certain that he has used such material. Here his indebtedness is manifest. I have indicated above that the idea of Paradise bears a resemblance to the home of Utnapishtim and his wife (the Sumerian Dilmun). Here we have an instance of an idea which the author could easily have known; and coincidence is not an attractive explanation. The incorporation of this idea, which had no connection with any creation account, into this narrative as the scene of the action of Chapters 2–3 must be attributed to the author of the Paradise narrative, not to the original stories.

The trees of Paradise have been much discussed, recently by J. Coppens. Coppens understands the knowledge of good and evil to mean ". . . to desire to sin, to desire to know good and evil at once, to desire to ignore and to tread underfoot the distinction between good and evil, to desire to establish the self in moral autonomy above good and evil, claiming to be like the gods."[66] In the concrete, he understands the sin of Chapter 3 to be a sexual transgression, and identifies it as the submission of conjugal life to the patronage of licentious cults.[67] The narrative is, in his interpretation, a polemic against Canaanite fertility and fecundity rites. In the theory of two independent stories which I have outlined, the tree of knowledge is not original in Chapter 2; but in the present form of the story it is one of the links between the two chapters, and its presence must be due to the author of the Paradise narrative. Some kind of symbolism is surely to be sought in the trees; and Coppens has done well to point out how, from rabbinical and patristic exegesis down to modern times, the theory of sexual symbolism has constantly recurred. This is due, as Coppens shows, to the obvious "sexual milieu" of the story. If, however, the expected climax of Chapter 2 has been suppressed, the theory of Coppens raises an interesting speculation; for it has been suppressed in favor of the narrative of the sin in Chapter 3. Consequently, I think Coppens is substantially right, and the author replaced the original climax, which must have been an epithalamion, by the story of the sin, which is in some way a perversion of the intended union of the sexes.

The symbolism of the tree of life is obvious. It occurs only in Proverbs 3:18 outside this passage, with no obvious dependence on Genesis. The tree in Ezekiel 47:12 is even less obviously dependent. The literary relationship of the tree of life to the rest of the story has caused much difficulty. Many critics believe that it is secondary, or that it belongs to a parallel narrative, or that it is a doublet of the tree of knowledge. Such hypotheses are scarcely possible now in the light of a pattern which Geo Widengren has been tracing in ancient Near Eastern religion, a pattern which will without doubt prove to be of no small interest in the interpretation of the Paradise story.[68] Widengren points out the importance of the tree of life, Mesopotamian myth and ritual, and believes that the tree of life, growing beside the water of life, stood in a garden in each Mesopotamian sanctuary. Of this tree the king is the gardener and the "Keeper." The garden represents the mythical garden at Eridu between the mouths of the two rivers (see my remarks on Dilmun above). Life is not communicated by eating the fruit of the tree but by contact with its branches; Widengren, arguing from plastic representations, supposes that the royal scepter represented a branch or twig from the tree of life. The tree is actually a mythic-ritual symbol of both god and king. Widengren himself establishes no connection between the tree of life and Genesis 3, but believes that the mythic-ritual pattern is alluded to several times in the Old Testament, and lies at the base of some of the ritual paraphernalia of the temple of Solomon. The differences between this conception of the tree of life and the tree of life of Genesis 2–3 are at once apparent: for instance, there is no "water of life" in Genesis, and the fruit of the tree is eaten. The similarities are equally apparent; and if the pattern which Widengren is tracing is correctly drawn — and one cannot question his documentation — we shall find more features of ancient Semitic mythology from which the author of Genesis 2–3 drew the imaginative vesture of his story, in accordance with the manner of composition which we have found in his work. The tree of life can symbolize nothing but immortality. This symbolism is put beyond all doubt by 3:22, and it is the symbolism of the "plant of life" of Gilgamesh and the "food and water of life" of Adapa.[69]

I do not believe we can exclude the possibility that the author has, in the two trees, amalgamated two conceptions which did not appear together in the original stories. The tree of knowledge is certainly original in Chapter 3, and may have come from there into Chapter 2. The tree of life, on the other hand, is most probably original in Chapter 2, and may have passed from there into Chapter 3. It has no place in the narrative of the sin, nor is it mentioned in the curse of 3:17–18.

Coppens has presented a large amount of material on the symbolism of the serpent; we cannot escape symbolism here. It is quite true, as many critics have remarked, that talking animals are a recurrent feature of folklore; but it is also true that we are dealing with an author who has handled folklore in a remarkably subtle manner. Coppens is certain that the symbolism of the serpent is non-Israelite.[70] The serpent he finds to be a phallic symbol, often associated with male and female fertility deities. The fact of this symbolism should not be denied; and it is one of the arguments on which Coppens leans most heavily for his interpretation of Genesis 3.[71] But the serpent appears in other forms in the Bible, and I do not believe that these should be left out of consideration. In Isaiah 27:1, Job 25:13, the serpent is a monstrous adversary of Yahweh. The serpent on the floor of the sea in Amos 9:3 must be the same mythological monster, although it does not appear to be perfectly identical with the Ugaritic monster Yamm.[72] I do not think this significance of the serpent was altogether absent from the author's mind. It would not be difficult for the Hebrew to identify the chaotic monster of evil with the serpent of those rites which he found so offensive to his moral sense. The origin of this symbolism, whatever it is, is beside the point here; what matters is that the author accepted a common and easily understood symbolism, drawn from Semitic mythology, and incorporated it into his story.

The threefold curse, 3:14–19, is called by Abraham Menes the key to the narrative.[73] I am not so certain that these difficult verses are a key that fits; one is likely to explain the obscure by the more obscure. The verses have been neatly joined into the structure of Chapter 3. The order of the sin is: serpent — woman — man. The order of the inquisition is: man — woman — serpent. The order of the curse is once again: serpent — woman — man. One cannot help wondering whether the preliterary story had a question addressed to the serpent. The threefold curse supposes not only the sin of Chapter 3, but certain elements of Chapter 2. The antithesis between the glorification of woman in Chapter 2 and the curse in 3:16 is evident.

The curse of the serpent refers no further back than Chapter 3. If one accepts Coppens' interpretation of Chapter 3, however, some interesting speculations arise once more which the learned Louvain doctor did not take into account. If the serpent is a phallic symbol, what are we to understand by the "enmity" of 3:15? It can mean nothing else but that sexual life is a curse to the woman; and this is stated expressly in 3:16. The seed of the woman, however, should not be limited to offspring of the female sex; the opinion suggests itself that the seed of the woman is doomed to an unending struggle against sexual sin, symbolized by the serpent. In a "sexual milieu" such as Coppens has suggested, this symbolism is quite in place. On the other hand, it may force the author into a too narrow conception of the symbolism which he has employed; and the general character of the story, as I have analyzed it thus far, shows greater freedom in the handling of the material. Perhaps, therefore, the curse, like the serpent itself, should be understood more broadly, with sexual sin in the foreground, but with sin in the general sense as the proper term of the symbol. Should this be predicated of the present form of the story, it would not necessarily be predicated of the preliterary form of the story.

In no theory has an entirely satisfactory symbolism been found for the curse of the serpent. The mistake, perhaps, lies in searching for too recondite a significance. Symbolism which is not fairly obvious loses its point; and farfetched symbolism, as the preceding examination shows, is not characteristic of this writer. The serpent itself suggests, in the popular mind, a degraded, stealthy, malicious being; and no more is necessary to understand the terms of the curse. J. Chaine gives substantially the same explanation; in addition, he finds in the curse a reaction against the Semitic cult of the serpent.[74]

The curse of the man is more difficult. It cannot be denied that the expression is somewhat redundant. There are three different references to the food of man: you will eat the soil (i.e., its products), you will eat the grass of the field, you will eat bread in the sweat of your brow. It is thought by many critics (Menes, Meinhold, Begrich, Simpson) that 3:18 is secondary or belongs to a parallel account. I have rejected, in general, the theory of parallel accounts, and so I cannot invoke it here. Mere redundancy is not enough to mark a verse as secondary. I must confess that I have not found a satisfactory explanation of this verse. Its language is reminiscent of 2:5, and of no other verse in the two chapters. If it is omitted, the formula of the curse loses much of its displeasing redundancy; a twofold repetition of a solemn formula is characteristic of Hebrew style. On the other hand, 3:17, 19 contain an allusion to Chapter 2: *'ādām-'ªdāmāh, 'āpār.* I have already noticed that agriculture cannot be considered a curse if man is represented in Chapter 2 as agricultural; but he is so represented, and hence the curse must draw a difference between types of agricultural conditions. Now the garden, as we have seen, suggests a Mesopotamian background; and Mesopotamian agriculture was carried on by irrigating a fertile alluvial plain. There was no small difference between this and the struggle of the Palestinian peasant to wring a living from his rocky soil. In default of any other explanation, I suggest this as the background of the curse. It indicates once more the fusion of different ideas.

The curse of the man, as critics have pointed out, does not refer back to the narrative of 3:1–7 at all. There is a reference in 3:17a, but this line lies outside the metrical structure of the curse, and appears to be a literary seam. Begrich has concluded from this that the sin story originally had only two actors, the woman and the serpent.[75] This is too much to draw from a single piece of evidence. But there are other factors to be considered. As the story of the sin stands, it has, in reality, only two actors; the man is silent and performs no independent action. Furthermore, the curse of the man is entirely free from any sexual motif. These, taken together, do suggest that the curse of the man and consequently the man himself were not present in the preliterary sin story. We have in Ezekiel 28 a conception of the sin of a man alone, which supports the assumption that Hebrew folklore knew the story in this form. If the author has assimilated this account, he has harmonized the stories in an artistic manner; and by doing so has given both breadth and depth to his conception. Even if the story of the woman and the serpent had a sexual motif, the amalgamation of the story of the man has broadened the idea of sin, so that the story in its finished form shows the effects of sin not only in the sexual field, but in human life in general. As the affliction proper to woman is sexual life and chattel ownership by the man, so the affliction proper to man is the struggle for food — especially if we view this against a Palestinian background.

Now if these considerations have any validity, the material appears to fall into three independent pieces of popular tradition: the creation of the sexes; the sin of the woman; and the sin of the man. In the form into which the story has been put in Genesis, the role of the woman is more significant than the role of the man in both chapters. This I do not propose as something new; but I do not find that commentators have emphasized its importance. If we are to understand the Paradise narrative this feature must be given it due weight.

The expulsion of the pair from Paradise is mentioned twice (3:23–24), and this should not be disputed. Unfortunately, the textual corruption of 3:24 does not permit us to form any conclusions. The correction of the Greek is too suspiciously harmonizing to be easily accepted. The two verses have been linked by the mention of the garden and Eden in both; the allusion 'ādām-'ªdāmāh appears in 23, but not in 24. The kᵉrūbîm of 24 are undoubtedly of Mesopotamian origin; the winged genii which guard gates are a characteristically Mesopotamian conception. This is not true of the flaming whirling sword; other biblical parallels suggest that lightning is meant here (Ps 104:4; Dt 32:22). This is a Syrian and Canaanite rather than a Babylonian idea, and such a conjunction of diverse ideas should be attributed to the author who gave the story its final form.[76] Due to the corruption of the text, I admit the activity of the redactor here and in 3:18; his restoration failed to give back what must have been as smooth a fusion of diverse ideas as we find elsewhere in the story.

These considerations show us that the author has, by skillful creative imagination, woven into a unified whole popular traditions and background elements drawn from highly diversified sources. Paradise is, geographically speaking, nowhere. Man is described as a primitive agriculturist; this is not only historically impossible, but was known to be impossible by the ancient Semitic peoples. The biblical conception of the pre-Canaanite inhabitants of Canaan, fragmentary as are our notices, did not regard them as urban-agricultural. The formation of man from clay is not only imaginative, but is paralleled in Mesopotamian literature. The order of creation — man, beasts, woman — is evidently an imaginative arrangement, invented for the purpose of the narrative. The serpent is symbolic on the basis of allusions alone, without invoking Coppens' hypothesis of the sexual motif. The trees are symbolic, as is their eating; and the curses reflect a social and cultural milieu which is not that of primitive man, but of Mesopotamian and Palestinian civilization in the first or second millennium B.C.

Scope of the Narrative

The preceding analysis is in general agreement with the opinion of the majority of commentators that the Paradise story is a unified narrative with a climactic structure. I have rather attended to the provenance of the elements of this narrative. Many of the conclusions which may be formulated as a result of this analysis are, in the present state of exegesis, extremely hypothetical; and, while I desire that they be accorded their due meed of probability, I do not wish to propose them for more than they are worth.

There can be no doubt that the Paradise story is, as it has long been interpreted, anthropocentric; it is a story of human sin, of a fall from a primitive state which was free of sin and its consequences. There is no doubt likewise that the narrative in its present form is intended to signify that the ills of mankind arise from sin. Sin, as Chaine remarks, disturbs the order of creation.[77] This is evident if we take the Paradise story in its present context, preceding the account of the spread of sin and the degeneration of mankind in the following chapters; if the Paradise story existed independently of this context, this meaning would be less evident, but it would still be present.

The possibility of foreign influence can be traced in a number of details. I can say no more than "possibility," because the extant literary remains do not permit us to argue dependence. But there are two facts to be taken into account. In the first place, the author of the Paradise story was endowed with a creative and subtle mind.

What foreign material he employed was assimilated into his account; there is no "borrowing," in the ordinary sense of the word. Hence foreign material is so transfigured that it is less easily traced. In the second place, the literature of the Hebrews manifests a wide acquaintance with the mythology and folklore of both Mesopotamia and Canaan. It is no longer possible to assert that the Hebrews ignored them or refused to allude to them. Where such an allusion appears, it must be assumed that the author was aware of the source of the allusion.

Now the details in which such allusions may be traced are not to be found in any single Mesopotamian composition; the author has not drawn his narrative from any single source. We find that the idea of man from clay mixed with a divine element, of a single pair living in solitary beatitude, of a man living alone with the brutes, of Paradise, of the tree of life, of the serpent, of the genii guarding the gates, are all certainly or very probably of diverse origin. Their present position and function in the narrative is due entirely to the creative imagination of the writer, and they indicate his capacity to assemble scattered strands from many sources into a compactly unified narrative. They form the ideal background of the narrative. On the other hand, the essential features of the narrative not only reflect no foreign influence, but are out of harmony with any foreign material which deals with similar subjects.

The importance of the woman in both chapters is, I think, the key (if we may speak of a key) to the narrative. Her position in Chapter 2 at the climax of the creative process has led me to conclude that the account of the process must have ended in an epithalamion, which the author of the Paradise story has suppressed. This immediately implies that the creation account of Chapter 2 was not original with the author himself, and that it must have existed in Hebrew folklore as an independent unit. Furthermore, the variation between 'ādām-'ᵃdāmāh and 'iš-'iššāh suggests that in Chapter 2 itself there may be a fusion of two accounts of the origin of man. In the present form of Chapter 2, the preexisting materials have been fused into an account, not of the creation of man, but of the origin of the sexes.

I do not believe that we can understand the prominence accorded

to the woman unless we view it against the background of comparative religion; and here I follow a line of thought suggested by the
work of Coppens. Let us recall the prominence of the female principle in the religion and mythology of Mesopotamia and Canaan.
The female principle is deified — Inanna, Ishtar, Astarte, Anath —
and is the object of the licentious cult in which sexual excess is
sanctified as an act of worship. Yet the human beings of which
Ishtar and Anath are the representatives were socially inferior, the
property of man and the creatures of his pleasure. May we not
conceive that the Hebrews, revolting against this, composed this
account of the origin of sex, of such striking dignity and chastity,
in which the female principle is put in its proper place? Here the
woman is, like the man, a creature of God, his partner in life as
well as in the sexual act, of equal dignity with him. The distinction
of sexes is a divine creation; there is no distinction of sex on the
divine level. The woman is the center of the family; and the Hebrews had a strong sense of family solidarity. Here, certainly, we
meet a profound mind, which sensed that both the deification of
the female principle and the social depression of woman (which he
could observe in his own people) were contrary to nature and, even
more, that the second evil grows out of the first: that the woman
who is a goddess of pleasure, worshiped for her sexual attractive-
ness, must of necessity be socially depressed in the world of reality.
Such a conception of the narrative of Chapter 2 shows how it could
exist as an independent unit of Hebrew tradition, with its own significance, before it was incorporated into the Paradise narrative.

The prominence of the woman in Chapter 3 is also evident. The
drama of sin has really only two actors: the serpent and the woman.
It is not by chance that the woman is the first to fall; the preliterary
story expressed, beyond doubt, the popular belief that the weaker
sex is the morally feeble side of the race. In view of the symbolism
of the serpent, it is altogether likely that the moral weakness of the
woman which is here indicated is sexual; this also is in harmony
with popular belief. But we must, I think, look deeper than this
platitude; for, as we have noticed many times, we are dealing with
a subtle mind. We may suppose that the preliterary pieces of folklore told no more than this, that the moral weakness of woman is

the cause of man's troubles; but it is extremely likely that the writer who united it with other materials to form the Paradise story meant it to signify more here. And I think Coppens is right in seeing here an allusion to the licentious cult of the female principle. It is not merely the alleged moral weakness of woman that is responsible for the troubles of man; it is precisely her sexual attraction that has ruined both him and herself, has made the man the slave of the goddess of sex, and the woman the slave of the man. And, in this sense, the forbidden fruit has a sexual significance. But the author has broadened the scope of the preliterary story beyond the merely sexual field by the addition of the curse of the man.

Coppens' interpretation suggests still another line of thought. He does not believe that "knowledge of good and evil" has of itself a sexual significance. The repetition of the phrase, "like 'elōhîm, knowing good and evil," in 3:5, 22 is very striking. It certainly does not mean the same thing in the mouth of the serpent and in the mouth of Yahweh. Yet there must be some fundamental idea which permits this play on the phrase. In referring to the fertility cults, M. Coppens has, I believe, indicated the key to this repetition. The fertility rite was a mystic communion of the worshiper with his gods; by intercourse under the auspices of the rites he shared the divine prerogative of procreation; he became, in a sense, the master of the force of life. This mastery, this communion with 'elōhîm, is what the serpent promises. In a writer of such consummate artistry it is not mere coincidence but supreme irony that, when the fruit which holds such promise is consumed, the man and the woman know — that they are naked. The promised communion has issued in shame. The promise is false, and the words chosen to express this have an obvious allusion to sexual life. The knowledge of good and evil, in the concrete, is the knowledge that they are naked, i.e., that they are the slaves of sexual desire. The promise of the knowledge of good and evil held out the alluring prospect of rising to the divine level of independence by mastery of the life force; the reality is shame. By the fertility cult the sublime power of procreation has been debased.

We may conclude, then, that the ancient Hebrews who told and heard this story viewed it as an idealized account of the origin of sex and of the perversion of sexual life from its primitive integrity. It is composed of many threads from many fabrics, carefully and skillfully woven into a new account. The religious and moral transcendence of the story, thus understood, needs neither explanation nor apology, and it fits into the basic categories of Hebrew thought. The central fact upon which the writer has constructed his story is the moral degeneration of man and of society. This degeneration, in his mind, comes to a focus in the perversion of sexual relations, but it is not limited to this. Coupled with this idea is his awareness of man's struggle with nature itself, which he sees as an inevitable consequence of the breakdown of personal and social integrity. This condition he traces back to the beginning of the race — ultimately, to man's attempt to arrogate to himself divine prerogatives, of which the fertility cult is a horrible example. With M. Chaine, we must attribute this profound and lofty view of human origins and sin to the influence of divine revelation.[78]

We think of folklore as simple and unsophisticated; have we overreached ourselves by this complex analysis? We should not forget that the simplicity of folklore is sometimes deceptive, and that this folklore comes to us through the genius of the author of these chapters. Folklore, in the hands of writers such as Homer or this author, can be elevated to a lofty level of wisdom. There is subtlety in the conception of Gilgamesh and Enkidu in the Gilgamesh epic; there is irony in the portrayal of Ishtar in the Gilgamesh epic which rivals that of Homer's Ares and Aphrodite — attributed, in the epic, to a wandering bard. There is irony in the story of the Tower of Babel. Let us not think that wit and irony, profundity and wisdom were beyond the reach of the ancient Hebrew storytellers; there was genius before Homer.

CONCLUSION

This paper is, perhaps, an essay in the history of interpretation rather than an essay in interpretation itself. It attempts to recover some of the significance which the narrative of Paradise and the fall must have had for the Israelites. This significance has not received much attention in modern theology and exegesis; the development of doctrine and the necessities of controversy have led theologians — if not forced them — to place the emphasis upon other elements. Probably a study of the meaning of the story in its original historical and cultural *Sitz im Leben* will contribute little to the necessities of modern theological discussion; at the same time there is no antinomy between the meaning which we suppose the ancient Israelites perceived in this narrative and the meaning which it has come to have in modern theology. Exegesis itself is a sufficient justification for recalling — or rather attempting to reconstruct — this meaning, in the hope that a clearer understanding of the historical, cultural, and literary background of the passage will deepen our appreciation of its content and enable us to draw from it a fund of truth which is not irrelevant for Catholic doctrine and Catholic life in the modern world.

The pursuit of this meaning has led me into the literary characteristics of Genesis 2–3 — a question which has always fascinated exegetes. Where so many renowned interpreters have run their heads against a stone wall, it would be the height of temerity to claim that I have found the clue which has escaped them. But I have enjoyed the advantage of their work. All the same, it is unfortunate that the significance of the text which I propose depends so largely upon a literary analysis which is the most novel feature of all that I have written here. I can, consequently, do no more than present these ideas to my colleagues in theology and exegesis with the proper diffidence, knowing that they will try them and hold fast to what is good.

Note on the Mythological Allusions in Ezekiel 28:12–18

In commenting on the literary characteristics of Genesis 2–3 I took the position that Ezekiel 28:12–18 contains a variant form of the tradition which appears in Genesis 2–3.[79]

A number of authors, both older and contemporary, have asserted that Ezekiel here either recounts a foreign myth or alludes to one.[80] This consensus is remarkable when one observes that no myth is cited upon which the allusions are based. Older authors identified the myth as Mesopotamian; more recent authors appeal to Phoenician or Canaanite mythology. Fohrer, for instance, the newest of the commentators on Ezekiel, says that the myth of the garden of Elohim is originally Mesopotamian, identified with Eden in Hebrew tradition.[81] In my own study I dealt with possible allusions to Dilmun in the descriptive details of Eden.[82] Fohrer also finds a reference to a Canaanite-Phoenician myth of Mount Ṣapon and Ashtar, also alluded to in Isaiah 14:12–14. Ezekiel, Fohrer thinks, has perhaps enriched the Canaanite-Phoenician myth with Babylonian motifs, or vice versa. One could scarcely treat the question more casually. The existence of mythological allusions in the Old Testament cannot be denied; all the same, very few of them were correctly recognized before the comparative material was discovered, and experience shows that it is rarely possible, if ever, to reconstruct these myths from biblical allusions alone with any degree of accuracy.

The mythological pattern of the king and the tree of life traced by Geo Widengren bears a closer resemblance to Ezekiel than any other source which has been alleged; but it must be noticed that this scholar's reconstructions and method are the subject of considerable criticism by the best qualified students of Mesopotamia.[83] Widengren finds a hero "whose body is shining splendor," placed in the garden of the gods and adorned with precious stones. These are descriptive allusions, and we should not neglect the substantial differences. The dominant features of the tree of life and the water of life are absent from Ezekiel; there is no indication of a fault and an expulsion in Widengren's pattern; and the hero of the Mesopotamian pattern is identified by Widengren as a god. Widengren also finds an allusion to the tablets of destiny. The hero of Ezekiel in the LXX is adorned with the stones of the breastplate of the high priest (Ex 39:10–13), which contained the Urim and Thummim; these, Widengren thinks, "play the same role as the tablets of destiny in being the instrument by which the will of the deity is communicated to the leader of the people." Hence he believes the Septuagint preserves the original reading in Ezekiel 28:13.[84]

It is important to determine whether the hero of Ezekiel is a divine being or not. Hebrew monotheism is not an operative factor. Allusions to the cosmic combat between the creative deity and the monster of chaos are found in the Old Testament, despite the divinity of the monster of chaos in mythology. Were it not for extrabiblical material, we could not tell from the biblical allusions that the monster of chaos is divine in mythology. The mythological divinity of Ezekiel's hero could be just as easily disguised. The hero is called a $k^e r\hat{u}b$ in the Massoretic text Ezekiel 28:14, but most commentators think this vocalization is false.[85] The second appearance of the word in 28:16 is syntactically and metrically clumsy and is questioned by many commentators. We cannot, of course, dismiss the traditional text too glibly; but these observations should caution us against a facile assertion that the hero of Ezekiel is a $k^e r\hat{u}b$. The being is not clearly a god, not clearly one of the $b^e n\hat{e}$ '$^el\hat{o}h\hat{i}m$, not evidently more than human. This feature I must leave indistinct, and conclude that the mythological coloring of the passage can have been derived from Mesopotamian sources, either in the popular story itself or in Ezekiel's recension, recalling once more that the "coloring" is limited to two or three descriptive features.

Marvin H. Pope, working on the Ugaritic texts, has made the most serious effort to find a parallel to Ezekiel 28, and he is the only author I have found besides Widengren who bases his opinion on the examination of comparative material.[86] Pope has reconstructed a myth of the displacement of El in the Ugaritic pantheon, and it is this myth to which he finds allusions in Ezekiel: "The allegory of the downfall of the Prince of Tyre is in terms of the aforementioned fate of El rather than of some lesser deity supposedly designated here as a cherub." Pope finds the associations with Ugaritic mythological motifs in 28:12–18 "especially striking."

It is, fortunately, unnecessary here to evaluate Pope's theory in general; it is ingeniously constructed and well argued, and it is in harmony with the widespread myth of a theomachy. I am less convinced that Pope is right when, following Morgenstern, he believes that the myth of the vanquished gods is found in the Old Testament.[87] Neither is it necessary to examine this theory as a whole, since we are interested only in whether such a myth is reflected in

Ezekiel 28:12 ff. Nor am I certain that the affinities of Ezekiel with the alleged myth are "especially striking." Pope mentions the "stones of fire" (Ezek 28:16) and the mountain of Elohim; this latter, he believes, is identical with the palace of Baal, which must have been located on the mountain of the gods, Mount Ṣapon. This identification, in the light of our knowledge of the mythological significance of Mount Ṣapon, is easily accepted.[88] But this allusion is fairly common in the Old Testament, is elsewhere much more explicit, and it is not especially striking here; Ezekiel could allude to the mountain of Elohim as he does here if he had never heard of the palace of Baal.

The "stones of fire," on the other hand, are one of the most obscure details of the passage; perhaps I identified them too quickly as precious stones in my study of Genesis 2–3, although this is still as probable as any other interpretation. Pope invokes both Ugaritic *abn brq*, suggested by Cassuto, and Akkadian *aban išāti*, which is also obscure, and thinks that smelting is involved in the production of these stones. This he compares to II AB (Gordon 51) VI 22–35, in which a fire burns in Baal's house for seven days:

> This suggests that smelting is involved in the production of *'abnē 'ēš* and recalls the description of the marvelous construction of Baal's mythical abode on Mount Ṣapān. The house was made of silver and gold, lapis lazuli, and perhaps some other kind of precious stones (*ilqṣm*) and the materials were apparently fused by a fire set inside the structure. . . . The saga of Baal's bizarre house-raising, we suggest, affords a plausible and withal very striking explanation of the enigmatic *'abnē 'ēš* of Ezek. xxviii 14, 16. The end product of this prodigy of metallurgy performed by the Ugaritic Hephaestos, *Ktr wḤss*, which is apparently referred to as *abn brq* in V AB C̄–D 23, could quite appropriately have been termed *abn išt*, in keeping with the process by which it was produced. This quite novel explication of the possible connection between the Ugaritic *abn brq* and the Hebrew *'abnē 'ēš* is in no way incompatible with Cassuto's plausible explantation. The *'abnē 'ēš* and the *abn brq* may very well refer to the notion that lightning is the flashing of the precious metals and jewels of which the heavenly dwelling was made and the Ugaritic building saga tells us how the divine architect and craftsman achieved this marvel in precious metal and stone.

Pope admits that the passage deals with Baal's palace, not El's; but we need not take mythological coloring so strictly. Still, if we are to go from Ezekiel's hero to El through the palace of Baal, we could go more expeditiously if a palace were mentioned in Ezekiel. The correspondence would be closer if the residence of El, as Pope himself points out, were in the garden of Elohim or on the mountain of Elohim, and not "at the springs of the (two) rivers, midst the channels of the (two) deeps."[89] Pope, it is true, has ingeniously located the abode of El in the mountains of Syria at Khirbet Afqa, 23 miles northeast of Beirut, where there is a spring.[90] One may also think of the rivers of Paradise; but this feature is not mentioned in Ezekiel just as no palace is mentioned. Since the actual points of contact have to be supplied, I do not find the parallel striking; if Ezekiel uses mythological allusions from this source, no distinct pattern emerges.

Pope, with many others, takes Ezekiel 28:1–10 and 12–18 as a single mythological complex.[91] With this I find it difficult to agree. No explicit mythological allusion appears in the first part of the chapter except the dwelling of Elohim in the midst of the seas and the wisdom of Danel.[92] The claim of the prince of Tyre to divinity is scarcely more mythological than the words of Jacob to Rachel (Gn 30:2). The passage may be compared to Isaiah 14:12–14, but the allusions, if present, are much less explicit, and do not pertain to the pattern of Ezekiel 28:12–18, as I hope will appear more clearly below.

Ezekiel 28:12–18 is connected with Isaiah 14:12–14 by a number of writers, including Fohrer. A detailed comparison runs as follows: the hero of Isaiah falls from heaven, the hero of Ezekiel is expelled from Eden, the garden of Elohim on the Mountain of Elohim. The hero of Isaiah is named Hêlēl ben Šaḥar, the hero of Ezekiel is unnamed. Hêlēl desires to ascend to the heavens, to set his throne above the stars of El, to sit on the mountain of assembly in the recesses of Ṣapon; the hero of Ezekiel has no ambition to ascend a height, but he is already on the mountain of Elohim. The hero of Ezekiel is the seal of perfection, perfect in wisdom, adorned with precious stones, perfect in his ways from the day of his creation until he fell into sin. Most of these differences are not significant;

but it is decisive that Hêlēl ben Šaḥar unsuccessfully attempts to
scale the heights of heaven, while the hero of Ezekiel, established
in Eden by Yahweh, is expelled for his sin. A story of an unsuccess-
ful attempt to ascend to the seat of divinity and a story of an
expulsion from Eden cannot be the same story, even if the holy
mountain appears in both stories. Mythological patterns are more
precise than this.

There remains the parallel which I suggested earlier: that Ezekiel
here preserves a piece of Hebrew tradition concerning the first man,
a tradition which differed in detail and probably, with Gunkel,
should be called "more mythological."[93] I thus summed up the
points of contact between the two passages: "There are some
indisputably common features in the two passages: Eden, the
garden of God, primeval perfection and bliss, a fall. But there are
some even more remarkable divergences: in Ezekiel the garden is
full of precious stones; there are no trees; the being is clothed, he is
endowed with marvelous attributes; he does not keep and till the
garden, which is located on the mountain of God; there is no
serpent; and, most important of all, there is no woman."[94] To this
I should have added that the motif of "likeness to Elohim" does
not appear in Ezekiel. From this I deduced the existence of an
account of a fall of a man alone which may be included in the
earlier traditions which lie behind the Paradise story. To the
authors who put Ezekiel 28:12–18 in the same pattern with Genesis
2–3 we can now add Fohrer, although I do not, with him, include
Isaiah 14:12–15 in the same pattern. In addition to these considerations we may add that the wisdom of the first man seems to have
been proverbial (Jb 15:7). This feature is not mentioned in
Genesis 2–3, although the naming of the animals implies it; from
this we might suspect that a form of the tradition existed in which
this feature was explicit, as it is in Ezekiel. Neither is the first man
in Genesis called the "seal of perfection . . . complete in beauty,
perfect in his ways." But the primeval conditions described in
Genesis, while simpler, are altogether in harmony with Ezekiel's
conception.

The sin of Ezekiel's hero is not specified; it is not seeking
"likeness to Elohim," and authors cite Ezekiel 28:2, 9 and Isaiah

14:13 in this connection. On the other hand, nothing in Ezekiel excludes this motif. Ezekiel does, indeed, speak of the sin of "traffic"; but here he is evidently mixing his metaphors, as he does in verse 18, where fire bursts out from the midst of the being and reduces him to ashes. This suits the city much better than its ruler. If this be the proper explanation of verse 18, then the fate of the hero is not mentioned beyond expulsion from the garden, as it is not mentioned in Genesis 3. Procksch has noticed that Ezekiel places Eden in the north, where the mountain of Elohim is found, while Genesis places it in the east; but this is no more than a modal difference.[95]

In conclusion, it appears that Ezekiel 28:12–18 has more points of contact with the Paradise story than with any other biblical passage or with any known mythological pattern. That it has derived mythological allusions from other sources is very probable; I pointed out such allusions in the Paradise story, and the allusions need not be the same in the two forms of the story. In each passage, they do not indicate that we have anything else but a piece of native Hebrew tradition. But I also tried to point out that the Paradise story itself leads one to wonder whether there might not have been a form of the tradition in which a man appears alone; this, taken together with the features mentioned above, suggests that we have such a piece in abbreviated form in Ezekiel. The conclusion which I drew that the variation illustrates the marvelous flexibility of Hebrew oral tradition still appears justified.

. 9 .

Myth and the Old Testament

I. Definition of Myth

The initial difficulty in our topic is the definition of myth. The *Oxford English Dictionary* defines myth as "a purely fictitious narrative usually involving supernatural persons, actions, or events, and embodying some popular idea concerning natural or historical phenomena." This definition does not represent an opinion which is gaining strength in contemporary scholarship. Some deny that it defines the thing to be defined; others regard it as composed *a priori* and too incomplete to be of much value. This scholarly trend is a recent development in philosophy and anthropology. Most contemporary exegetes, it seems, accept the saying of Hermann Gunkel that there is no myth in the Old Testament. Myth, according to Gunkel, was by its nature polytheistic, and it frequently represents the deity in close connection with nature.[1] If this is the proper understanding of myth, then there is no room for further discussion of the topic.[2] But the question has been raised because of the efforts of philosophers and anthropologists to define myth in such a way as to remove the note of falsehood, which popular opinion places in the very definition; and exegetes ought to face the question.

One cannot review or even mention all the writers who have attacked this problem; but one cannot ignore the work of Ernst Cassirer. Cassirer treated the problem in more than one of his works, but his opinions remained substantially the same in his

182

various writings. He defined myth with art, language, and science as a symbolic form of expression. These four have in common that they are "forces each of which produces and posits a world of its own."[3] The mythic mind is not the abstract analytical mind of discursive thought.[4] Myth is an intuition, not an abstraction or a discourse, and the peculiar quality of mythical intuition is that its object, which is the momentary experience, becomes substantial and permanent.[5] Myth differs from art in that it is an act of belief.[6] It perceives physiognomic, not objective characters; its world is a world of actions, forces, and conflicting powers.[7] To mythical and religious feeling nature becomes one great society, the society of life.[8] For Mircea Eliade myth is an autonomous act of creation of the mind which translates an event into a mode of being.[9] Myth expresses in action and drama what metaphysics and theology express dialectically.[10] Myth is not merely story or tradition, because the object of myth is an archetype, which survives in an eternal Now. Myth is not history but exemplar history, the meaning and value of which lie in its repetition.[11] Johannes Hempel calls myth a form of expression of belief, with no judgment about its veracity implied.[12] Myth claims a correspondence with reality.[13] The element common to all myths, according to Eduard Buess, is that they deal with the knowledge of the unknowable.[14] The unknowable here signifies not the absolutely unknowable or mysterious, but that which is unknowable to man in a given concrete stage of intellectual development. The reality which he perceives but cannot recognize and define is inadequately defined by myth.[15] Ultimately myth reduces all causality to the mysterious divine causality which lies beyond perception.[16] Henri Frankfort distinguished mythical thought from logical thought in this, that where logical thought confronts the world of phenomena as an "It," mythical thought confronts it as a "Thou," and mythical thought is dominated by the "I-Thou" personal relationship. Frankfort defines myth as "a form of poetry which transcends poetry in that it proclaims a truth; a form of reasoning which transcends reasoning in that it wants to bring about the truth it proclaims; a form of action, of ritual behavior, which does not find its fulfilment in the act but must proclaim and elaborate a poetic form of truth."[17] Frankfort, generally following Cassirer, has set forth the characteristics of mythopoeic thought: it does not distinguish the subjective and the objective, reality and appearance, life and death, symbol and reality, part and whole, impersonal and personal causality.[18] Myth is not discursive thought, which operates on general principles and accepted laws of thought and being. Admitting that reality cannot be apprehended adequately by myth, mythical thought accepts the validity of more than one avenue of approach. These avenues may be contradictory in their form of expression, but mythical thought dismisses the contradiction, since reality can be expressed only by manifold images. The contradiction lies not in the manifold images of reality but in reality itself. E. O. James writes: ". . . the conception of myth in popular thought and language cannot be sustained since it is not primarily a fictitious narrative setting forth the exploits of supernatural persons and the unusual and fantastic behaviour of natural phenomena, or of historical occurrences."[19] "The chief purpose of . . . myths has been to stabilize the established order both in nature and in society, to confirm belief, to vouch for the efficacy of the cultus, and to maintain traditional behaviour and status by means of supernatural sanctions and precedents."[20] "Myth . . . gave expression to the fundamental experience of a divinely ordered world in which a conflict of supernatural powers and forces was immanent, the one hostile and the other beneficial to their well-being. To fulfil its proper functions it must always be a symbolic representation of the ultimate reality, however this may be conceived and interpreted, concerning the essential meaning and facts of existence and of human destinies. . . . Enshrined in it are the deepest realities, the things by which men live. . . . It is a reality lived. Consequently, every vital religion must have its mythology because myth is the natural language of religion just as ritual is its dramatization in worship."[21] M. Leenhardt describes myth as reality apprehended in images, words, and deeds, and notices that myth and rational knowledge coexist not only in ancient but also in modern society, since neither form of mental operation can do the work of the other nor entirely supplant it.[22] G. van der Leeuw has said: "Doctrine can never completely discard the mythical if it wishes to avoid falling to the level of a mere philosophical thesis."[23]

Millar Burrows has summarized the new view of myth as "a symbolic, approximate expression of truth which the human mind cannot perceive sharply and completely but can only glimpse vaguely, and therefore cannot adequately or accurately express. . . . Myth implies, not falsehood, but truth; not primitive, naïve misunderstanding, but an insight more profound than scientific description and logical analysis can ever achieve. The language of myth in this sense is consciously inadequate, being simply the nearest we can come to a formulation of what we see very darkly."[24] And

G. Henton Davies writes: "Mythology is a way of thinking and imagining about the divine rather than a thinking or imagining about a number of gods. . . . Myth is a way of thinking, independently of a polytheistic setting."[25] Hence it is legitimate to raise the question of myth and the Old Testament once more. The usual denial of myth in the Old Testament does not touch myth as it is understood in these recent studies. These studies may make it possible to accept myth as a vehicle of truth, and as such it is not by definition excluded from the literary forms of the Bible.

In answering the question of myth in the Old Testament we must remember that the concept of myth in modern scholarship is not strictly univocal. There is no generally accepted definition, and the forms of expression which are covered by the term are too diversified to be easily brought together. Much of the constructive work on mythology has been done by anthropologists. When we deal with the peoples of ancient Mesopotamia and Canaan we are not dealing with primitives. The men who built the cities, the industries, and the commercial networks of the ancient world, wrote its literature and created its art cannot be placed on the same level with the Semangs of the Malay peninsula.

I do not think that the difficulty of elaborating a precise and comprehensive concept of myth makes it impossible to give some answer to the question of myth and the Old Testament. This question touches a definite and known collection of literature which has been closely studied: the myths of Mesopotamia and Canaan. It is to this body of literature that we must turn for the answer to our question. We need not create a philosophy of myth in order to answer it. If we can identify certain patterns of thought and expression in this literature, we should be able to tell whether there is anything in the Old Testament which corresponds to these patterns. What we must avoid is a definition of myth so broad that myth ceases to be a distinct intelligible concept. It seems that one can say with Aage Bentzen that myth is not an independent literary type,[26] hence when I employ the word "myth" in this discussion, a more precise term would be "mythopoeic thought," a phrase which is used by Frankfort.

We find it easier to say what myth is not than to say what it is.

Myth is not mere metaphor; myth so understood has no identity of its own.[27] Nor is myth mere poetry, poetic apprehension and expression. Myth is not history, even in the sense in which we use the word history of ancient literature; nor is it the story, popular tradition in the usual sense of the word. It seems most unlikely that the Assyrians would have regarded the story of Ishtar's descent to the underworld as the same type of story which might be told of Sennacherib's victorious campaign in western Asia. It is doubtful that myth should be identified entirely with nature myth, although the connection between myth and nature is very close. Here we do well to remind ourselves that in the ancient Near East there was no concept which corresponds to the modern concept of nature.[28] The world of nature was phenomena: numerous, diverse, and often conflicting, hostile or beneficent to man, exhibiting what we call personal traits and understood as a world of personal beings. But myth was not an allegorical view of nature. Nature deities like Aleyan Baal and Anath represented no particular force or phenomenon of nature, unless one wishes to call such things as life, death, and sex natural forces or phenomena. But there are in Mesopotamia myths which deal with the relations of man with the gods, and these cannot be classified with nature myths.

Myth is not logical discursive thought; hence it is not strictly true to say that myth is a philosophy or a theology. Neither is myth a substitute or an alternate for discursive thought. It does not really do the work of discursive thought, the work of analysis, organization, and synthesis. Those who employed mythical thought did not employ it because they preferred it to discursive thought, at least for some questions, or because they believed it achieved a deeper insight than discursive thought; they employed it because they had no other mode of thought. When discursive thought arose among the Greeks, the conflict between discursive thought and myth at first led to a self-conscious employment of myth as poetic ornamentation or allegory, then to a rationalization of myth and a conversion of myth into the terms of discursive thought, and finally to an abandonment of myth in its classical form. The remark of Leenhardt is true of Greece, however, as it is in general; myth continues to coexist with discursive thought even in advanced civilizations.

What is called the myth-ritual pattern school identifies myth as the discourse, the *hieros logos,* which accompanies ritual.[29] Some anthropologists say that the rite comes first and that the myth is added to explain the rite and to determine its validity explicitly. The importance of the ritual myth in the ancient Near East has been indisputably established by modern research; as a universally valid principle to explain the origin of myth it is not so definitely established. There is much Near Eastern mythology for which no place has been found in the cult; until a place has been found for it, it seems that we ought to leave open the possibility that the single explanatory principle of myth, if there be such a principle, is to be sought outside the myth-ritual pattern.

Can we draw up a positive definition of myth as it appears in the ancient Near East, or at least a description? Our discussion up to this point encourages us to go beyond the common popular conception and the dictionary definition if we can. But we ought to note first that the central and essential character of myth cannot lie merely in its opposition to logical discursive thought; this, again, would make its definition so broad that it would comprehend perhaps most of the human ideational process.[30] We should note also that while myth seems always to be associated with religious belief and practice, myth should not be so closely associated with religion that the two become identical. If myth is identified simply with polytheism, we shall find it difficult to explain some biblical passages. It is not within the scope of this paper to do that which a generation of scholars has not yet done: to present a philosophy of myth which is organized and comprehensive. I present the remarks which follow as no more than a description of some common traits which emerge in the mythical literature of the ancient Near East and are generally so recognized by the scholars who have studied this literature. I cannot say that this description is complete, or that any single feature is to be regarded as the essence from which the other features are derived as properties.

In the first place, it seems that we must with Cassirer identify myth as symbolic expression. The writers of myth do not pretend to attain and describe as immediately perceived in its concrete existence the reality with which the myth is concerned. They intend to present the reality in a symbolic form. The necessity for symbolic conception arises, as Buess has pointed out, because myth deals with the unknown. To avoid the paradox of knowing the unknowable, we go on to explain that the unknown is recognized as existing and operative; but it escapes definition through the intellectual processes of the myth-making man. The myth is intended, in the words of van der Leeuw, to attain mastery over the external world by endowing it with form — that is, with intelligible form.[31] The unknown remains unknown; but the mythopoeic mind has attained by intuition a fleeting grasp of the unknown reality, and it gives this reality the only expression of which it is capable: the expression of the symbol. The unknown reality which is thus expressed is in general the reality which escapes sense observation and the simple deductions of an intellectual process which has not attained the skill of logical discourse or does not know how to apply this skill to the unknown reality.

If we give this reality definition we remove it from the area of myth; hence it is not strictly accurate to say that this reality is the gods, or the divine, or nature, or impersonal force. All such terms give the unknown a definition, the lack of which is precisely what elicits mythopoeic activity. A general term which seems as innocent as any other is transcendental reality. This reality is more than nature, since, as we have observed above, the ancient Near East had no conception of nature as a unified process, a *kosmos*. Now this underlying reality, perceived but unknown and unrecognized, is presented in myth as a personal or a personalized reality. Primitive animism is no longer defended as a theory by contemporary anthropologists even for primitives; it certainly cannot be predicated of the civilized peoples of the ancient Near East. They could distinguish between the "It" and the "Thou." But when they dealt with this unknown reality expressed through mythical symbols, the reality was not identified as an "It." Neither did Near Eastern mythology define this reality as a single personal "Thou"; the complexity of reality, the interplay of numerous obviously distinct forces, and the beneficent or maleficent effect of the play of these forces on man suggested to them the presence of a personal activity like the unpredictable activity of human beings. In this reality were rooted the phenomena which they observed.

The concept of cause and effect is so different in mythical thinking from what it is in philosophy and science that the terms are almost equivocal.

Cassirer has written: "Isolating abstraction, which singles out a specific factor in a total complex as a 'condition,' is alien to mythical thinking. Here every simultaneity, every spatial coexistence and contact, provide a real causal 'sequence.' It has even been called a principle of mythical causality and of the 'physics' based on it that one take every contact in time and space as an immediate relation of cause and effect. The principles of *post hoc, ergo propter hoc* and *juxta hoc, ergo propter hoc* are characteristic of mythical thinking."[32]

"Whereas empirical thinking speaks of 'change' and seeks to understand it on the basis of a universal rule, mythical thinking knows only a simple metamorphosis. . . . When scientific thinking considers the fact of change, it is not essentially concerned with the transformation of a single given *thing* into another; on the contrary, it regards this transformation as possible and admissible only insofar as a universal law is expressed in it, insofar as it is based on certain functional relations and determinations which can be regarded as valid independently of the mere here and now, and of the constellation of things in the here and now. Mythical 'metamorphosis,' on the other hand, is always the record of an individual event — the change from one individual and concrete material form to another."[33] "Science is content if it succeeds in apprehending the individual event in space and time as a special instance of a general law but asks no further 'why' regarding the individualization as such, regarding the here and now. The mythical consciousness, on the other hand, applies its 'why' precisely to the particular and unique. It 'explains' the individual event by postulating individual acts of the will."[34]

Causality in mythical thought is the intuition of a cosmic event which is reflected in the succession of events in the phenomenal world. Without the cosmic event the phenomenal event would not happen or would cease. The succession of phenomena was not governed by the known laws and properties of natural bodies and natural forces; natural bodies and natural forces as such were not known, and no laws of their behavior had been established. The succession of phenomena was achieved by the interplay and sometimes by the conflict of personal wills on a cosmic scale.[35] This does not mean, as I have remarked, that the various personalized forces, whether gods or demons, which the myth-maker saw in the unknown reality were merely allegorical figures of wind, rain, and so forth. The gods are distinguished from the phenomena, and the symbolism is more subtle than the crass allegorism which would identify Hadad with the storm. Were there no Hadad, there would be no storm; were Hadad not a personal being, the storm would not exhibit the capricious behavior which makes it for man both a blessing and a curse. The great seasonal myth of fertility is an expression of the mysterious fact that life as man experiences it comes only from death. Hence the distinction between the two is blurred. The world is annually re-created; were it not for the original creation annually renewed, the cycle of fertility would not endure in the world of phenomena, and the monster of chaos would secure lasting dominion. But the gods of fertility are not merely symbols of natural forces; the succession of phenomena depends on the perpetual life-death cycle on a cosmic scale, and these gods make the cycle. Now the concrete cosmic event can be expressed only in the form of a story.[36] Without discursive thought the myth-maker cannot elaborate the abstract universal concept and deduce general principles. Both the story and the concrete cosmic event are removed from time as it is known in the phenomenal world; they become eternally recurrent.

When we say that myth is wider than nature myth, it is necessary to define our extension lest it become unintelligible. Some classifications of myth made independently by several writers will indicate the area covered by the mythopoeic faculty. Paul Tillich distinguishes myth as cosmological, anthropological, soteriological, and eschatological.[37] Johannes Hempel classifies myth as cosmogonic, soteriological, and the revelation myth.[38] René Largement classifies Akkadian and Canaanite myths as myths of origins, myths of the quest of life, and myths of deliverance.[39] There is substantial agreement in these classifications.

The pattern of myth is used to formulate not only the origins of the universe and of man but also the origins of human institutions, the ideals and desires and ambitions of man, and his success or failure in achieving them.[40] In all these the myth ultimately goes to the unknown underlying reality, whether this reality be explicitly identified as a divine personal being or not. Hence the description of myth as a *Göttergeschichte,* "a story about gods," is not entirely adequate.[41] This pattern of thought and language was intended in the minds of those who employed it not as a vehicle of falsehood or of fiction for the sake of entertainment, but of truth. Does its failure to express truth come from the thought pattern itself or from some other cause working defectively? Is myth so essentially vitiated by the polytheism of the myths which we know that myth cannot be so defined as to exclude polytheism, while the pattern of thought and language remains? Is there any more reason to call myth an essentially defective thought pattern because of its errors than there is to call philosophy an essentially defective thought pattern?

I suggest, with the writers cited above, that in defining myth in such a way as neither to include polytheism nor to exclude it we do no violence to the mythical literature of the ancient Near East nor to any pattern of thought which logical discourse imposes upon us. If the myth-makers were striving for an intuition and an expression of truth, we must give them credit for what they strove to do. Their failure to express the truth about the transcendental reality which lies beyond the phenomenal world is not of necessity to be explained as due to the essential inadequacy of the thought and language processes which they employed. In attempting to tell stories which symbolized the transcendental reality they succeeded only in telling the story of the phenomenal world over again on a larger scale. They did not break through the limits of the observation of phenomena, and their symbols symbolized the unknown without signifying its "wholly other" character. They did not attain the divine; they brought the divine down to their own level, and doubtless they thought they had attained it in reducing it. I submit that they were satisfied with their view of the divine because it was an easier view which made few demands upon them; the ultimate root of their error was not in their thought patterns but in their will.

II. Mythical Patterns in the Old Testament

So much, then, may be said in explanation of one of the two terms of our topic, and it seems necessary to say it. Turning to the other term, we may state at once and without any need of demonstration that the Old Testament certainly makes extensive use of mythical language, imagery, and conception; this is generally accepted by modern scholars. In an earlier chapter I treated Genesis 2–3 as an original composition of the Yahwist tradition largely made up of fugitive pieces of mythological allusion drawn from various sources.[42] In connection with this passage I also treated Ezekiel 28:12–18 as a variant form of the story of the first man which is likewise an original piece of Hebrew tradition but is more mythical in character.[43]

Hermann Gunkel pointed out as examples of mythical conception and language: the treatment of natural phenomena as the action or the experience of personal beings (Ps 19:6; Is 14:12 ff.; the rainbow, Gn 9:12 ff.); the description of the eschatological period as a return to conditions of the primitive period of creation; etiological stories such as the creation of woman from the rib (Gn 2:21 ff.); the origin of human toil and the pains of childbirth (Gn 3:16 ff.); the union of the sons of God and the daughters of men (Gn 6:4 ff.). In addition Gunkel finds mythical elements in poetry and prophecy: an allusion to the story of the first man (Jb 15:7 f.); poetic variations on the creation story; eschatological events such as the world catastrophe, which is a reversal of creation and a return to chaos (Is 24:19; 17:12 ff.); the sword and judgment of Yahweh upon the nations (Is 34:5); the return to chaos (Jer 4:23 ff.); the golden age (Is 11:6 ff.); the imagery of prophetic visions, such as the enthroned Yahweh (Is 6) and the chariot of Yahweh (Ez 1).[44] Johannes Hempel has adverted to what he calls the historicization of myth, by which he means the use of mythical conception and imagery to describe a historic event, such as the fall of the great king represented as a descent into Sheol (Is 14:5–15); Israel as the bride of Yahweh, a response to the myth of fertility (Hos 2; Yahweh has no divine spouse, He has chosen Israel; cf. also Is 62:1–5). Hempel also sees mythical language and conception in eschatology, especially in such features as the Day of Yahweh (Jl 2:10 ff.; 3:3 ff.) and the final victory of Yahweh over His enemies (Is 51:9–13; 1:21–27) and in particular in the tension between history and eschatology in the prophets, which frequently permits them to describe contemporary events in terms of the Day of Yahweh.[45] Edmond Jacob also has adverted to the historicization of myth.[46] In this conception the mythical event, the importance of which lay originally in its character as "exemplar history" (Eliade) and its eternal Now by which it sustains the succession of phenomena, loses its transfiguration and becomes important as a single event. Geo Widengren alleges the assembly of the holy ones (Ps 89:18; 16:3; Dn 8:13; Ex 15:11; Ps 82); the identification of Jerusalem with the mountain of the north, the mountain of assembly (Ps 48:3); Gn 2–3 and Ez 28; the imagery of the theophanies (Ex 19; 33:19–23; Jgs 5:4–5; 1 Kgs 19:9–18; Hb 3).[47] Evidently these instances are not all of equal value, and the scope of this paper does not permit an analysis of each pattern. Equally evidently, however, some of them do bear the stamp of the mythopoeic pattern; cf. my own treatment of some of these passages cited in notes 42, 43, 47, 48.

In some instances the mythical character of the thought and language is evident. The conception of creation as a victory of Yahweh occurs in several passages.[48] Edmond Jacob says that these passages reflect a history of creation, not a myth of creation; the characteristics of myth, especially repetition, he finds absent.[49] It is true that the passages appear to be no more than echoes of the creation myth of the Near East. But Jacob has not defined the characteristics of myth; and not all of the characteristics which I have outlined above are absent from these passages. I am now no longer ready to accept these passages as mere poetic imagery and embellishment; I would rather say that Hebrew religious belief was broad enough to admit more than one symbolic form in which the belief in creation could be expressed.[50] One, which is found only in fragments in the Old Testament, is the victory of Yahweh over the monster of chaos; the other and more reflective account appears in Genesis 1, but this passage too has a relation to myth. The creative combat includes a characteristic of mythical thinking which is rarely verified elsewhere in the Old Testament: the conception of the event as eternally recurring. The creative victory is constantly achieved anew. Yahweh continually slays the monster, but in some passages He keeps it under restraint; thus He removes the perpetual danger that it may break loose and the world may return to "void and waste." Creation is thus a continuing achievement.

Besides these instances of mythical conception, we are able by comparison of the Old Testament with extant literature to see how the Hebrews could revise an existing myth. It is quite impossible to suppose that Genesis has any source of the story of the deluge besides the Mesopotamian myth. By this I do not mean that Genesis knew precisely the myth in the literary form in which we know it, but that it possessed the same source in tradition and no other. The use of the tradition in Genesis gives it no more and no less historical value than it had in Mesopotamian tradition. The Hebrew here was not dealing with history. Now what did Hebrew literary art do with this myth? It removed the gods of Mesopotamia and with them the dissension among the gods which was the moving factor in the myth. As a motive of the deluge it replaced the capricious anger of Enlil with the righteous anger of Yahweh aroused by the deep and total guilt of all mankind. It omitted the passage in which Ea rebuked Enlil for inflicting a punishment which exceeded the guilt. Both the Mesopotamian and the Hebrew faced the problem of destructive natural catastrophes. In common they sought an explanation of these disasters not in the operations of natural forces according to physical laws but in the will of a personal being behind the phenomena. For the Mesopotamian this being was divine — not supreme, but powerful enough to impose his will upon his associates. His will — and this is important — is like the human will in this, that its movements sometimes defy a reasonable explanation, and man is ultimately the victim of catastrophe because he cannot be altogether certain of what the will of the gods may be; like him, the gods may act unreasonably and he suffers their anger without knowing why. For the Hebrews this view of divinity was intolerable. If God exhibits anger it must be reasonably motivated, and there is no reasonable motivation of His anger except the sin of man. When men sin, He punishes them through the operations of nature. The Hebrew neither affirmed nor denied the historical character of the deluge of Mesopotamian myth. What he affirmed was that, if such a catastrophe occurred, it had an adequate motivation. In the world of experience in which the Hebrews lived such cosmic catastrophes did not occur, and this he attributed to the kindliness of God, who spared man the extreme punishment which his rebellion might well deserve.

The creation account of Genesis 1 is another example of a re-treatment of a known myth. Here, however, the writer has excised the mythical elements more radically; he has written an explicit polemic against the creation myth.[51] Polytheism is removed, and with it the theogony and the theomachy which are so vital in the Mesopotamian form of the myth. Even the creative combat is removed, and the author has very little left of the myth except the structure of the universe, which is not strictly a mythical concept. The act of creation is achieved in entire tranquillity, and it is achieved simply by the creative word — an element which is paralleled in the Memphite theology of Egypt.[52]

Now what are we to call such compositions as the creation account of Genesis 1 and the deluge story? The Hebrew did not replace myth with history; it is impossible to suppose that he had historical knowledge of either of these events. He retains too many traces of the myth for us to suppose that he had another source on which to draw. Some might wish to call the Hebrew version a theological reconstruction or interpretation. Theology, however, is logical discourse: a synthesis of abstract concepts which are obtained by the analysis of phenomena. Discursive thought does not appear in the Old Testament, and to call such passages theology is to use the term improperly. It may be necessary to use some term improperly, but why should it be theology? Actually, the Hebrews displaced the objectionable story only by telling another story; and whether this other story is to be called myth depends ultimately on the definition of myth.

Extending the question to other passages where mythical thought and language appear, we may ask whether the Hebrews chose deliberately to portray the unknown reality with embellishments drawn from the wealth of mythical imagery, although they were able, if they wished, to describe the reality in more sober and less figured language. We have no right to say that they proceeded in this manner. They had no abstract discursive thought, and I believe we may say of them, as we say of the myths of other ancient peoples, that they regarded such passages as apprehensions of reality. It was not, indeed, a total and immediate apprehension; but they apprehended the unknown reality in single events, which were symbols, and single events for them too must take the form of a story. And since no single story, no single intuitional apprehension, can exhaust the unknown reality toward which it strives, the Hebrews, like others, were ready to admit a multiple approach to the unknown reality and to describe it in symbols which were diverse or even contradictory in their imagery. Speculatively viewed, the creation account of Genesis 1 and the creative combat of allusions elsewhere in the Old Testament cannot stand together; but the Hebrews did not view them speculatively. They are images, each having its value as an intuition of the reality of creation, neither of which apprehends and describes the reality in its fullness. In the same way we have indications that the story of the fall of man was told in more than one form.

The passages which are cited above all seem to exhibit the features of mythopoeic thought which I have enumerated. They are symbolic representations of a reality which is not otherwise known or expressed. This reality reposes upon a divine background which is represented as personal. This background is apprehended in concrete events on a cosmic scale from which the succession of phenomena arises. This reality is apprehended and described in images, words, and deeds. In the Old Testament we find these forms used of such subjects as cosmogony, soteriology, eschatology, and human origins. Lest it be thought that I have sketched the characteristics of mythopoeic thought in such a way as to establish my proposition, I wish to say simply that these characteristics do not of themselves define a literary form. If we doubt that myth exists or must exist as an independent literary form, we may be satisfied with saying that Hebrew thought and language, when it deals with questions with which other ancient peoples dealt in mythical compositions, has in common with these compositions certain characteristics which we are accustomed to designate as mythical or mythopoeic. Whether these characteristics are enumerated exhaustively, so that we should apply the term myth without any reservation to the Hebrew pattern, is a question which demands further study.

Some recent writers exhibit an inclination toward an affirmative answer. Adolf Kolping: ". . . We should not fail to see that the categories of expression in Israel, like the non-Israelite ancient oriental representations, have the same peculiarity. If the word *myth* were not so objectionable in our own speech, we could speak without hesitation of a similar formally mythical type. . . . The truth of a proposition consists obviously in the correspondence of the content of expression, mediated by the categories of expression, with objective reality. . . . The inspired author of the Pentateuch has incorporated into Genesis the old narratives with their peculiarity of unreflecting unity of attractive means of expression and purposeful content of expression. Here he found ideas preconceived and preformulated which corresponded to that which he wished to say."[53] A.-M. Dubarle: "These different considerations lead to the admission that the story of Eden, and more generally the entire primitive history, proceed from the faith of Israel by the means of mental activities which, in religions less clearly linked with history and lacking the same knowledge of the true God, have arrived at mythical stories. This solution, which admits the close union of matter and form in the mind of the sacred writer, recognizes in these chapters a literary form which is very largely symbolic, without the necessity of distinguishing the historical portions from the fictional portions. . . . [This biblical history] reaches the fact in literary productions related to myth, but in which the content and the orientation of mythical thought have been profoundly modified by the historic faith of Israel."[54] M. Leenhardt: ". . . rationalism has never been able to expel religious thought from human preoccupations. Religious thought is concerned with those human realities which can be apprehended only by mythical knowledge." The same writer explains his application of the term "myth" to the fall of Adam and the redemption in these words: "It is self-evident that the word 'myth' is employed here in the sense of a circumscribed event indicated in these pages, a manner of apprehension intended to seize a reality which escapes the senses."[55] J. Henninger: "So it is seen how revelation, which is not a mythical event but a precise historical event, could utilize the language of myth, granted that this is the most adequate way for the divine pedagogy to reach man. It is seen also how the most profound tendencies of the mythical attitude — among others, the actualization of the primordial events — could find their accomplishment and their sublimation in Christianity."[56] H. Cazelles: "However transcendent the biblical message is, it is too deeply immersed in the oriental literary world not to be expressed in the forms used in this world. . . . The myth is the literary form which expresses the need of man to know the divinity, not under an abstract and metaphysical form but in a personal and concrete manner. . . . The myth expresses the personal character of the forces which operate upon man in and through nature. Biblical religion always remains a religion in which man has personal relations with God, knowing him as will and spirit."[57] Cazelles would limit the word to the earliest portions of Hebrew literature.

It should be stated emphatically that no one who has followed the recent discussions of myth and mythical thinking will be in danger of placing the biblical conception of these things on the same level with the myths of ancient peoples, against which Pius XII warned in *Humani Generis*.[58] The recent literature on the subject, viewed *in globo*, brings out more sharply the difference between the Hebrew treatment of the material of myth from the treatment of other ancient peoples.

Eduard Buess places the difference in the idea of God, which is the unique feature of the Bible.[59] The Yahweh of the Old Testament is not a form posited by mythical thinking; the mythical thinking of the Near East, as far as we know it, showed itself incapable of producing any such form. The unique character of this God is so evident that it needs no discussion. Is the concept so unique that it shatters myth beyond repair? Certainly not to the extent that mythical patterns of thought and language are entirely excluded from the Bible, as we have seen. But the conception of God affects very seriously one of the characteristics of mythopoeic thought which I have enumerated; for God is the unknown reality recognized as unknown and symbolized by mythological forms, the divine background which is conceived as personal. Hebrew religion is unique precisely in that the unknown is not totally unknown. In their own belief the character of this God was known through His revelation of Himself. Their treatment of mythical pieces such as the deluge and the creative combat is to remove anything which is out of character with the God who revealed Himself to them. This knowledge of God through the revelation of Himself they possessed. But the unknown remained unknown and mysterious; man was incapable of a total revelation. When the Hebrews touched upon the questions of the relations of God with nature, with man, and with society, what resources were available to them to give expression to the impact of this mysterious reality upon phenomena and upon their own minds? They had no logical discourse of science and philosophy through which they could express these relations. It is not a tenable view that God in revealing Himself also revealed directly and in detail the truth about such things as creation and the fall of man; the very presence of so many mythical elements in their traditions is enough to eliminate such a view. All they could do was to represent through symbolic forms the action of the unknown reality which they perceived mystically, not mythically, through His revelation of Himself.

III. CONCLUSION

Whether this Hebrew representation of reality is to be called mythopoeic may appear to be merely a question of terminology. Since the recent discussions of myth are known only in the world of scholars, and not even throughout that world, the application of the terms myth, mythical, and mythopoeic to the Old Testament will certainly be misunderstood. My colleague R. A. F. MacKenzie has suggested the term "religious prehistory" to designate the material of Gn 1-11.[60] This term is probably an echo of the term "primitive history" coined by Père Lagrange in 1902. I am doubtful that this term is altogether acceptable. If history must in some sense mean a human witness of past events, the application of the term to this material stretches the term at least as far as it will go. The term is not applicable at all to the mythical patterns of eschatological passages or to the creative combat. These passages have such a distinctive character that it is very difficult to classify them with any recognized literary forms. I remarked above that perhaps some term must be improperly applied; if it is not to be theology or history, why should it not be myth? And is not myth a less improper term than these others? No doubt something should be added to distinguish these passages from the myths to which the name has so long been exclusively applied. Tentatively and as no more than a step in the right direction I suggest that mythopoeic pieces be classified under the general heading of wisdom rather than history; this has already been suggested by A.-M. Dubarle for the Paradise story.[61]

But the question is perhaps deeper than terminology; it may even be a question of the honesty and integrity of scholarship. The studies of the past generation have brought all exegetes to a realization of the kinship of Israel with the ancient Near East in civilization and literature. The theological and religious significance of the Old Testament, we know, has gained, not lost, by this broadening of perspective; this is less well known and realized outside of professional circles. Certainly we have an imperative duty to make this truth better known. Our studies of the Near East have taught us to understand the language of Israel better, to enter its mind, and to share its experience. The more deeply we share its experience and its cultural milieu, the more overwhelming becomes our awareness that Israel's experience of God was like nothing else in the ancient world. Surely there now ought to be little room for timidity and misunderstanding if we call Hebrew literature in some passages mythical, or wisdom discourses couched in mythopoeic patterns. Even if the rigorous ethics of scholarship do not clearly demand the adoption of this terminology, they do demand the recognition of Israel's community with the ancient Near East in patterns of thought and language. We shall never understand the Old Testament unless we learn to read its language. To make it speak our own language is ultimately necessary if we are to make it intelligible; but we cannot do this unless we have first apprehended its meaning in its own literary, cultural, and historical *Sitz im Leben*. The Hebrew intuition of the ineffable reality which revealed itself to man as the personal reality behind the succession of phenomena, the agent of the great cosmic event which we call creation, the reality from which all things came, in which they exist, and to which they must return, was not the creation of mythical form or of logical discourse, but a direct and personal experience of God as the "Thou" to whom the human "I" must respond. But they had no media through which they could enunciate the ineffable reality except the patterns of thought and speech which they inherited from their civilization.

PART IV

MESSIANISM

. 10 .

Royal Messianism

I PRESUPPOSE an idea of messianism which is accepted in substance by all exegetes of all shades of opinion and belief. As Joseph Klausner has stated it, messianism is "the prophetic hope for the end of this age, in which there will be political freedom, moral perfection, an earthly bliss for the people Israel in its own land, and also for the entire human race." Klausner describes the belief in the Messiah as "the prophetic hope for the end of this age, in which a strong Redeemer, by his power and his spirit, will bring complete redemption, political and spiritual, to the people Israel, and along with this, earthly bliss and moral perfection to the entire human race."[1] Exegetes are not entirely in agreement on the extent to which messianism should be called eschatological: that is, whether the messianic hope is to be realized within history or outside history. In either case, however, messianism is understood to be a divine intervention in history and the establishment of the kingdom of God over all men. Later on I shall state the meaning which I think should be attached to the word "eschatological." Here at the beginning we must notice that the future kingdom of God is conceived and described in terms of the historical kingdom of Israel as the primary term of analogy; consequently, the messianic hope rarely appears entirely deprived of national features. In this, as A. Gelin emphasizes, the messianic hope has its roots in history.[2]

My subject is royal messianism as it is seen in 2 Samuel 7 and its parallel passage in Psalm 89 and in those passages which depend upon the oracle of Nathan.[3] I omit from this paper any discussion of the theories of the king in the cult which have been proposed by writers of the Scandinavian school. The arguments raised against this theory by many scholars I accept as decisive, and hence I interpret the messianic character of the Israelite king without any reference to his place in the cult. I must, however, presuppose certain ideas about the kingship of Yahweh which need no demonstration here. That Yahweh is king of Israel is clear, particularly in the Psalms. And while it is not necessary at this point of the paper to define more precisely the meaning of the kingship of Yahweh, we shall have to point out that the human ruler cannot be understood as king except as associated with Yahweh. Israelite theology would not permit the kind of king who appeared in Mesopotamia and Egypt. There was similarity, and we shall point out some similar features; but Hebrew kingship and its ideology cannot be explained as a derivation or a borrowing from foreign ideologies because of its connection with the kingship of Yahweh, which is a distinctive Hebrew belief.[4]

I must presuppose also that the king has a unique position in the religion of Israel. He is a charismatic officer, the successor of the judges; this appears most clearly in the narratives of the installation of Saul as king and in some of the stories of David, although we must grant that this feature appears rarely in the stories of their successors.[5] To the king is attributed superhuman strength and wisdom and the possession of the spirit of Yahweh.[6] The ritual of anointing, which the king shares with the priests and the altar, indicates his sacred character; in him Yahweh dwells. He is, with the help of Yahweh, the defender of his people against external enemies and the support of the social order. Upon him and his relation with Yahweh the national welfare primarily depends. He is the incorporation of his people, and in him are recapitulated the covenant of Israel and the promises and obligations which flow from the covenant.[7] The survival of Israel as a people and the endurance of its hopes both national and messianic were essentially dependent upon the king during the period of the monarchy. After the fall of the monarchy, the national and messianic hopes of Israel had to take a new form.

Hence we must notice that, as G. E. Wright puts it, the line of division between historical and eschatological kingship is somewhat difficult to draw.[8] The historical king appears with traits which are sometimes superhuman, or very near it. He is, at least in the widest sense, a messianic figure. The accession of a successor of David was a new sign that the national hope of a historical or an eschatological future persevered, that the blessing of Yahweh still rested upon the figure of Israel through the king. And this can be proposed without recurring to the theory of a royal Sion festival, as presented by H.-J. Kraus.

I have not included in this study the oracle of Balaam (Nm 24:17). W. F. Albright has shown that this line should be translated: "When the stars of Jacob shall prevail, and the tribes of Israel shall arise," and that it belongs to the thirteenth or twelfth century.[9] Consequently, it contains no reference to the monarchy or to any individual king.

2 SAMUEL 7 AND PSALM 89 (88)

Our point of departure is the oracle of Nathan in 2 Samuel and Psalm 89. In my earlier article on these passages I made the point which many other writers have made both before and since that this oracle is the root of the royal messianic hope.[10] Few modern scholars deny the early date of the oracle. All those mentioned in the preceding note place it in the reign of David or shortly afterward. I have proposed that Psalm 89 is nearer to the original form of the oracle. This hypothesis has been rejected by A. van den Bussche in favor of his own hypothesis.[11] I am not convinced by van den Bussche's defense of his hypothesis, so I retain my own. Some other writers have quoted it without any discussion. From the three forms in which the oracle is preserved I made a reconstruction in which the following elements appear: (1) The election by Yahweh of David as king. (2) Yahweh's protection of David against enemies (the enemies of David must be understood here as the enemies of Israel as well). (3) A father-son relationship based upon the divine adoption of David. This should be compared with the adoption of Israel as the firstborn of Yahweh,

Exodus 4:22. This native Israelite conception makes it unnecessary for us to appeal to the father-son relationship in foreign king ideologies. (4) An eternal covenant with David and the promise of an eternal dynasty. (5) Sin in the successors of David will not destroy the eternity of the dynasty.[12]

On the basis of this reconstruction one can point out some theological development both in 2 Samuel and in the Psalm. In 2 Samuel the father-son relationship, which I attributed originally to David, is transferred to the entire dynastic line (in 1 Chronicles to Solomon). The greatness of the king of the Davidic dynasty, who is like the great ones of the earth in 2 Samuel, has become supreme over the kings of the earth in Psalm 89:28, and in the Psalm the dominion of the Davidic ruler extends from the sea to the rivers. A similar phrase occurs in Psalm 72, which we shall discuss below.[13] In this oracle Yahweh becomes the God of David — something new in Israel, as Johannes Pedersen remarks.[14] But Yahweh cannot be understood as the God of David unless we recall that He was the God of Abraham, Isaac and Jacob, and the God of Israel. The term indicates the covenant relationship; but since David was the king and the incorporation of his people, the covenant with David is not a merely personal covenant. The union of the people Israel with its God now takes the form of a monarchy; the dynastic principle is added as a principle of stability, in harmony with ancient Oriental ideas of the state and the people. If the dynasty is to endure eternally, then Israel as a people and its relationship with its God are to endure eternally.

Psalm 89, which I dated near the fall of the kingdom of Judah in 587, was written at a time when the hope uttered in the oracle of Nathan was submitted to a severe strain. The dynasty appeared to be near collapse. Others, who place the psalm somewhat earlier (Eerdmans, for instance, at the beginning of the reign of Rehoboam), have pointed out that there were several occasions between the reign of David, or at least the reign of Solomon, and the fall of the kingdom of Judah when the hope of an eternal dynasty, or certainly of a world rule, might seem to be vain.[15] The psalm expresses the faith of the devout Israelite that the promise of Yahweh cannot be frustrated, whatever may be the conditions, at the moment, of Israel and its dynasty. If it should fall, a restoration must be expected. No such limitation, however, is present on the horizon of the oracle of Nathan except the vague condition that if David's successors sin, they will be punished as other men; but the dynasty must endure.

Hence it may be said, with Albrecht Alt, that the covenant of David tends to absorb the ancient covenant of Israel.[16] It is difficult to see how Henri Frankfort can call this oracle the dissociation of the people from its leader in relation to the divine.[17] The promise to maintain the greatness of the house of David, a royal house, can scarcely be understood as dissociated from the people ruled by the royal house. Frankfort's desire to refute the cultic-religious interpretation of the king ideology as proposed by many scholars, especially of the Scandinavian school, has here led him to far. We cannot make the Davidic monarch a purely secular figure; neither this oracle nor subsequent royal passages permit this. Israel and the house of David are now by the oath of Yahweh associated beyond the possibility of separation. From the time of the oracle of Nathan no form which the messianic expectation might take could reject the idea of the kingdom and the king, the successor of David.

We find a clear allusion to the oracle of Nathan in the oracle called "The Last Words of David," 2 Samuel 23:3–5. Here the eternal covenant is associated with the righteous rule which is expected of the convenanted ruler. Another clear allusion appears in Psalm 132:11–12. A. R. Johnson has pointed out that "testimonies" (CCD translation "decrees") which appears in v. 12 probably refers to the royal duties involved in the acceptance of the Davidic covenant and not merely to the "testimonies" which occur so frequently in the legal codes of the Old Testament.[18] Otherwise these two passages add nothing substantial to the oracle of Nathan itself.

As a messianic passage, therefore, the oracle of Nathan is neither directly nor indirectly eschatological. It envisages a worldwide rule under a just monarch (and the universality of the rule may be questioned); but this is scarcely the kingdom of the end-time. And no individual ruler besides David himself is presented; the messianic dynasty as eternal is seen, not any single member of the line of which David himself is the head. The oracle supposes no more than a continuation of the Davidic qualities of rule in the descendants of David. It is indeed the root and the Magna Carta of the messianic expectation, but it is susceptible of considerable development; this development we must now consider.

The first passage which comes to our attention is Psalm 2.

PSALM 2

Why do the nations rage
  and the peoples utter folly?
The kings of the earth rise up,
  and the princes conspire together
  against the LORD and against his anointed:
"Let us break their fetters
  and cast their bonds from us!"

He who is throned in heaven laughs;
  the LORD derides them.
Then in anger he speaks to them;
  he terrifies them in his wrath:
"I myself have set up my king
  on Sion, my holy mountain."

I will proclaim the decree of the LORD
  The LORD said to me, "You are my son;
  this day I have begotten you.
Ask of me and I will give you
  the nations for an inheritance
  and the ends of the earth for your possession.
You shall rule them with an iron rod;
  you shall shatter them like an earthen dish."

And now, O kings, give heed;
  take warning, you rulers of the earth.
Serve the LORD with fear, and rejoice before him;
  with trembling pay homage to him,
Lest he be angry and you perish from the way,
  when his anger blazes suddenly.
  Happy are all who take refuge in him!

Many modern interpreters, if not a majority, understand this psalm as directly messianic and eschatological.[19] At the other extreme are interpretations such as that of Gressmann, who finds the psalm messianic in no sense, and takes it as a description of a contemporary king in terms borrowed from the *Hofstil* of Mesopotamia and Egypt. There is in Gressmann's view no eschatological outlook in the Psalm.[20] Gressmann does, however, find in this psalm the "Mutterboden" of the messianic hope; and his explanation of this is similar to the explanation I have already given of the oracle of Nathan — a passage which, strangely enough, is almost entirely passed over by Gressmann in his otherwise very complete discussion of the messianic passages.[21] Aage Bentzen also denies that the psalm is messianic or eschatological. Here, as elsewhere, Bentzen finds the king described as the Primeval Man; and this psalm is an enthronement hymn for a ritual which Bentzen identifies as a repetition of the enthronement of the primeval king.[22] Other interpreters have attempted a third type of interpretation which combines both the messianic and the historical. Artur Weiser, for instance, believes that the psalm celebrates the enthronement of a post-Davidic king; but in the historical event of the enthronement the divine will is revealed as moving towards a universal and final judgment. History and eschatology are joined.[23] In Kissane's interpretation the psalm conceives the oracle of Nathan as fulfilled and addresses the historical king as the ideal king of the future, endowing him with typically "messianic" traits.[24]

The psalm opens with a rebellion of the nations of the earth and their kings and princes against Yahweh and His anointed. The anointed of Yahweh is here, as generally, the historical king; nothing in the psalm indicates any other identity. In response to this rebellion Yahweh Himself speaks; it is He who has set up His own king on Zion, His holy mountain. At the time of the psalmist the messianic-eschatological ruler had not been established on Zion; and unless we are to suppose that the psalmist, without any warning, has leaped into the eschatological future, we should take verse 6 as referring to the establishment of the Davidic dynasty on Zion, as I pointed out in discussing the oracle of Nathan. The king himself then becomes the speaker, repeating the oracle of Yahweh. This oracle is an oracle of divine adoption; it is clearly interpreted as such in the light of the oracle of Nathan, and no suggestion of metaphysical divinity is implied in the phrase in the light of this context, in spite of the efforts of de Fraine (275–276) to find true divinity in the oracle.

The oracle continues with the promise of Yahweh that the king shall rule the nations and the ends of the earth and concludes with an address to the kings and rulers of the earth to give heed and serve Yahweh with fear. Nothing in the text of the passage indicates directly another ruler than the contemporary Davidic monarch. I have pointed out that divine adoption is most easily understood in the light of the oracle of Nathan.[25] What Psalm 2 adds to the oracle of Nathan is a wider outlook, although such a wider outlook may also be found in Psalm 89:28. It is possible to understand in Psalm 2 the kings of the earth, the rulers of the earth, and the ends of the earth in terms of the little empire of David and Solomon, which extended from the Euphrates to Egypt, and from the sea to the boundary of the Desert and the Sown. Such exaggerated expressions of its extent are not out of harmony either with Mesopotamian *Hofstil* or with the poetry of the Old Testament At the same time, whether we understand it as *Hofstil* or as hyperbole, the words of the text actually look beyond Palestine and even beyond the empire of David proper to the world as the Hebrews knew it; the Davidic kingdom has here become co-extensive with the kingdom of Yahweh Himself. And the ultimate establishment of the kingdom of Yahweh on a worldwide scale under the Davidic ruler with whom Yahweh has a covenant is here envisaged. This cannot be predicated of any historical ruler of Israel; it expresses the assurance that the dynasty, represented by the contemporary monarch, will see the realization of the promises which Yahweh has given to the king and to the people. Thus the psalm is better understood as not directly messianic, except in the sense that the king has become a messianic figure, himself the living pledge of the hope of the eternal dynasty of David, the eternity of Israel, and the final establishment of the kingdom of Yahweh within the framework of the kingdom of Israel and its monarchy.

Most modern commentators think the psalm is early rather than late; some put it within the reign of David or of Solomon. The psalm seems to celebrate either the accession of the king or its anniversary. If the accession of any particular monarch is the occasion, the psalm is most easily understood as composed for the accession of Solomon; the language of the psalm fits him better than it fits any of his successors. Since the psalm presupposes the oracle of Nathan, we can hardly understand it of the accession of David himself, which did not occur on Zion; but it could be written for an anniversary of David's accession after the conquest of Zion and the oracle of Nathan. Robert (97) supposes that the psalm is postexilic; this opinion is losing ground among modern interpreters.

In summary, then, this psalm repeats the promise of an eternal dynasty and the adoptive father-son relationship of Yahweh and the king. It adds to this promise an element drawn from the Hebrew belief in the universal kingship of Yahweh, with which the Davidic ruler is associated by covenant. The hope of the eternal dynasty now demands that the kingship ultimately become coextensive with the kingship of Yahweh Himself, from whom the Davidic ruler has received his commission to rule.

PSALM 110 (109)

The LORD said to my Lord: "Sit at my right hand
    till I make your enemies your footstool."
The scepter of your power the LORD will stretch forth from Sion:
    "Rule in the midst of your enemies.
Yours is princely power in the day of your birth, in holy splendor;
    before the daystar, like the dew, I have begotten you."

The Lord has sworn, and he will not repent:
    "You are a priest forever, according to the order of Melchizedek."

The LORD is at your right hand;
    he will crush kings on the day of his wrath.
He will do judgment on the nations, heaping up corpses;
    he will crush heads over the wide earth.
From the brook by the wayside he will drink;
    therefore will he lift up his head.

Psalm 110 is understood as directly messianic by Heinrich Gross (93). This view, common among older authors, has been modified by contemporary scholars. The idea of divine filiation which appears in the Greek text is not found in the Masoretic Text, and among modern interpreters the Septuagint is followed by scarcely any one except the new Latin Psalter and the Confraternity of Christian Doctrine translation. Lagrange said in 1905 that it was better to leave the two redactions of the psalm each in its own character as an attestation of two different messianic conceptions. The same opinion is repeated by Podechard (18–19) and by Gelin (1189). The reasons for accepting the Greek text of verse 3 appear insufficient to me, and therefore I follow the Masoretic Text as commonly emended. If, however, the Greek is accepted, the meaning of divine filiation does not differ here from that which we have found in the oracle of Nathan and in Psalm 2. It denotes the covenant relationship between Yahweh and the royal house.

Modern scholars generally assign to this psalm an earlier date than did older scholars. Ringgren,[26] for instance, thinks that it is not only preexilic, but possibly pre-Israelite Canaanite. It is regarded as preexilic by Artur Weiser (II, 459) as well as by Kissane and Podechard. Gressmann (24) also regards it as early, but thinks that the priesthood mentioned in the psalm comes from a priestly reworking; the psalm itself is monarchic. Gressmann (3) denies any messianic character to this psalm; furthermore, he rejects for this psalm as for all others any comparison of the reigning monarch with the Messiah or any conception of David as a messianic figure. The psalm, he thinks, is entirely political. Aage Bentzen (24–25) believes that the cultic situation of the psalm belongs immediately before the ritual combat. Hans Schmidt[27] also proposes a cultic interpretation: the king here takes his seat on the divine throne during the festival of the enthronement of Yahweh. Kissane interprets Psalm 110 according to the principles which I have sketched above for Psalm 2. Podechard (170–177) takes it as an enthronement psalm. The hero of the psalm is David, who is here attached to the past as the successor of Melchizedek. The psalm is an echo of the Davidic covenant as it is proposed in the oracle of Nathan. Weiser (459) also takes the psalm as referring to a historical king who is here divinely authorized as God's representative.

The psalm does not contain an explicit reference to the oracle of Nathan; but the covenant of Yahweh with David and his house is presupposed. We find in Psalm 110 the elements of a personal and intimate relationship between Yahweh and the king, the perfection of the king, and divine assistance to conquer his enemies. The combat here is presented in more concrete terms than it is in the passages previously discussed. If the obscure verse 3 contains a reference to divine filiation, as I have already pointed out, it is most easily understood in terms of the oracle of Nathan. What is new in Psalm 110 is the association of the monarch with Yahweh in verse 1, where the monarch is invited to sit at Yahweh's right hand. I have already indicated that Psalm 2 introduces a closer association of the monarch with the kingship of Yahweh than we find in the oracle of Nathan. Here the king takes a position which the satellites of the great king might be invited to take. The ritual of putting the enemies at or under one's feet is represented in Mesopotamian art.[28] The title *'adoni*, "my lord," given to the king in verse 1, is the usual polite formula of addressing the Hebrew monarch. Therefore there is nothing in the text of the psalm itself which imposes upon us the conclusion that the psalmist is looking beyond the reigning Israelite king. But, as I have already noticed, the Israelite king is not viewed as a simple historical figure but as a religious figure who incorporates in himself the kingdom of Israel and its hope for a future in which the kingship of Yahweh will become universally effective. In this sense the psalm is messianic, since it repeats the messianic outlook of the dynasty of David.

A second new element introduced is the priesthood of the king according to the order of Melchizedek. The Israelite monarch is not described in the Old Testament as the kind of priest-king which we find in Mesopotamia, Egypt, and Canaan. In Israel the sacral character of the king was suppressed rather than emphasized. This passage stands alone in this respect. A suggestion made by Gressmann and accepted by others seems to offer the simplest explanation of this singular feature. If the psalm is placed early in the reign of David or of Solomon, the reference to Melchizedek is most easily understood as uttered at a time when the connection of the dynasty of David with Zion, the city of Melchizedek, was still new, and when most of the inhabitants of Jerusalem were not themselves Israelites. In the psalm the monarch presents himself to the people of Zion as the legitimate heir of Melchizedek: his successor in the rule of Zion and in his character as priest-king. Such a conception, it is true, did not fit with the Hebrew conception of kingship, and therefore finds little or no echo in subsequent passages. But in David's reign or even in Solomon's such an utterance could find a place in the situation of the monarch, and hence this suggestion appears quite probable.[29]

PSALM 72 (71)

O God, with your judgment endow the king,
    and with your justice, the king's son;
He shall govern your people with justice
    and your afflicted ones with judgment.
The mountains shall yield peace for the people,
    and the hills justice.
He shall defend the afflicted among the people,
    save the children of the poor,
    and crush the oppressor.

May he endure as long as the sun,
    and like the moon through all generations.
He shall be like rain coming down on the meadow,
    like showers watering the earth.
Justice shall flower in his days,
    and profound peace, till the moon be no more.

May he rule from sea to sea,
    and from the River to the ends of the earth.
His foes shall bow before him,
    and his enemies shall lick the dust.
The kings of Tharsis and the Isles shall offer gifts;
    the kings of Arabia and Saba shall bring tribute.
All kings shall pay him homage,
    all nations shall serve him.

For he shall rescue the poor man when he cries out,
    and the afflicted when he has no one to help him.
He shall have pity for the lowly and the poor;
    the lives of the poor he shall save.
From fraud and violence he shall redeem them,
    and precious shall their blood be in his sight.

May he live to be given the gold of Arabia,
    and to be prayed for continually;
    day by day shall they bless him.
May there be an abundance of grain from the earth;
    on the tops of the mountains the crops shall rustle like Lebanon;

the city dwellers shall flourish like the verdure of the fields.
May his name be blessed forever;
    as long as the sun his name shall remain.
In him shall all the tribes of the earth be blessed;
    all the nations shall proclaim his happiness.

Psalm 72 is a prayer for a king. We find a similar division of opinion concerning the messianic character of this psalm. Procksch (594) takes the psalm as messianic-eschatological with the historical king as its point of departure. It is understood as directly messianic by Gross (91–92), Ceuppens,[30] and Roland Murphy (98). A. R. Johnson (6) understands it as a prayer for the ruling member of the dynasty at the time of his accession. Gressmann (16) denied any messianic or eschatological character to the psalm. De Fraine (374) does not think the psalm is messianic; the same opinion is held by Hans Schmidt (136). Weiser (329) believes that the psalm belongs to the ritual of the royal enthronement. It describes the king as the ideal king and confers upon him eschatological traits. These traits are drawn from a common tradition of God's kingship. In a wider sense, then, Weiser understands the psalm as messianic. Kissane's (315) interpretation follows the principles already set forth for Psalms 2 and 110. The king is an historical king with messianic features. Podechard (309) likewise believes that it is an accession psalm, but he believes that it has in its present redaction received messianic additions.

This psalm, again, presupposes the oracle of Nathan, although it contains scarcely any explicit allusion except the endurance of the dynasty in verses 5 and 17. The idea of worldwide rule is stated more clearly than it is in the passages considered above. In verse 8 the king's rule extends from sea to sea and from the river to the ends of the earth. This geography is called "cosmic" by A. R. Johnson (9–10) while Podechard (311) takes the words as describing the ideal limits of Palestine. Kraus[31] takes the limits of the kingdom as worldwide, while Gressmann (19) believes that the geographical terms are derived from Mesopotamia. Weiser (330) takes the boundaries to be those of God's kingdom, by which he must mean the eschatological kingdom. Whatever is to be said about the geography, it is wider in extent that it is in any passage hitherto considered. *Hofstil* does not seem to be the only reason for these terms. They are most probably, as Weiser says, the boundaries of the kingdom of God. These boundaries are the ideal boundaries of the kingdom of the Davidic ruler, who here, as in the preceding passages, rules over a kingdom which is coextensive with the kingdom of Yahweh.

More clearly than in the passages considered above, a transfer of power, as Kraus (73) calls it, is affirmed in verse 1, where the psalmist prays that Yahweh will grant the king His own *ṣᵉdaqah* and *mišpaṭ*, His own judgment and justice. These are the qualities by which a ruler is enabled to govern according to the will of Yahweh. The motif of justice in government is dominant in this psalm compared with the others which we have considered. In addition, a motif appears here which has not appeared in earlier passages, and this is the connection between the king and the prosperity of nature. This is seen in the comparison of the king with the sun, moon and rain in verses 5–6 and in the prayer for abundant crops in verse 16. Here the king is a mediator between Yahweh and the fertility of the soil; the prosperity of the kingdom is conditioned upon the king's justice and righteousness in government. This may be an implicit allusion to the oracle of Nathan; here, however, if the ruling king fails to fulfill the conditions of the covenant, the people who are incorporated with the king in the covenant shall also suffer for his failure.

The prayer is most easily understood of a reigning monarch; this monarch, again, is not seen as a merely secular figure, but as the representative of the dynasty with which Yahweh has an eternal covenant. He is described therefore not in terms of his actual reality, but of the expected fulfillment of Yahweh's promises.

PSALM 45 (44)

My heart overflows with a goodly theme;
   as I sing my ode to the king,
   my tongue is nimble as the pen of a skillful scribe.

Fairer in beauty are you than the sons of men;
   grace is poured out upon your lips;
   thus God has blessed you forever.
Gird your sword upon your thigh, O mighty one!
   In your splendor and your majesty ride on triumphant

In the cause of truth and for the sake of justice;
    and may your right hand show you wondrous deeds.
Your arrows are sharp; peoples are subject to you;
    the king's enemies lose heart.
Your throne, O God, stands forever and ever;
    a tempered rod is your royal scepter.
You love justice and hate wickedness;
    therefore God, your God, has anointed you
    with the oil of gladness above your fellow kings.
With myrrh and aloes and cassia your robes are fragrant;
    from ivory palaces string music brings you joy.
The daughters of kings come to meet you;
    the queen takes her place at your right hand in gold of Ophir.

Hear, O daughter, and see; turn your ear,
    forget your people and your father's house.
So shall the king desire your beauty;
    for he is your lord, and you must worship him.
And the city of Tyre is here with gifts;
    the rich among the people seek your favor.
All glorious is the king's daughter as she enters;
    her raiment is threaded with spun gold.
In embroidered apparel she is borne in to the king;
    behind her the virgins of her train are brought to you.
They are borne in with gladness and joy;
    they enter the palace of the king.

The place of your fathers your sons shall have;
    you shall make them princes through all the land.
I will make your name memorable through all generations;
    therefore shall nations praise you forever and ever.

Psalm 45 is less clearly messianic. Lagrange spoke of a "messianic tincture" which comes from the enthusiasm of the psalmist on the occasion of the royal wedding.[32] The psalm illustrates what we called above the charismatic character of the king, his superhuman strength and wisdom, and here also his beauty. The psalm contributes to our understanding of the Hebrew conception of the monarch; but the messianic interpretation of the psalm rests chiefly, if not entirely, upon verse 7, in which the king possibly is addressed as *'elohim*. This is not the only possible interpretation of the verse. C. R. North,[33] for instance, suggests that the verse may be rendered "thy throne is *'elohim*," a construction identical with Canticles 4:1:

"thine eyes are doves." Such an interpretation is quite in accord with the Hebrew appellative use of 'el and 'elohim. North's suggestion is superior to that of Lattey and others (which I accepted in the article cited): "thy throne is the throne of 'elohim." In North's interpretation the line means, "thy throne is divine." Other writers have pointed out that even if the word 'elohim is understood as addressed to the king, it implies no divinity in the metaphysical sense. Sigmund Mowinckel,[34] for instance, points out that the king is the son of Yahweh. He has the spirit of Yahweh and possesses superhuman qualities; for this reason he can be called 'elohim. Gelin (1179) refers to the superhuman power of the monarch, which is the basis of this superhuman title. Weiser (I,234) translates it as *göttlicher*, "divine," and sees in it a reference to the function of the king as a just ruler, while Kissane (I, 112) understands 'elohim as magnate or noble, "great one." Podechard (I, 181) accepts the conjectural emendation of *yihyeh* for Yahweh. The original reading *yihyeh* was corrupted to *Yahweh*, which was then altered to 'elohim in the redaction of the elohistic Psalter. Podechard translates the verse: "thy throne shall be forever."

These considerations make it extremely difficult for us to affirm that the psalm is directly messianic. On the other hand, we have more than the messianic tincture mentioned by Lagrange. The king is here viewed in his superhuman character as one who has a covenant relationship with Yahweh and is endowed by Yahweh with the qualities to rule. These traits are messianic. They reach their fulfillment in the dynasty and are expected to appear in each individual member, although in fact he may not exhibit them.

There is nothing in the psalm to suggest a date; most modern writers place the psalm in the monarchic period. In its emphasis upon justice and righteousness the psalm resembles Psalm 72; this emphasis does not appear in the oracle of Nathan, which is certainly early, and Psalms 2 and 110.

ISAIAH

From the Psalms we turn to the royal Messiah in the prophetic literature. Here our earliest passage is Isaiah 9:1 ff. It is unnecessary to justify the attribution of this passage to Isaiah himself; most modern interpreters take the passage as original.[35] In interpreting the passage I presuppose the king ideology already found in the Psalms. The passage is regarded as directly messianic by Edward J. Kissane.[36] Ceuppens (234 ff.) finds here an attribution of metaphysical divinity to the Messiah. This attribution, as we shall see, is not well founded in Hebrew idiom.

The identity of the child is closely linked with the Emmanuel oracle of Isaiah 7:14 ff., which is discussed elsewhere in this panel, and hence need not be taken up here.

We point out, however, some of the opinions proposed by recent writers. Helmar Ringgren (133), for instance, thinks the child is possibly a son of the reigning monarch who is described in colors which are not novel in king ideology and are messianic in character. This opinion is in harmony with the conception of the king which we have described. Gressmann (245) sees the king here as a kind of demigod. If this be accepted, the king or the Messiah is here raised to a level which we have not seen in the royal Psalms. Jean Steinmann[37] takes the oracle as referring to Hezekiah at the time of his birth; but Hezekiah is described in messianic terms. The Messiah of the moment becomes the prototype of the perfect Messiah. This opinion is substantially identical with the opinion of Ringgren and others.

The passage begins with a vision of victory over enemies. This victory contains an element which we have not seen in the passages discussed above: the victory comes after a period of tribulation and defeat. The sign of this victory is the birth of a child, a son. This child is without question a scion of the royal house; he shall sit upon the throne of David and over his kingdom. This was the historical situation of the time in which the Emmanuel oracle of Isaiah is to be placed; consequently, it is not entirely without probability that Alt explains the oracle in exclusively political terms. But Herntrich is sure that the passage is eschatological.[38]

It seems that the passage is best understood as we have understood the royal Psalms. The child mentioned is historical, but again he is viewed as the representative of the dynasty, the bearer of the covenant promises and of the messianic hope of the future. The titles which are given him surpass what we have read in the passages mentioned above. He is wonderful counselor, *'el gibbor,* the father forever, the prince of peace. Two of these titles demand some special attention. *'El gibbor,* literally god-hero, is not understood by most recent writers as expressing divinity in the metaphysical sense (Herntrich, "Prachtheld"; Steinmann, "divine hero"; Kissane, "god of a warrior"). In my own article I pointed out a number of instances where the common nouns expressing divinity are applied to persons or objects because of wonderful or superhuman qualities.[39] No more is required for the understanding of the word here. Even if it be granted that it is applied to Yahweh as an appellative in 10:21, it is not alien either to Hebrew idiom or to Hebrew theology to apply the title to the king in virtue of his charismatic qualities and his covenant with Yahweh. Similarly, the title "Father forever" (rather than "father of booty") indicates the eternity of the king no more than does the usual polite form of address to the king, "O king, live forever."

In summary, then, the four titles do not go substantially beyond the king ideology which we have seen in the royal Psalms, and nothing in the passage or in the proximate or remote context indicates that the prophet looks beyond his time for the appearance of this marvelous prince, the new representative of the dynasty of David, the bearer of the covenant promises and of the hopes of the messianic future.

Isaiah 11:1–9 is understood as directly messianic by Feuillet[40] and Kissane (I, 133–134; 142) Feuillet (200–201) describes the king as a charismatic person endowed with wisdom and strength from on high; he is the antithesis of the great king of Assyria, who was the supreme threat to the Hebrew state during the career of Isaiah. His reign is eschatological, depicted in terms which recall cosmic origins. Other modern interpreters understand the passage as referring to a historical monarch. Gressmann (246) seems to refer the passage to David himself; the sprout of Jesse, he says can be no other than David. Klausner (64–65) believes that this passage, together with Isaiah 9:1 ff., refers to Hezekiah, who is here described as the supreme man, politically, spiritually, physically, and ethically. But the passage is messianic in a certain sense. The wish and longing of the prophet, says Klausner, to see his ideal completely realized are his messianic expectations. Steinmann (170–171) understands the passage of Hezekiah in the sense explained above for Isaiah 9:1 ff. Herntrich (208) does not believe the oracle refers merely to a *David redivivus.* More is seen by the prophet here, and this more is a messianic person. Procksch (187) likewise understands the oracle of the historical descendant of David, but the kingdom is here described as the *Urbild der Endzeit;* a Davidic ruler is a historical type of the Messiah.

When the passage is compared with the royal passages already discussed, some new elements appear. The first verse, the shoot from Jesse and the sprout from his roots, perhaps suggests a more remote time than the oracle of Emmanuel or 9:1 ff., which to all appearances are in the immediate present. This remoteness, however, is no more than suggested here. The king is fully endowed with the charismatic qualities of the spirit of Yahweh. Gelin (1182) asserts that there is nothing here which is not connected with the royal Psalms; and if we limit ourselves to the charismatic gifts and the justice of his rule, described in verses 3–5, this assertion will stand. But with verse 6 elements appear which are not found in the royal Psalms. Here we have what is usually called a return to the conditions of Paradise. This suggests the establishment of the final kingdom of Yahweh, in which the conditions of origins are restored.[41] I hesitate to date the passage so understood in the same historical context as Isaiah 9:1 ff.; these developments suggest a later point in the prophet's career. It has become clearer to him that neither under Hezekiah nor under any other historical ruler would the covenant of Yahweh with the house of David reach its fulfillment in the establishment of the kingdom of Yahweh. This was an event which could not be foreseen in the historical context of Isaiah himself. Here, it may be suggested, his vision passed beyond this context, dwelling upon the eternity of the dynasty to look forward to a ruler who would give it the ideal qualities which were expected in the dynasty and which could now be seen only in David himself, the founder. While the passage does not expressly speak of a *David redivivus,* the ruler who is foreseen will once again exhibit in Israel those qualities of government which, by the time of Isaiah, tradition had associated with David, the ideal king of all Israel.

MICAH

The other prophetic passages which we have to consider are substantially no more than echoes of the oracle of Nathan and the king ideology of the royal Psalms. There are, however, a few new elements to be noted. The first passage to be considered is Micah 5:1 ff. The king here is not a present but a future monarch. He comes from Bethlehem to rule over Israel, and his origins are "from old, from days of old." No doubt Micah is here influenced by the Emmanuel oracle, as Procksch (210) suggests. Quite likely also the reference to Bethlehem simply signifies that this king is to come from the royal line of David, not necessarily that he will be born in Bethlehem.[42] By the time of Micah the Davidic monarch was much more closely associated with Zion than with Bethlehem. The reference to his ancient origins can be understood in Micah's time as referring to the time of David himself; it was remote enough to be called "days of old, ancient days."[43] This king also shall feed his flock in the strength of Yahweh and the majesty of the name of Yahweh, and he likewise will be great unto the ends of the earth.

It cannot be established from this passage that Micah sees anything beyond the historical future and the historical line of David. The passage is easily understood in harmony with the oracle of Nathan and the royal Psalms, and needs no further messianic or eschatological explanation.

JEREMIAH

After Micah we must wait for Jeremiah before we meet another prophetic allusion to the messianic king. These occur in Jeremiah 23:5 ff.; 30:9; 30:21. The passage in Jeremiah 23 is probably more eschatological than any passage we have hitherto considered; the introductory formula, "Behold, days are coming," suggests the eschatological future. In the time of Jeremiah the dynasty collapsed. We cannot date this oracle precisely before or after the fall of Jerusalem; it can easily come from the difficult days which followed the death of Josiah. At this instant hope in the dynasty of David as a historical reality was vain. It was not possible to hope for a continuation of the dynasty, but only for a restoration; Jeremiah himself asserted without any doubt that the dynasty would fall. In 22:30 Jechoniah is described as childless, a man who has no success with his sons; none of his race shall sit on the throne of David or rule Judah. Hence the righteous shoot whom Jeremiah sees raised up in 23:5 must be a new David, a new founder of the line. He is described as ruling with success (or wisdom), with justice and righteousness, and as the one in whose days Judah shall be saved and Israel shall find security; and his name is *Yahweh-ṣidqenu*, Yahweh is our righteousness, or Yahweh is our vindication. Outside of the transfer of the prophet's vision to the eschatological future (in the sense of metahistorical) the king is not described in terms which go beyond those found in the royal Psalms.

In Jeremiah 30:9 the Israelites of the future will serve Yahweh their God and David their king. Here we meet the concept of a *David redivivus,* unless the king of the future is called David merely as the new founder of the monarchy. Klausner (101–102) believes that we must distinguish the individual Messiah in Chapter 23 from the collective Messiah — the entire line — called by the name of David in Chapter 30. Klausner does not accept either passage as original, an opinion held by many older scholars; modern critics, however, are more willing to attribute it to the prophet himself — Procksch (247), for instance. Both Procksch and Ernst Sellin[44] have emphasized the nonpolitical character of Jeremiah's concept of the Messiah. This follows from the historical developments of which Jeremiah was a witness. Not only was hope in the dynasty of David vain in his day, but hope in any political future for Israel which could be foreseen. No human power would be able to restore Judah as a political force. The kingdom of the Messiah, therefore, is described in terms of its moral and religious qualities rather than in the political ideas which persist even in the messianic concepts of Isaiah.

EZEKIEL

In Ezekiel, the younger contemporary of Jeremiah, we find four allusions to the Davidic ruler. Like Jeremiah, Ezekiel lived in the period of the collapse of the dynasty. In the ordinary arrangement of his discourses, two of these allusions come before the fall of Jerusalem, two after. In 17:22–23 the prophet foresees a revival of the house of David. It is a cedar which has been cut down; but it has not died. A twig has been planted in the mountains of Israel, and it will once again grow to a noble cedar. Here without explicit reference we have the belief in the eternity of the dynasty of David. Gressmann (255) believes that the new ruler will be David himself *redivivus*. In 21:32 Ezekiel, like Jeremiah, clearly predicts the downfall of the monarchy of Judah. It will be a ruin, and a ruin it will remain until he comes to whom the *mišpaṭ* belongs (American translation, "to whom it rightfully belongs"). This seems to be, as Gelin (1185) points out, a clear allusion to Genesis 49:10. The prophet foresees not only the downfall of the dynasty but also its future restoration; and for the terms of this restoration he returns to the language of one of the oldest oracles concerning the ruler of Israel which remain.

Ezekiel 34:23–24 and 37:24–25 are clear references to a *David redivivus* who will once again be king over Israel. Here, however, Klausner (126) once again sees the collective Messiah, the entire line of David. Klausner also believes that after the fall of the monarchy the royal ideal was abandoned. It is true that Ezekiel does not call the future ruler a king; on the other hand, he certainly does speak of a ruler, and it seems that the word is taken too narrowly if we call this an abandonment of the royal ideal. Possibly, as Gelin (1186) suggests, the name David had by this time come to have a meaning like that of Caesar in the Roman Empire; it designates not only the founder of the dynasty but also any succeeding member.

LATER TEXTS

An allusion to the covenant of David is found in Isaiah 55:3–4; the covenant which Yahweh will make with Israel is like the covenant which He made with David, here called the kindness granted to David. The position of the restored Israel among the peoples is likened to the eminence of David; here nothing is added to the king ideology, but the expectation of the restoration of the people is couched in terms of royal messianism. Zechariah 9:9–10 also contains an allusion to the restoration of the monarchy.[45] The character of the king here is the same as that which we have described already, except that he is here described as "humble." The word probably does not refer to humiliation or defeat, since he is called victorious in the preceding verse, but rather to the absence of the pomp of royalty: a return, we may imagine, to the simplicity of the early kingdom of Saul and David. The king of this restored monarchy is also a king who brings peace and whose dominion is worldwide; the language here is borrowed from Psalm 72.

Finally, we have the prediction of the restoration of the fallen hut of David in Amos 9:11. With the majority of commentators, I do not believe this passage is original with Amos. Gressmann (233) finds the statement entirely political in character, and verse 12, as it stands, is so understood, but the passage should be read in the light of the earlier passages which we have considered. And while the emphasis is political, the restoration of the Davidic dynasty implies also the kingdom of righteousness, justice, and peace which is so often described.

SUMMARY AND CONCLUSION

Messianism in Israel in its earliest form appears in the patriarchal promises and the Sinai covenant. With the monarchy there appears royal messianism, which is monarchic in form.[46] We have seen that this form of messianism contains the following elements: (1) the covenant of Yahweh with David and the promise of an eternal dynasty; (2) a kingdom of righteousness and justice; (3) safety from external enemies and internal security and prosperity; (4) ultimate extension of this kingdom to the entire world; (5) an intervention of Yahweh to accomplish this. We must now answer a few questions about the origin of this conception and its relation with other Israelite beliefs.

We have adverted more than once to opinions which would derive messianism from some foreign source. Gressmann, for instance, and others believe the royal messianism is derived from Mesopotamian conceptions of the world empire and savior king and of the king as a divine figure, a demigod intermediate between gods and men. This opinion admits no positive refutation; we can only examine the evidence adduced and decide, with the majority of modern interpreters, that whatever similarities may be pointed out do not compel us to conclude that Israelite beliefs depend upon Mesopotamian ideas. In addition, we are able to point out peculiar Hebrew elements which are in no way derived from foreign sources. The same argument is valid against the theory of H.-J. Kraus (67) that the Amorite kingship is the point of contact at which foreign king ideology entered into Israelite belief and became the source of the messianic expectation. The arguments of Kraus are ingenious, but the evidence in nonbiblical sources upon which they rest is extremely slender and carries no more conviction than the opinion that Hebrew king ideology comes from Mesopotamia. This opinion has been refined by Gerhard von Rad,[47] who, while he does not believe that the royal Psalms are messianic, finds in Mesopotamian *Hofstil* a bridge between king ideology and messianism. This refinement is subject to the same criticism. Of itself, Oriental court style is hardly a sufficient explanation of such a remarkably distinctive and original idea as Hebrew royal messianism.

We cannot deny certain literary similarities between the formulae addressed to the Hebrew king and the court formulae of Mesopotamia. At the same time, the employment of these formulae in Israel indicates a basis of belief which we cannot find in Mesopotamian literature. If we can find other factors in Hebrew belief which furnish a basis for *Hofstil*, it is these factors which lie at the roots of messianism, and not mere literary forms.[48]

The basic Israelite ideas which are presupposed in the king ideology and which cannot be explained as derived from foreign belief are the Sinai covenant and the kingship of Yahweh. It is unnecessary for me to elaborate here any defense of the originality of these ideas; this is accepted by the majority of exegetes.[49] These ideas enter essentially into the idea of a covenant of Yahweh with David and the ultimate realization of the worldwide kingdom of Yahweh under His chosen king. This concept cannot be explained as derived from the world kingdom of Mesopotamia, either in its ancient form or in its concrete realization under the Assyrians. It might be explained in the eighth century as a reaction to the

Assyrian expansion, which seemed to be the supreme threat to the universal kingship of Yahweh; if so, it is a native Hebrew reaction, a genuine development of the oracle of Nathan and the early royal Psalms as I have explained these passages. Belief in Yahweh's power demanded that this aggressive godless empire must yield; and since the Assyrians had realized concretely the ideal of a world empire found in the second millennium B.C. in Mesopotamia, it no doubt opened the eyes of the Hebrews to the possibilities of a concrete realization of a world empire of Yahweh, where they saw this less clearly before Assyria.

But the world empire which the Hebrews see under Yahweh is not the world empire of the Assyrians of the eighth and seventh centuries. It is transfigured by Hebrew belief not only in the power of Yahweh, but also in His righteousness and justice. As Procksch (596) points out, the universality of the kingdom of Yahweh is not an imitation of the great world empire, but is derived from faith in Yahweh's cosmic dominion. Similarly, the covenant of David is inconceivable without the Sinai covenant preceding it, even though the royal covenant seems to absorb the Sinai covenant, as we mentioned above, when the king becomes the mediator of the covenant.[50] In virtue of the royal covenant, a personal and intimate relationship arises between Yahweh and the king which may be compared to the relationship between Yahweh and the people of Israel as a whole in the covenant of Sinai.

The Messiah may be called, with H. W. Wolff,[51] an *Erscheinungsform* of Yahweh. Here, however, we must be very careful to distinguish this view from the Mesopotamian view of the relation between the king and the god. The Hebrew king is not regarded as a demigod, although he is, as we have seen, a charismatic figure. The Mesopotamian king was the visible representation of the divine power; as such, he was a kind of divine image. Hebrew belief would not admit that the king was an image of Yahweh any more than it would admit that Yahweh could be represented by any image at all. Hence the king is a manifestation of Yahweh not in the sense that he is a visible representation of Yahweh, but rather that in him the power of Yahweh appears. The manifestation of this power is called the spirit of Yahweh, and its effect in the king is to endow him with wisdom, strength, prudence, judgment, courage beyond that of ordinary men.

The question of royal messianism as usually posed is really a question of eschatology: a passage is not taken to be messianic unless it is eschatological. If it refers to a historical king, then by definition it is not taken as eschatological or as messianic.[52] In contrast to this rigid view, other writers assert that the passages are messianic either directly or indirectly, by which they mean that the passages refer not to a historical ruler, but to a future ruler and a kingdom of the end time. This seems to be a false position of the question. In the passages which we have considered, we find features which are applicable only to historical Hebrew kings, others which are applicable to no historical ruler. These additional features may be explained either on the basis of *Hofstil* or as a part of a larger complex of ideas. This larger complex, as we have seen, is ready to hand in the Sinai covenant and the kingship of Yahweh. Gressmann (202) himself has stated this presupposition exceptionally well, in spite of his subsequent explanations, as Israel's consciousness of its own dignity, which rises to a conviction of a call to greater things. This conviction, Gressmann says, is a genuine Israelite concept not derived from foreign ideologies.

But the features which are not applicable to any historical monarch need not, it seems, imply eschatology in the ordinary and strict sense of the word. Indeed it is a question whether in the earlier books of the Old Testament eschatology is found at all in this sense. Certainly there is no well-developed scheme such as one finds in the writings of Judaism. One finds rather a vague belief in a great future. If eschatology is capable of definition at all, I take it that it means a future which lies outside history in the sense that it will not be determined by historical factors. It is an intervention of God outside history and independent of historical factors which will effect this future. The Hebrews believed in the intervention of Yahweh not only in the remote future but also in the present course of their history; consequently, to draw too precise a line between history and eschatology seems to make a distinction which, at least for the early books of the Bible, has no basis in belief.

I have said elsewhere that for the Hebrews the present moment could be conceived as recapitulating the whole past, just as it could be conceived as pregnant with the whole future. But I do not wish to say this in such a way as to make Hebrew thought unintelligible. The Hebrews could speak in this manner because they perceived a reality which persevered through the succession of events and which therefore could be conceived as present and active in each of these events. This reality was the dynasty of David, promised eternal endurance in the oracle of Nathan. In this dynasty they saw the future: a universal kingdom of Yahweh, a kingdom of justice and righteousness, whose ruler by the covenant was placed in a personal and intimate relation with Yahweh, through which he received the spirit of Yahweh and by which he was endowed with superhuman qualities which enabled him to rule. Each successive king was in his turn the bearer of the promises and the pledge of the hope; he was a messianic figure in virtue of his office. However far he himself might fall from the ideal of the king as conceived in David or in his descendants, through him and through no other the ideal of Yahweh's kingship remained living and capable of realization. It was not, therefore, unreal to invest him with the hopes and promises of the dynasty, and to speak of him in terms which in some instances had very little relation to his own personal qualities.[53] This conception suits the Hebrew concept of corporate personality as explained by H. Wheeler Robinson, which can be illustrated also in the patriarchs and in the Hebrew conception of the family and of the state. David in a sense is identified with his seed which he bears in his loins, and in a way he continues to live in each of his descendants, eminently in the one who will realize the ideal of the kingship. His qualities can be attributed to them. The whole line of David is conceived as a single corporate personality.

Such a conception does not of itself imply an eschatological development, nor a view of the future which transcends the historical king and looks to an end time, and to an individual who is not identified with the historical king. In the passages which we have considered such a conception does not appear before Isaiah 11:1; we think we see it in the messianism of Jeremiah, Ezekiel, and

Zechariah. If one compares these passages with the earlier messianism of Isaiah and the royal Psalms, one sees that there is in the earlier passages no reference equally clear to a future ruler. What appears there is the present ruler who is endowed with the ideal traits of the future. The basis for this identification is the collective personality of the whole line and the historical reality of the present ruler as the bearer of the covenant of David and the promises of an eternal dynasty and a worldwide kingdom.

As it seems unnecessary to speak of eschatological messianism in the strict sense, so likewise is it unnecessary to appeal to such views as that of von Rad: that the royal Psalms represent the divine *Urbild* rather than the historical king. Neither is it necessary to recur to the myth of the returning king, as Schmidt has done.[54] In later passages, perhaps, we may have the idea of a *David redivivus*, although we have seen in the discussion of these passages that they may be understood of the dynasty as a whole or of the king of the future identified with David as his descendant and endowed with his qualities in an even higher degree. But the myth of *Urzeit* and *Endzeit* and of the *Urzeitskönig* and the *Endzeitskönig* is a creation of exegetes rather than an explanation of the royal Psalms.[55]

In conclusion, then, we can state that royal messianism is a conviction that Yahweh has promised the dynasty of David an eternal duration. With this eternal duration Israel is inescapably connected. The Davidic king and the kingdom of Israel are to extend their sway over the entire world, and to be the medium through which the kingship of Yahweh will realize itself for all men, a kingship not of conquest and oppression like the world empire of the Assyrians, but a kingdom of justice, righteousness, peace, and security. This hope in its earliest form focuses upon the dynasty as a whole, represented in each successive historical king. As time goes on and the historical perseverance of the dynasty becomes uncertain, and it finally comes to an end, the hope turns to an assurance that the promises of Yahweh will find fulfillment only in a restoration of the dynasty. Attention is then focused not upon the dynasty as a whole — for it no longer exists, or is shortly to perish — but rather upon the ruler who will restore the dynasty. This founder of the new dynasty will be another David, he will exhibit the qualities of the ideal king. In him the fullness of the spirit will be realized, upon him will rest the gifts of the spirit, and through him the power of Yahweh will establish His reign over the entire world, which will submit in peace to the rule of a righteous God.

. 11 .

Messianism and the Catholic College Teacher of Sacred Doctrine

IN MODERN biblical theology messianism is the name given to a complex of ideas which, in the words of Joseph Klausner, contain "the prophetic hope for the end of this age, in which there will be political freedom, moral perfection, and earthly bliss for the people Israel in its own land, and also for the entire human race."[1] The belief in the Messiah himself is described by Klausner as "the prophetic hope for the end of this age, in which a strong Redeemer, by his power and his spirit, will bring complete redemption, political and spiritual, to the people Israel, and along with this, earthly bliss and moral perfection to the entire human race."[2] Once one goes beyond this somewhat neutral definition there is an amazing variety of opinion among interpreters on what is and what is not messianism. It is impossible to settle all these discussions here; our task is to discuss the place of messianism, understood as generally as possible, in the college course in sacred doctrine. Perhaps the first service we can render the teacher of sacred doctrine is to remind him that when he deals with messianism he is handling a topic which escapes facile definition and which can be simplified only by distortion.[3]

If anything deserves the name of traditional, it is the apologetic use of messianic texts to vindicate the messianic character of Jesus. By an easy extension many of these texts were also employed to demonstrate His divinity in the metaphysical sense of the word —

that is, in the Nicene, Ephesian, and Chalcedonian sense. This use can be traced to the third century A.D., and it is attributed to the apologists, especially to Justin. The principle of this apologetic use was and is that a number of predictions in detail of the life and personal characteristics of any individual person can be explained by no coincidence of happy conjecture but only by the divine revelation of these details. Now the Old Testament, it was argued, presents some seventy-five allusions to the life and personal characteristics of Jesus which can be verified in no other person; hence His life and personal characteristics were revealed to the Old Testament prophets by God, and Jesus is recognized as the Messiah of whom they spoke. The argument seems simple and effective. It is not. The primary question: Of whom do these passages speak? was never answered by any serious exegesis. Isaiah 7:14 appears in the Greek and Latin (not in the Hebrew) to speak of a child born of a virgin; it is quoted by Matthew in connection with the conception of Jesus, presumably in illustration of its virginal character; there is no other individual of whom a virginal conception is affirmed or even suggested; therefore Isaiah must predict the virginal conception. All the steps in the argument except the last are doubtfully valid. Every one of the seventy-five texts can be submitted to a similar examination. We are left with a vacuum where we used to have a demonstrated thesis; and in addition we are left with serious doubt whether the Old Testament has any relevance whatever to Christian doctrine, and a skepticism about the meaning of the Old Testament which may never be replaced with certainty. This you call progress?

This I do call progress. As it stands it is purely negative, but even this can be progress. It is not, and we trust never will be, necessary and proper to explain and defend our faith by anything else but the truth. If biblical science has advanced at all in the seventeen hundred years since Justin — a development which ought to surprise no one — then there are some things we know better than the apologists did. This is one of them. And we need not end with a vacuum. We have lost some messianic texts — or rather we recognize that we never had them; we have gained understanding of others. But we have gained far more. Modern biblical studies have given the messianic belief a breadth and a depth which we never perceived in earlier generations, and they have shown us that messianism influenced the composition of the New Testament far more than we realized. Jesus was the Messiah, the fulfillment of the hope of Israel, not by verifying predictions of isolated episodes in His life but by bringing the reality for which Israel hoped.

This introduces us to the idea of "fulfillment," which has been so important in the traditional messianism of apologetics; indeed it is still important, and that is why I dwell upon it briefly. In the traditional apologetics fulfillment was one term of a duality of which the other term was prediction. This is one view of fulfillment; it scarcely seems to be the understanding of the New Testament writers (most frequently Matthew) who use the term. One's hope can be fulfilled. One's personality or destiny can be fulfilled by the realization of the potentialities which lie within one's person. One's desires can be fulfilled. In all of these the common element is the emergence of some reality which in some way is foreshadowed, demanded, needed by that which precedes it: a reality without which the preceding reality remains unfulfilled and to that extent unreal. Jesus is the reality which gives fullness to the reality of the Old Testament; He satisfies its desires, realizes its hopes and potentialities, gives it intelligibility. He is the fullness of Israel.

This, I think, sums up in one word better than any other what is meant by the messianic character of Jesus: He is the fullness of Israel. And here also, I think, lie the importance and value of messianism for the college teacher of sacred doctrine. What Jesus Himself said and did, the manner in which the primitive preaching of the Church presented Him, were principally determined by the recognition that He was the fullness of Israel. The words of the New Testament concerning the person and mission of Jesus are not intelligible without constant reference to the hopes, the desires, and the destiny of Israel whose fulfillment He was. It is doubtful that the course in college theology offers time and opportunity for a full-scale study of Old Testament messianism in itself; but it seems that it must offer time and opportunity for that understanding of messianism which makes the New Testament meaningful.

There is a caution to be entered at this point. Jesus, in realizing the hopes and the destiny of Israel, transformed them. The messianism of the New Testament is not simply the same as the messianism of the Old Testament. One must not only recognize the difference, but one must try to see as well as one can why these differences exist. Old Testament messianism was at best an imperfect apprehension of the destiny of Israel. The full reality of Jesus was something which was not described in the Old Testament because it could not be described. The reality of Jesus is not truly intelligible without reference to the Old Testament; and the Old Testament is not truly intelligible without reference to its fullness. The Old Testament raises questions which it never answers and arouses hopes and desires which it never fulfills. When the reality is fulfilled, it grows into new dimensions, exhibits new features and qualities. The man who fulfills the promises of his boyhood is the same individual person; but without a change of identity he has educed personal powers and performed achievements which were not perceptible in the early stages of his development.

Modern interpretation raises some questions concerning this transformation of Old Testament messianism which are difficult and complex; but the teacher of college sacred doctrine cannot afford to ignore them in his own studies at least, and it now seems impossible that he should not acquaint his students with these questions. I speak of the literary origins and formation of the Gospels. New Testament scholars of our generation accept the principle that the Gospels are the products of faith; that they are compilations of the *kerygma* and the *didache* of the primitive Church. In the Gospels, that is, Jesus is presented as the object of faith and never as the object of detached historical investigation. The historian now asks himself how much the transformation of Old Testament messianism comes from the words of Jesus Himself and how much from the faith of the primitive Church which perceived in the light of its pentecostal experience that Jesus was the fullness of Israel. To this question the historian has not and probably never will have an entirely satisfactory answer. To the believer and to the theologian, who accept the continuity of the teaching of the Church with the teaching of Jesus Himself, the question is interesting but not peremptory. They believe that Jesus lives in the Church, revealing Himself still further and in a particular way to that generation which had personal experience of Him. They know that the fact that the Gospel narratives are propositions of belief does not make them less what they were intended to be: a true presentation of that reality which was Jesus Christ. In this discussion we have neither the time nor the occasion to enter into any detailed investigation of the literary origins of particular Gospel passages.[4]

I remarked above that Old Testament messianism has been broadened and deepened by modern biblical studies. We have learned that a number of elements should be included in messianism which had no place in the traditional apologetics. I omit, not without regret, the hotly debated question of the eschatological character of Old Testament messianism, not because it is irrelevant, but because the time available would permit the discussion of nothing else.[5] There is no doubt about the eschatological character of New Testament messianism, whatever be its origins; this is sufficient for our present purpose. What is lacking in Old Testament messianism is a synthesis of its elements, which are so varied as to seem discordant; indeed, some modern scholars would exclude some elements which are usually included. Sigmund Mowinckel, for instance, argues very ably that messianism is eschatological by definition, and that the king-savior motif, which is not eschatological in the Old Testament, is not to be included in the messianic complex. In synthesizing these elements the New Testament effects the transformation which we noticed above. Disparate and even apparently irreconcilable elements are fused into unity.

Since the messianism of the Old Testament is so fluid, one should be wary of conclusions hastily drawn from the use of the word *christos* in the New Testament. The Hebrew word *mašiaḥ*, which *christos* represents, means "the anointed one," and in the Old Testament designates almost always the king, rarely the priest. It is never used in the Old Testament of the figure called the Messiah; this use of the term arose in later extrabiblical Judaism. The word *christos* consequently refers to the entire complex of messianic ideas; what it means in any given passage can be defined more precisely, if it can be defined at all, only by a study of the context and its ideological background.

Under the general heading of "messianism" one may distinguish several streams of thought in the Old Testament. The king motif is basic in messianism, so we may consider this first.[6] In the ancient world the rule of a king was the only political factor which assured an ordered, peaceful, and strong society, possessed of the resources to resist external aggression and internal corruption. The two functions of the king are said by George Mendenhall to be war and law; and these are the functions which resist external and internal attack. The royal messianism consisted in a belief in the eternity of the dynasty of David, and, after the fall of this dynasty, a restoration of the dynasty under a new and greater David.

The idea of a kingdom often appears without any explicit reference to the Davidic ruler. This idea is rooted in the kingship of Yahweh rather than in the kingship of David. The kingship of Yahweh is worldwide and His effective dominion demands that all men acknowledge His sovereignty and submit themselves to His will. This kingdom is, of course, centered upon Israel, to whom Yahweh has revealed himself; His rule, when it is exercised over all men, will go out from the place which He has chosen as the scene of His manifestation. Nevertheless, there is no clear identification of the kingdom (or *reign*) of Yahweh with the kingdom of the dynasty of David, nor does the Davidic ruler clearly appear as the human instrument through whom the reign of Yahweh is to be established. The themes of king and kingdom are related but not integrated.

The theme of the Son of Man is late and not prominent in the Old Testament. There are many obscurities in the origin and development of this concept, much of which lies in extrabiblical literature, and scholars have not yet come to an agreement on the solution of these difficulties. But the roots of the New Testament are most properly placed in Daniel 7:13, where one "like a son of man" appears before "the ancient of days" and receives from Him a kingdom. Exegetes commonly agree that the son of man here is a personification of the Jewish people; thus the Son of Man theme is related to the messianism of the king and the kingdom. The word "son of man" in Aramaic signifies no more than a man, an individual human being; but the word in popular usage certainly acquired overtones which as yet are not entirely clear to us.

The prophetic theme in Old Testament messianism is less clear. It was the belief of Judaism that prophecy ceased with Malachi and that a prophet would not again appear until the prophet came who would immediately precede and announce the coming of the Messiah. The Messiah-king is not represented as a prophet. Judaism, however, never included in its messianism the Servant of Yahweh, who appears in four passages of Isaiah (42:1–4; 49: 1–6; 50:4–9; 52:13–53:12). In the first three of these passages the prophetic mission of the Servant is at least strongly suggested. In the fourth the Servant becomes one who delivers by an atoning death; the idea is original and unparalleled elsewhere in the Old Testament, and it is not surprising that Judaism failed to find any room for this theme in its messianism.

These are the common messianic themes; but messianism as a whole is much wider. Israel itself is a messianic entity, a society moving toward a life under the will of God but never achieving it, a society which will find its consummation, its "fulfillment" in the dwelling of God among His people. It is a society living in a covenant with Yahweh under the law of Yahweh, worshiping Him in His temple through the priesthood which He established. All of these are institutions through which Israel approached Yahweh; they are all institutions which look to a fulfillment of some kind. Jeremiah 31:31–34 sees a new covenant in which personal knowledge of Yahweh will make law and priestly instruction unnecessary. The same prophet (3:16–17) sees the symbolic presence of Yahweh in the ark of the covenant yielding to His real presence. The redemption of Israel, according to Hosea 2:14–23, cannot be accomplished without another passage through the desert. It is a new creation and a new passage through the sea (Is 51:9–11).

This, we may suggest, is the reality underlying the New Testament synthesis of messianic themes: Jesus is the new Israel who fulfills the destiny of Israel. And since He lives in the Church which He founded, this Church also is the new Israel. Israel's historic encounter with God tends to the "decisive eschatological event," as Rudolf Bultmann has well called it, of the coming of Jesus, where Israel finds its true identity. In Him Israel lives eternally. And in unfolding itself it reveals Jesus Christ in His true identity.

Is this, one may ask, the key to the mystery of salvation which I seem to imply that it is, the comprehensive principle which will answer all questions and solve all problems? I really intend to suggest no facile comprehensive answer to anything, most of all to the mystery of salvation, whose dimensions always remain too large for us. But I do suggest that this is a fruitful approach which will remove some obscurities and afford some new insights. The new Israel which outgrows the old as new wine bursts its bottles is a paradox; but whatever we do, to understand the adult we must study the child — but not exclusively.

To begin, let us take the theme of kingship. There can scarcely be any doubt, although we have no time to argue the point, that Jesus Himself did not emphasize this feature of His mission; if anything, He dismissed it. There are too many Gospel passages which indicate this, in spite of the fact that the early Church did not hesitate to give Him the titles of royalty. We have all heard the traditional explanation that it was politically dangerous to claim royalty, and I am sure we have all felt that there is something wrong with this explanation; Jesus as we know Him made no decisions on the basis of political prudence. If He had a claim to kingship He would have asserted it. Let us ask whether His dismissal of royal messianism did not come from the inner character of His mission. Kingship, we noticed, indicated an ordered and peaceful society, and Jesus certainly intended to move toward such a society. But He had to deny that such a society is possible by political means; it comes from the inner regeneration of each man. Jesus is the initiator and agent of this process of regeneration; He is the king-savior by offering a principle of salvation more certain and effective than the warmaking and the lawmaking of a king. Readers of the Gospels cannot but notice that the allusions to kingship are more common in the infancy Gospels of Matthew and Luke than elsewhere; interpreters with some probability credit this emphasis to the Church herself. Surely the authors of these accounts were as well aware of the paradox which they created as we are; they could recognize, we think, the entirely unroyal character of the circumstances of the birth which they narrated, and in so describing it they succeeded, whether they intended it or not, in describing what is called in John "a kingdom not of this world."

A similar paradox appears in the triumphal entry of Jesus into Jerusalem before His passion, an event related by all four Gospels (Mt 21:1-9; Mk 11:1-10; Lk 19:28-38; Jn 12:12-15). The paradox is attributed to Jesus Himself, who deliberately reenacted the scene described by Zechariah (9:9). The king appears "lowly," a term which is almost technical in much of the late Old Testament literature; it designates the great mass of the poor, the helpless and oppressed. The king-savior identifies himself with those who are most in need of the deliverance which he brings. Here again the placing of this event at the beginning of the passion narratives could scarcely have escaped the notice of the authors of the account.

John contains the only explicit claim of Jesus to royalty in the dialogue between Jesus and Pilate (18:33-37). The account is a final and effective disclaimer of any secular royalty; the allegiance which Jesus demands is allegiance to the truth which He proclaims. Pilate was perhaps a bit hasty in concluding that such allegiance was no threat to the secular government which he represented; other and later Roman administrators saw that the issue between Christianity and the empire was a combat to the death of one of the parties, for even the empire owed allegiance to the truth.[7] But Pilate spoke for many men of his time, if not for most, in believing that the pursuit of truth was such an airy and elusive occupation that it did not deserve the serious concern of practical men of affairs.

Again, we do not believe that the Gospel writers were unaware of the implications of the narrative which finally synthesizes the themes of kingship and the suffering Servant of Yahweh, another event related by all four Gospels (Mt 27:27-31; Mk 15:16-20; Lk 23:42-43; Jn 19:2-7): the mock salutation of Jesus as king by the Roman soldiers and the proclamation of His kingship on the placard of His execution. Here the Gospels present the recognition and proclamation of the kingship of the Son of David. The post-resurrection narrative of the two disciples on the road to Emmaus attributed to Jesus Himself the explanation of this theme: the Christ had to enter His glory through suffering (Lk 24:26).

This development of the theme of kingship is constant in the apostolic preaching as it appears in Acts and in the Epistles. By the quotation of Psalm 2:7, "You are my son, this day I have begotten you," and Psalm 110:1, "Yahweh said to my lord, Sit at my right hand" the Apostles proclaimed that Jesus acceded to His kingship when He was seated at the right hand of God after His resurrection and ascension (Acts 2:30–35; 4:25; 13:33–37; Rom 1:2–4; 1 Cor 15:24–27; Eph 1:20; Col 3:1; Heb 1:3, 5, 13; 10:12–13). By so modifying the theme of the ancient messiah-savior-king Jesus made it complete; the idea of kingship has been "fulfilled."

The theme of the reign of God does not experience the same eschatological transformation. The common designation of the preaching of Jesus is the announcement of the reign of God, and in one passage He declares that the reign of God is "among you" (Lk 17:20–21); it is a present existing reality. The dispute about the meaning of this passage illustrates well the tension between history and eschatology which we experience constantly in the New Testament. Indeed, it suggests that our division between history and eschatology should not be too schematic. Whether we translate Matthew 4:17 and Mark 1:15 as "The reign of God has arrived" or not, the word certainly means nearness, imminence; it cannot refer to a vague and distant event. This arrival of the reign of God is indicated in the parables of the kingdom (Mt 13; Mk 4; Lk 8), where the reign of God is described as an existing reality which passes through a period of testing toward its eschatological fulfillment. But it is an existing reality; wherever men accept Jesus, the reign of God is effective. Indeed, the kingdom contains those who do not accept the reign of God; it is nonetheless the kingdom. The idea of the reign of God as an existing reality in a small beginning is as much a transformation of Old Testament conceptions as the synthesis of the royal messiah and the suffering Servant. As Jesus merited His royalty by His passion and death, so the reign of God merits fulfillment by a process of growth and struggle. In this it faithfully reproduces the lineaments of the life and death of Jesus Himself.

The first generation of the primitive Church perceived that the Church herself, the community which they formed, was the existing reality of the reign of God in the world.[8] In the Old Testament the reign of God was established by the manifestation of Yahweh on "the Day of Yahweh," when He appeared to deliver His elect and smite His enemies. The Day of Yahweh, as we shall try to set forth below, also experienced a transformation in the New Testament; but here again we may borrow Bultmann's lapidary phrase to point out that the early Church saw the death and resurrection of Jesus as the "decisive eschatological event" which established the reign of God. The description which Paul gives of the successive stages of the subjection of all creation to the reign of God (1 Cor 15:20–28) is one of the most profound and mysterious passages of this great ambassador of Christ, and one of the most moving. Here, he seems to say, the resurrection and exaltation of Jesus begins the eschatological process which is now going on and continues until "fulfillment." The salvation process has entered its final and ineluctable phase; all the principles are established which are necessary to bring it to its conclusion. It is for the Church herself to be conscious of her role as the existing reign of God and to recognize in herself the vital force of growth and development which has been instilled in her through the communication of life from Jesus dead and risen and seated as king.

The theme of the Son of Man, we observed, is in Daniel a theme of kingship, and it appears as such in the New Testament; but it also is transformed. Jesus alone uses the title; He used it when He claimed power to forgive sins (Mt 9:6; Mk 2:10; Lk 5:24) and authority over the Sabbath (Mt 12:8; Mk 2:28; Lk 6:5). But the feature of the Son of Man theme which appears most frequently is the coming in the clouds; this feature commonly appears when the Second Coming of Jesus as judge is mentioned (Mt 16:27; 24:26–31; 25:31–46; Mk 8:27; 13:26–27; Lk 9:26; 17:24; 21:27). In the three synoptic Gospels Jesus appeals to the motif of the Son of Man when He is asked directly at the critical hour of His trial before the high priest whether He was the Messiah (Mt 26:64; Mk 14:62; Lk 22:69), and by employing this motif He furnished the court with a basis for His condemnation. The theme of the Son of Man is the principal source of the apocalyptic features of the eschatology of the synoptic Gospels; here as much as anywhere modern interpreters ask to what extent this application of the Son of Man theme is due to Jesus Himself and how much to the *kerygma* of the apostolic Church. The Second Coming, the Parousia, relates the Son of Man theme to the theme of Jesus constituted king by His resurrection. It is the New Testament modification of the Day of Yahweh, a sudden coming of God as deliverer and as judge; the term used in Luke 17:24, "the day of the Son of Man," applies the Old Testament phrase to Jesus Himself.

The transformation of the phrase is somewhat obscure, but it seems possible to trace it. The title is used by Jesus in two contexts where He speaks of His human condition: His homelessness (Mt 8:20; Lk 9:58) and His ordinary manner of life and His associations with the common people (Mt 11:19; Lk 5:34). These might be merely coincidental, were it not for the imposing list of passages in which the title appears in allusions to the passion (Mt 12:40; 17:12, 22; 20:18, 28; 26:2, 24; Mk 9:31; 10:33, 45; 8:31; 14:21, 41; Lk 9:44; 11:32; 9:22; 18:31; 22:22; Jn 3:14; 8:28; 12:34, and in particular Jn 12:23 and 13:31, where the glorification of the Son of Man is identified with His passion). Here again Jesus transformed the theme of the Son of Man by merging it with the theme of the suffering Servant. The emphasis which He placed upon the title brings out the humanity of the Son of Man and His identification with the common condition of man as much as it brings out the ideas of the kingdom and the coming in the clouds.

The theme of the prophet, we noticed, is not prominent in Old Testament messianism. But the prologue of John (1:1–14) sees Jesus as the "fulfillment" of prophecy in a most magnificent way. The word of Yahweh made Yahweh Himself known, for the dialogue of the word is a personal encounter. In hearing His word Israel knew Yahweh as the personal reality which His word expressed. The word in Israelite thought was more than a symbol of the concept; it was a distinct reality, and when it expressed the will of a person it was a dynamic reality whose dynamism was measured by the power of the speaker. The word of Yahweh was creative, for He produced the world by His command. It was destructive, for at His word kingdoms fall. It was the hinge on which history turned, for it brought to pass each crisis which it announced. To Jeremiah it was a fire burning within him. The word of Yahweh never returns to Him without doing its work; the world passes but His word endures forever. Against this rich background of the word as the revelation of God and His operative force in the world John proclaimed that this word, given to the prophets, the agent of creation and the mover of history, is a personal reality who is incarnated and pitches His tent among men. Here is the self-revelation of God through the spoken word, the new creation, the crisis of history which this Word announces and brings to pass.

We have frequently had occasion to refer to the theme of the suffering Servant of Yahweh. The importance of this theme cannot be measured by the number of quotations of Isaiah 53 in the New Testament, of which H. B. Swete counts eight.[9] It lies in the implicit reflection of the passage in the large number of New Testament texts which speak of the death of Jesus as an atonement, a ransom, a deliverance. This conception of the death of Jesus is a constant theme in the synoptic Gospels, the Epistles, and the Johannine writings. The idea of the suffering Servant, we noticed above, had no place in Judaism. This is not surprising, for it is the supreme paradox of the Christian fact. It is the proclamation of success through failure, of creation through destruction, of life through death. Whether for oneself or for another, in the words of Jesus Himself, one who wishes to gain life must lose it. Does not Jesus here also reenact the history of Israel, which had to die as a nation in order to survive as a faith? It is basic in the soteriology of St. Paul that each Christian attains salvation by sharing in the experience of the redeeming death of Jesus; without death one does not pass to a new life.

It seems captious to attribute the theme to any other source than Jesus Himself, although it is not impossible, viewed in the absolute, to consider it as a result of the meditation of the Christian community upon the death of Jesus. The synoptic Gospels emphasize several times the fact that the disciples did not grasp before the resurrection the truth that Jesus had to accomplish His mission by His death. The understanding of the mystery of the atoning death was a part of their pentecostal enlightenment. That Jesus Himself never even attempted to explain the character of His mission nor to show how He "fulfilled" the theme of the suffering Servant is a proposition which does not admit critical and exegetical demonstration. One who believes that Jesus contributed anything to the creation of Christian faith finds it difficult to accept the suggestion that He contributed nothing to the central truth of the Christian mystery of salvation. For the atoning death is the point of synthesis of the various streams of messianic thought in the Old Testament. Without it the other motifs of messianism lose all meaning and significance; they become pieces of ancient oriental mythology, interesting as stories of the adventure of the human spirit exploring the dark mystery of life and death, but no more relevant to modern man than the victory of Marduk over Tiamat. If the apostolic preaching was the creative agent of this synthesis, then the disciples were greater than their master.

Let us now return to what we said was the dominating theme of New Testament messianism: the theme of Jesus as the new Israel. It is this conception of Jesus as "fulfilling" in Himself not only the gifts and mission of Israel but also Israel's historic experience which permits the New Testament writers to employ allusions to the Old Testament which sometimes appear far fetched. Like Israel, Jesus came out of Egypt (Mt 2:15; Hos 11:1). His forty days in the desert and His temptation are reenactments of the forty years of Israel in the desert and its temptations (Mt 4:1-11; Mk 1:12-13; Lk 4:1-13). The storm of the Sea of Galilee gives Jesus an opportunity to exhibit the power over nature which was shown in the passage of Israel through the sea (Mt 8:23 ff.; Mk 4:35 ff.; Lk 8:22 ff.). The feeding of five thousand in the desert recalls the manna (Mt 14:13-21; Mk 6:30-44; Lk 9:10-17). John connects this episode both with the manna and with the bread of life which Jesus gives, His flesh and blood (Jn 6:31-35, 48-58).

John also presents Jesus as the new Moses who through faith in Himself produces the water of life (7:37–38). The transfiguration of Jesus presents Him between the two pillars of the Israelite community: the Law, represented by Moses, and prophecy, represented by Elijah (Mt 17:1–18; Mk 9:2–8; Lk 9:28–36). These were the two channels through which Yahweh spoke to Israel; they are joined by the Son, who "fulfills" them by completing the revelation which they initiated. Paul draws an antithesis between the brilliance of the religion of death and the greater brilliance of the religion of the Spirit (2 Cor 3:7–11). Jesus is the seed of Abraham to whom the promises were made (Gal 3:16), and the community which He created is the Israel of God (Gal 6:16). The Apostles shall sit on twelve thrones judging the twelve tribes of Israel (Mt 19:28; Lk 22:28–30); they rule the Church, the new Israel.

The Epistle to the Hebrews draws upon other Old Testament themes less prominent elsewhere in the New Testament. Jesus is the fulfillment of the priesthood and sacrifice of the Old Testament. The use of sacrificial terminology to describe the death of Jesus appears also in the synoptic Gospels and may go back to the Servant passage of Isaiah 53:10; but the author of Hebrews goes beyond Isaiah. By comparing the death of Jesus with the regularly repeated ritual of sacrifice the author of Hebrews is able to give a peculiar emphasis to the total efficacy of the atoning death.

The Epistle to the Hebrews also combines the themes of kingship and priesthood. The ancient Sumerian and Semitic priest-king represented the people whom he incorporated before the gods; he was the head of the cult as well as the head of the state. Melchizedek (Gn 14) was such a priest-king. This conception of priest-king did not appear in the Israelite monarchy; the reasons for the Israelite modification of the common ancient Near Eastern conception are not entirely clear, but it is clear that the Israelites were unwilling that the king should become a sacral figure. Now Jesus, a priest according to the order of Melchizedek, who was priest-king, and not of Aaron, who was priest alone, restores the ancient conception. The roots of this idea may lie partly outside the Old Testament. Jewish apocryphal literature in some places exhibited the idea of two Messiahs, one royal and one priestly, and the Qumran literature has again raised questions concerning this peculiar feature of messianism.[10]

The Epistle to the Hebrews also uses the theme of covenant to present Jesus as the new Israel. The word covenant (*diatheke*) appears in the synoptic Gospels only in the words of institution of the Eucharist (Mt 26:28; Mk 14:24; Lk 22:20; Lk 1:72 refers to the Old Testament covenant). Paul also uses the word in his formula of institution (1 Cor 11:25). But outside of Hebrews the new covenant is mentioned elsewhere in the New Testament only in 2 Corinthians 3:6. This is really not surprising, in spite of the fact that the covenant theme is so basic in the Old Testament. For the idea of covenant carried with it the correlative idea of the Law, and the relation between God and the new Israel established by Jesus was such that the word "covenant" with its implications of law could hardly be an accurate designation. Where the ideas of fatherhood and adopted sonship enter, the covenant is "fulfilled" in such a way that it can no longer be mentioned. Thus for Paul in Galatians law and covenant are fulfilled in freedom and sonship. The occurrence of the word in the formula of the Eucharist is an allusion to the sacrificial victims of the covenant rite of Exodus 24:8; the application of the blood of the same victim to the two parties of the covenant — Yahweh, symbolized by the altar, and the people present — signified their community in covenant. Jesus is the victim who established communion between the Father and the new Israel, to whom His blood is applied sacramentally. But the nature of the relationship is as different as the quality of the victim.

We ought to mention another factor which was active in the transformation of messianism, a factor which itself arose from messianism; and this was the preaching to the Gentiles. I say this arose from messianism itself, and in particular from the theme of the reign of God. It is evident that the apostolic church was slow to see the full scope of its mission. Jesus Himself had limited His activity to Judaism. When the question of admitting Gentiles to the new Israel arose, the response of many if not most of the community was that they could be admitted if they first became Jews. Not, it seems, until the question was put in these terms did the

Church see clearly that it was the fullness of the new Israel, and that it had to become as spacious as the reign of God itself, which knows no limits. Once this became apparent the Church, by reflecting on the Old Testament, perceived that this fullness was a legitimate development of another biblical theme, and that to make Jesus and His Church, the new Israel, depend upon the old Israel, was to deny the newness and the fullness of the Christian fact. If the Judaizers were right, then Jesus and His Church were not a "fulfillment," but simply another stage in the development of the synagogue. Thus the Church recognized her identity with Jesus as Messiah-Savior, and her mission as a continuation of His.

But in taking the world as the unsubdued kingdom of God the Church transformed the concept of messianism still more. The peculiarly Aramaic title of "Son of Man" does not appear in the Epistles, although the theme of the coming derived from it remains. The words "savior" and "salvation" occur twice in John, more frequently in Luke, Acts, and the epistles, and in Matthew and Mark not at all. The title "savior" (*soter*) is given frequently to Hellenistic kings and to the Roman emperors, and it is hardly doubtful that this Hellenistic conception of kingship influenced the presentation of the royal dignity of Jesus to the Gentiles; it was a conception more familiar to them than the Old Testament conception of kingship. The most important modification is the appearance of the title of "Lord" (*kyrios*). Vincent Taylor has shown, I believe, that this is a title conferred upon Jesus after the resurrection and ascension; the occurrences in the synoptic Gospels as a form of address mean no more than "Sir." He also shows that the origin of the title cannot be explained from the terminology of Hellenistic mystery cults; it is an old title and was used by those who spoke Aramaic as well as by those who spoke Greek.[11] This does not imply that the influence of the Greek-speaking communities was not strong in the development of the term; the Aramaic world, after all, was itself subject to the pressure of Greek usage. As a royal title *kyrios* was extremely common, and its application to Jesus puts in a Greek form the transformation of the idea of kingship which we noticed above; the New Testament conceives kingship as received by Jesus in His resurrection and ascension.

It may seem that I have become so enraptured with my subject that I have forgotten the college teacher of sacred doctrine. It may seem also that I have forgotten messianism and wandered into ecclesiology and Christology, not to mention sacramental theology. But these excursions were not digression; our theological areas are divided by artificial lines which do not always hew to reality. The concept of messianism is complex, as I have observed; it is also basic and touches upon most of Christian revelation. To treat it as merely apologetic is to simplify it by distortion; in fact, this comes near to making it theologically irrelevant.

But what of our teacher of college theology? We have done our best, as others have done before us, to show that the traditional apologetic messianism has no place in a modern course of theology. I do not suggest that a synthetic treatment should simply be inserted in its place. I am aware that messianism as I have outlined it here does not belong to apologetic theology at all, but to dogmatic theology. I think I am aware also that the synthetic presentation of messianism fits into no scheme of dogmatic theology with which I am acquainted. But the college teacher of sacred doctrine is conscious of no compulsion to reorganize the material of theology, and it would be ungracious to leave him with the impression that I think this is all he can do.

It seems to me that such a broad and comprehensive theme can be introduced into our course in sacred doctrine at several points, and that it ought to enrich our presentation of this doctrine. This is perhaps superior to a schematic and synthetic study of the messianic complex which is more suitable to an advanced group of theological or exegetical students. The messianic character of Jesus and of His mission shows us the context of His historical reality. We shall not waste time on useless discussion of "messianic claims" which there is no record of His making, but try to see how His character as the new Israel gives sharpness of outline and contemporary urgency to His words. The incarnate Word is a timeless reality precisely because He is so deeply identified with time, with a definite history and a definite culture. We shall by the exploration of this theme perhaps reach a more profound insight into the identity of Jesus and the Church, an insight which is as necessary now as it always has been. Catholics have not always seen as well as St. Paul saw that a theology of the Church is a theology of the Incarnation. This truth may become clearer and more meaningful when both the Incarnate Word and the Church are seen as the new Israel.

Messianism, we have seen, is deeply involved in the theology of redemption and salvation. What the New Testament means by salvation is largely put in terms of the messianic hope, and we must explore the messianic themes if we are to comprehend its teaching. In our theology the social character of redemption and salvation will become clearer and more relevant to us and our times. Jesus as king is ruler of a society, not of a collection of unrelated individuals, and the reign of God is a social fulfillment, not a group of individual achievements. The tension between history and eschatology will remind us that the Church is an incarnation in history and culture as was the incarnation of the Word. Perhaps no greater falsification of the mission of Jesus and His Church was ever proposed than the theory which made Him the founder of a tight little eschatological group which was willing to let the world go to perdition while it awaited the coming of its redeemer on the clouds. And perhaps there is always a tendency to such eschatologism; it relieves us of our missionary obligations.

And here, in conclusion, may be the most fruitful effect of the treatment of messianism in sacred doctrine: a deeper awareness of the mission of the Church, and of the place of each of her members in that mission. If sacred doctrine in the colleges can contribute to this end, it will have justified itself beyond all demands.

Notes

NOTES FOR CHAPTER 1

1. LX, No. 12 (Sept., 1960), pp. 1109–1120.
2. *Ibid.*, p. 1117.
3. *Ibid.*, p. 1110.
4. *Ibid.*, p. 1117.

NOTES FOR CHAPTER 3

1. Vincent Taylor, *The Names of Jesus* (New York, 1953), p. 161.
2. Cf. for full treatments Oskar Grether, *Name und Wort Gottes im Alten Testament* (*Beihefte zur Zeitschrift für die alttestamentliche Wissenschaft,* 64; Giessen, 1934); Otto Procksch, *Theologisches Wörterbuch zum Neuen Testament* (Stuttgart, 1942), IV, pp. 89–100; R.-J. Tournay, A. Barucq, and A. Robert, in *Supplément au Dictionnaire de la Bible* (Paris, 1952), IV, pp. 425–465. The subject is also treated in most theologies of the Old Testament. Cf. Walther Eichrodt, *Theologie des Alten Testaments* (Berlin, 1948), II, pp. 32–38; P. van Imschoot, *Théologie de l'Ancien Testament* (Tournai, 1954), pp. 200–207; Edmond Jacob, *Theology of the Old Testament* (New York, 1958), pp. 127–135; Thorleif Boman, *Hebrew Thought Compared with the Greek* (New York, 1960), pp. 58–68.
3. Grether, *op. cit.*, pp. 139–143; Tournay, *op. cit.*, V, 424–433.
4. Cf. Walther Eichrodt, *op. cit.*, p. 32. G. van der Leeuw has written in his *Religion: Its Essence and Manifestation* (London, 1938), pp. 403–405: "The world of the primitive and of antiquity, and above all the religious world, knows nothing whatever of 'empty words,' of 'words, words'; it never says: 'more than enough words have been exchanged, now at last let me see deeds'; and the yearning no longer to have to 'rummage among words' is wholly foreign to it. But this is not at all because the primitive world has a blunter sense of reality than ours; rather the contrary: it is we who have artificially emptied the word, and degraded it to a thing. But as soon as we actually *live*, and do not simply make scientific abstractions, we know once more that a word has life and power, and indeed highly characteristic power. . . . Whoever speaks, therefore, not only employs an expressive symbol but goes forth out of himself, and the word that he lets fall decides the matter. Even if I merely say 'Good Morning' to someone I must emerge from my isolation, place myself before him and allow some proportion of my potency to pass over into his life, for good or evil. . . . the word, then, is a decisive power; whoever utters words sets power in motion."
5. Jacob, *op. cit.*, p. 128, seems to overstate the case when he says that the Hebrew mentality makes no distinction between thought and action. He could have adduced Mt 5:22, 28: "Any one who looks at a woman lustfully

has already committed adultery in his heart." The adultery, nevertheless, is committed in the heart. In Hebrew "to say in one's heart" is "to think." But the Hebrew mentality does distinguish between the word in the heart and the word which proceeds from the mouth; Isaac blessed Esau in his heart and Jacob in his mouth, but it was the spoken word which prevailed. There is an essential ambiguity in the word-thing-deed of *dābār*, and the Hebrew mentality was aware of this; if it were not, it would not have spoken of the "fulfilling" or the "coming" or the "establishing" of the word. The Hebrew mentality distinguished between thought and action, just as it distinguished the triple reality of word-thing-deed in *dābār*; but the distinction is not put in our terms, and it permits affirmations of identity between these realities which our logic rejects.

6. Cf. Procksch, *op. cit.*, 4, p. 92.
7. Translation by Speiser, in Pritchard, *op. cit.*, pp. 60–61.
8. In Gn 2:19 Yahweh introduces the animals to the man that the man may give them names. He thus "rules" them, as in Gn 1:26–28. In the 125th chapter of the Egyptian Book of the Dead the deceased is to say: "Evil will never happen to me in this land or in this Broad-Hall of the Two Justices, because I know the names of these gods who are in it, the followers of the great God" (the forty-two assessors before whom the deceased is tried). He then addresses each of the forty-two by name.
9. Cf. Boman, *op. cit.*, p. 68 f.
10. Cf. Grether, *op. cit.*, pp. 59–80.
11. J. L. McKenzie, in *Journal of Biblical Literature*, 74 (1955), 22–27; Gunnar Ostborn, *Tora in the Old Testament* (Lund, 1945); Joachim Begrich, "Die priesterliche Tora," *Beihefte zur Zeitschrift für die alttestamentliche Wissenschaft*, 66 (1936), 63–88.
12. Cf. P. A. H. de Boer, "The Counsellor," *Supplements to Vetus Testamentum*, 3 (1955), 42–71.
13. Quoted from *The Complete Bible: An American Translation* (Chicago, 1939).
14. Cf. Grether, *op. cit.*, p. 98; Procksch, *op. cit.*, 4, pp. 92–93.
15. Cf. Jacques Guillet, *Themes of the Bible* (Notre Dame, Ind., 1960), pp. 225–272.
16. Cf. Procksch, *op. cit.*, 4, p. 95.
17. Wis 18:14–16 demands special treatment (*The Complete Bible: An American Translation*):

> "For when gentle silence enveloped everything,
> And night was midway of her swift course,
> Your all-powerful word leaped from heaven, from the royal throne,
> A stern warrior, into the midst of the doomed land,
> Carrying for a sharp sword your undisguised command,
> And stood still, and filled all things with death,
> And touched heaven but walked upon the earth."

Here the word is the agent of the destruction of the first-born of Egypt (Ex 12:29–30). In Exodus the agent is Yahweh Himself (12:29) or Yahweh and "the destroyer" (12:23), not otherwise identified. Grether, *op. cit.*, p. 150, is right in saying that such a heightened personification is not found in the Hebrew books of the Old Testament. Bousset-Gressmann state categorically that the passage is more than a poetic personification; cf. *Die Religion des Judentums im späthellenistischen Zeitalter* (Tübingen, 1926), p. 347. Joseph Reider states with equal assurance that "the personification of *logos* here is purely poetical"; *The Book of Wisdom* (New

York, 1957), p. 210. I would incline to the opinion of Bousset-Gressmann, who include the passage among instances of the hypostatization of divine attributes as a substitute for God and the divine name which is characteristic of later Judaism. Where Exodus spoke of Yahweh Himself, the Alexandrian poet spoke of His word, as elsewhere the writers of this period spoke of the name or the presence or the angel. "Word" here has no particular force, although the antecedents of its conception as a distinct reality are found in a number of the passages cited in this article. But none of these passages suggest a personal reality like that of Wisdom. This new element is to be attributed to the general doctrine of hypostatization rather than to a development of the concept of word.

18. Cf. Grether, op. cit., pp. 126–135; Procksch, op. cit., 4, p. 94. Cf. also Johannes Hempel, "Wort Gottes und Schicksal," Festschrift Alfred Bertholet (Tübingen, 1950), pp. 222–232.

19. Boman, op. cit., pp. 63–65, insists with perhaps more energy than is necessary that there is no sermo operatorius in the Old Testament which corresponds to the divine word in Egypt and Mesopotamia. Boman does not include in the canon Wisdom, which reads (9:1): "Who made all in your word." Even Psalm 33:6, Boman thinks, is merely a conversion into the passive of the sentence: "And God said: Let there be a heaven." Boman is no doubt correct in insisting that the Israelite conception of the creative word is to be distinguished from the creative word of Egypt and Mesopotamia; but it is not easy to draw the distinction as sharply as he desires. Whether the Yahwist in the creation account of Genesis 2 deliberately rejected the foreign ideology (Egyptian) as implying emanation and chose instead the more primitive conception of creation by work is a challenging assumption. The mind of the Yahwist was more subtle and sophisticated than appears on the surface, and it is not impossible that he wished to convey this idea. Certainly it was foreign to his thought to conceive the divine word as a god, as it was conceived in the theology of Memphis.

20. Cf. Grether, op. cit., p. 137; J. L. McKenzie, in CBQ, 14 (1952), 26–33.

21. Cf. translation by Speiser, in Pritchard, op. cit., pp. 67–68.

22. Cf. A. Robert and A. Feuillet, Introduction à la Bible (Tournai, 1957), 367–371, 812–813.

23. Cf. Albrecht Alt, "Die Ursprünge des israelitischen Rechts," Kleine Schriften (Munich, 1953), I, pp. 278–332.

24. Boman remarks that the layman could easily misunderstand Deuteronomy 8:3 by thinking that the word of God is a substance which man can eat. The meaning of the verse, as is generally understood, is that man can live "by everything which the command of God makes." Here and in other passages in which the word of God appears as a distinct entity, he says, it is evident that the spoken word is conceived metaphorically. At the risk of being thought a layman and of running against a general consent, I must depart from Boman here. When he says metaphorical, he seems to dismiss the whole thing as not serious. I take it that metaphorical (bildlich) means the conscious use of metaphor to describe an object in terms of another object to which it is similar, but with which it is not identical; the cloud is not the daughter of earth and water nor the nursling of the sky, if one must be precise about it. But I object to the reduction of characteristic Hebrew patterns of thought and speech to mere metaphor, which is only an obstacle to the genuine insight of truth through dialectics. Poetry also expresses truth, and it often expresses it better than dialectics. To the Israelites, as to us, the reality of the word was more than a

flatus vocis. We have our way of affirming this reality, they had theirs. To us their way is metaphorical. But when the Israelite said that man lived by the word which proceeded from the mouth of Yahweh, he did not conceive it as an edible substance. He believed that life in its origin and continuance depended upon the word of Yahweh that life should exist and remain. For man, who can obey the word of Yahweh or resist, the word which gives him life is not a simple fiat, but a word which determines the manner in which he should live. The animals sustain their lives by food; man cannot sustain his by food alone, for to reject the word of Yahweh is death. This was not mere metaphor.

25. I cannot forbear from translating this paragraph from Eichrodt, *op. cit.,* II, pp. 37–38: ". . . The New Testament conception is rooted in the original characteristics of word and spirit. The word retains its proper function as revealer of the divine will, not only where, endowed with its own *dynamis,* it shows itself powerful as the joyous message of divine salvation, grows, expands, runs, cannot be bound, and as judge of the intention and thoughts of the heart, sets each man before the decision, but especially where, through its identification with Jesus, it becomes an independent person. . . . The designation of Christ as the *Logos* in John 1:1 is as closely connected with the Old Testament conception as it is in sharp contrast to the Hellenistic *logos,* in that it knows nothing of either a world-mind in the pantheistic sense nor of a 'saving idea' in the idealistic-mystic sense, but sees embodied in the personal life of a human being the will of a personal God for the world and the kingdom in all its dynamic movement. By the recapitulation of the main elements of biblical revelation in a 'Word,' the revelation, as the disclosure of the divine will, opposes the personal-spiritual mode of the divine dealing with men to all physical divinization or mystical union, and thereby preserves the mystery of the divine majesty while at the same time it brings into unity creation and salvation, order and new creation, the static and the dynamic, present and future; all this was possible only through the application of the Old Testament conception of the word of God in its fulness to the Saviour and can therefore be understood only in the light of the Old Testament."

26. Jacob, *op. cit.,* p. 129 (Eng. tr.).

NOTES FOR CHAPTER 4

1. *CBQ,* 20 (1958), 2.
2. Here I follow lines of thought opened by R. A. F. MacKenzie, *ibid.*
3. *From the Stone Age to Christianity* (New York, 1957), p. 64.
4. *ZKT,* 78 (1956), 137–168, in particular 151–152, 158–159. Cf. Rahner's, *On the Inspiration of Scripture* (New York, 1961).
5. In Robert and Tricot (Eng. translation), *Guide to the Bible* (2nd ed., New York, 1960), I, pp. 12–31; Coppens, Descamps, Massaux, *Sacra Pagina* (Paris, 1959), I, pp. 86–99.
6. *Sacra Pagina, op. cit.*

NOTES FOR CHAPTER 6

1. E. L. Allen, *Expository Times,* 57 (1945–1946), 132–133.
2. Sir James Jeans, *Physics and Philosophy* (Cambridge, 1943), p. 145.
3. "In all its phases religion stands in a relationship to nature and is especially determined, among other factors, by the conception of nature. It can truthfully be said that the religion of the primitives consists entirely of a

conception of nature, a certain manner of considering the processes of reality and of adjusting oneself to them." Edvard Lehmann, in Chantepie de la Saussaye, *Lehrbuch der Religionsgeschichte* (Tübingen, 1925), I, p. 29.

4. *The Intellectual Adventure of Ancient Man* (Chicago, 1946), pp. 62–63.

5. *Ibid.*, p. 127.

6. Cf. Dhorme, *Religions de Babylonie et d'Assyrie* (Paris, 1945), pp. 264–268; G. Contenau, in *Religions of the Ancient East* (New York, 1959), pp. 94–98.

7. *An Outline of Biblical Theology* (Philadelphia, 1946), p. 115.

8. *Inspiration and Revelation in the Old Testament* (Oxford, 1946), pp. 1–48.

9. *Ibid.*, 1. So also Heinisch-Heidt: "There is no special word in the Old Testament for 'world' corresponding to the Greek 'cosmos,' i.e., an ordered universe" (*Theology of the Old Testament* [Collegeville, 1950], p. 141).

10. *Inspiration and Revelation in the Old Testament, op. cit.*, pp. 4–6. But we should note that the *Song of Songs* is an exception to this.

11. *Ibid.*, pp. 6–7.

12. *Ibid.*, p. 11.

13. *Ibid.*, p. 16.

14. Eichrodt remarks: "But in this lively animation of nature, which ascribes to the non-human creation a relation to its divine lord similar to the relation of the people of God, there is seen the immediate and unbroken relation of the processes of nature to God, whose activity accompanies them in the history and the life of the people. Therefore one never arrived at the mythological individual life of natural powers, by which they could assert themselves as independent realities in opposition to God. Israel was acquainted with such mythological conceptions, partly from its own past and partly from neighboring peoples, but such mythological ideas could not proceed new from its view of nature as personified, in which this traditional mythical material was used only as poetic ornament" (*Theologie des Alten Testaments* [Berlin, 1948], II, p. 78).

15. *Intellectual Adventure of Ancient Man*, p. 4.

16. Cf. Irwin, *ibid.*, p. 244.

17. *Old Testament Theology* (Philadelphia, 1957), p. 85.

18. *Inspiration and Revelation in the Old Testament*, p. 2; cf. also *ibid.*, pp. 22–23.

19. *Intellectual Adventure of Ancient Man*, p. 244.

20. *The Call of Israel* (Oxford, 1934), p. 14.

21. So Dillmann, *Genesis* (Leipzig, 1882); Driver, *The Book of Genesis* (London, 1909); Ryle, *Genesis* (Cambridge, 1921), *ad loc.*

22. Cf. Gruenthaner, *CBQ*, 9 (1947), 49–50.

23. Deimel, *"Enuma Elish" und Hexaemeron* (Rome, 1934), pp. 83–84; Heidel, *The Babylonian Genesis* (Chicago, 1942), pp. 83–86.

24. Ps 74:13–15; 89:10–11; Is 27:1; 51:9–10; Jb 9:13; 26:12–13; 38:8–11; cf. *TS*, 11 (1950), 275–282.

25. This appears in English translation in Gordon, *Ugaritic Literature* (Rome, 1949), pp. 14–16, 47–48; cf. also Ginsberg in Pritchard, *Ancient Near Eastern Texts* (Princeton, 1950), pp. 131, 141.

26. Cf. *TS*, 11 (1950), 278.

27. *Old Testament Theology*, pp. 88–90.

28. Cf. Heinisch-Heidt, *Theology of the Old Testament*, p. 151; Eichrodt, *Theologie des Alten Testaments*, II, p. 78.

29. Dillmann, *Genesis*, and Gunkel, *Genesis (GHK)* (Göttingen, 1910), *ad loc.*

30. *Old Testament Theology* (Eng. tr., Edinburgh, 1895), II, p. 188.
31. The instrumental function of wisdom in creation appears much more clearly if, with the Greek, Syriac, and Vulgate, *'amman* is read in Prv 8:30 instead of the difficult *'amon*. The word, meaning "master craftsman," appears elsewhere only in Ct 7:2, and seems to be suggested by the ἁρμόζουσα of the Greek LXX and the Vulgate *componens*. The Syriac word is not given in Brockelmann; according to Toy, the word suggests "arranger." This meaning in Prv 8:30 is accepted, on the basis of the VV., in the older lexica of Brown-Driver-Briggs and König, and by Eichrodt, *Theologie des Alten Testaments* II, p. 40, among recent writers; but it is rejected by Gesenius-Buhl and in the newer works of Zorell and Köhler. Cf. also the defense of this sense by Moriarty, *VD* 27 (1949), 291 ff. The reading *'amun,* "foster child," "darling," is proposed by Toy, *Proverbs* (*ICC*) (New York, 1899), Wiesmann, *Das Buch der Sprüche* (*HSAT*) (Bonn, 1923), Gemser, *Sprüche Salomos* (*HAT*) (Tübingen, 1934), and Beer in *BHK*. The context appears to favor the reading *'amun;* the following words, "I was a delight day by day, playing in His presence, playing in the world," suggest not the craftsman, but rather the small child accompanying the workman. Against this weight of opinion, one should not too facilely educe the instrumental function of wisdom in creation from this text.
32. There is an undeniable similarity, in conception and execution, between Ps 104 and Ikhnaton's hymn to Aton. An English translation of the Egyptian poem may be found in Steindorff and Seele, *When Egypt Ruled the East* (Chicago, 1942), pp. 214–215, Wilson, in Pritchard, *Ancient Near Eastern Texts*, pp. 370–371, Breasted, *The Dawn Of Conscience* (New York, 1933), pp. 281–286. Breasted prints Ps 104:20–26 in a parallel column. Among recent writers Gressmann (in Simpson, *The Psalmists* [Oxford, 1926], pp. 18–20) and Oesterley (*The Psalms* II [London, 1939], p. 440) argue for a direct dependence of the psalm on the Egyptian poem. Schmidt (*Die Psalmen* [Tübingen, 1934], p. 191) thinks that it was "easily possible that the song was known to the Psalmist and influenced him." Buttenwieser vigorously denies dependence (*The Psalms* [Chicago, 1938], pp. 158–161). He notes that "in both poems creation is described as continuous, as renewed day by day." Calès (*Le Livre des Psaumes* II [Paris, 1936], p. 271) sees no reason to suppose that the Egyptian served as a model for the Hebrew. Buttenwieser's criticism of the alleged parallels seems valid. The similarity is primarily due to the identity of subject; and even those authors who defend direct dependence note that the Egyptian hymn is addressed to the solar disk.
33. *Inspiration and Revelation in the Old Testament*, pp. 10–11.
34. Eichrodt alone (*Theologie des Alten Testaments* II, pp. 79–83) seems to find in the Old Testament a view of nature as a whole — "the concept of the cosmos as an organism with its own laws of life"; and this concept he finds in Gn 1 only. He traces a development in the idea of regularity in nature from the ancient Israelite idea of the interplay of divine and human action to the idea of "law." But Eichrodt does not mean that this idea of nature as a whole is identical with the modern idea of nature; for in any Hebrew view "there is a constant relation to the creator as the cause and source of cosmic life." The "laws" of nature which are mentioned in the prophetical literature are not objective, like the modern "physical laws"; they are subjective, expressing the constancy and order of the creative will as opposed to the arbitrary will of man. Thus, except

for the interpretation of Gn 1, these pages of the distinguished theologian are not opposed to what is set forth here. As for the Hexaemeron, it seems to me, with all due respect to the learned author, that his interpretation does not justify me in removing this chapter from the general context of Hebrew thought — the same context which Eichrodt himself establishes — but that it is rather to be interpreted in accordance with that context. Eichrodt himself, in conclusion, treats the two ideas as complementary rather than antithetic: "It is distinctive of the Old Testament view of nature that it combines two fundamental types of consideration. It can pass from the recognition of the regularity of nature to the utter obscurity of nature to human understanding without giving up the immediate activity of God in natural events. Thus it meets on the one hand the dangers which are attached in a particular way to the formation of a closed world-view, the extreme division between God and the universe in the manner of the deism which recognizes only a God who 'pushes from outside,' and which leaves the universe to its own laws, and one of nature, which dissolves its regularity in divine arbitrary acts and no longer recognizes any revelatory value in the great ordinances of creation."

35. *Intellectual Adventure of Ancient Man*, p. 56; cf. also Frankfort, *Kingship and the Gods* (Chicago, 1948), pp. 27–30. Wilson's version of the text of the Memphite theology is available in Pritchard, *Ancient Near Eastern Texts*, pp. 4–6.
36. Heidel, *Babylonian Genesis*, p. 27; Speiser, in Pritchard, *Ancient Near Eastern Texts*, p. 66.
37. *Genesis*, p. 105.
38. Heidel, *Babylonian Genesis*, pp. 49–64; Speiser, in Pritchard, *Ancient Near Eastern Texts*, pp. 67–68.
39. Frankfort, *Ancient Egyptian Religion* (New York, 1948), pp. 20–22; cf. also C. Desroches-Noblecourt in Gorce and Mortier, *Histoire Générale des Religions* (Paris, 1948), I, pp. 213–216.
40. *The Religion of Israel Under the Kingdom* (Edinburgh, 1912), pp. 11–12.
41. Stade, *Biblische Theologie des Alten Testaments* (Tübingen, 1905), pp. 17, 94–95, and, more recently, Matthews, *The Religious Pilgrimage of Israel* (New York, 1947), p. 56. Eichrodt (*Theologie des Alten Testaments*, II, p. 1 ff.) submits this view to criticism as a "false isolation" of the incontestably remarkable fact that Yahweh appears not in the benevolent forces of nature, but in the storm.
42. Reading *rokeb ba'araphoth;* cf. Ginsberg, *JBL*, 62 (1943), 112; J. H. Patton, *Canaanite Parallels in the Book of Psalms* (Baltimore, 1944), p. 20. This reading is recommended by the Canaanite verbal parallel and by such passages as Ps 18:10; 104:3. It does not appear, however, even in the most recent commentaries.
43. *The Psalter* (Oxford, 1926), p. 39.
44. *Le Livre des Psaumes*, I, p. 230.
45. Tablet XI, pp. 97–98, 105–107; Heidel, *The Gilgamesh Epic and Old Testament Parallels* (Chicago, 1945), pp. 84–85; Speiser, in Pritchard, *Ancient Near Eastern Texts*, p. 94.
46. Rogers, *Cuneiform Parallels to the Old Testament* (New York, 1926), pp. 147–150; Ebeling in Gressmann, *Altorientalische Texte zum Alten Testament* (Berlin, 1926), pp. 248–250.
47. *Die Psalmen* (Freiburg, 1899), p 52 ff. Artur Weiser ("Theophanie in den Psalmen und im Festkult," *Festschrift für Alfred Bertholet*, Tübingen, 1950) agrees with this criticism of Duhm, and agrees also that the Sinai

theophany is the pattern of the Psalm theophanies. But he would find the explanation of the theophany in the *Gattung* of the Psalms; and he sees in them a cultic representation of the Sinai theophany, which was a part of the annual covenant celebration at the anniversary of the monarch's accession. I do not believe this theory can be discussed here; nor do I see that it should alter our consideration of the theophany as an expression of the Hebrew idea of God and nature.

48. A summary and discussion of the exegetical opinions on this passage is found in Tobac-Coppens, *Les prophètes d'Israel* (Malines, 1932), pp. 158–160. Coppens' conclusion is simple despair: "In our opinion, we do not yet possess a satisfying interpretation of the scene of Horeb."

49. The Ugaritic texts are published in transliteration with glossary by Gordon, *Ugaritic Handbook* (Rome, 1947). Two English translations of the mythological texts are now available: Gordon, *Ugaritic Literature* (Rome, 1949), and Ginsberg, in Pritchard, *Ancient Near Eastern Texts*, pp. 129–155. For a discussion of the religion of the Canaanites on the basis of the texts, cf. Albright, *Archaeology and the Religion of Israel* (Baltimore, 1942), pp. 68–94. The title of Julian Obermann's *Ugaritic Mythology* (New Haven, 1948) is somewhat misleading; it contains a very small selection of texts. On the Babylonian New Year's festival, cf. the full treatment by Frankfort in *Kingship and the Gods* (Chicago, 1948), pp. 313–333.

50. *Archaeology and the Religion of Israel*, p. 71.

51. *Israel*, I–II (Copenhagen, 1926), p. 204 ff.

52. *Op. cit.*, p. 182 ff., 211.

53. Cf. *TS*, 11 (1950), 275–282.

54. There seems to have been such an aberration in the Jewish military colony of Elephantine in the fifth century, where there was a temple to Yahweh, Anath-Bethel, and Ishum-Bethel, cf. Cowley, *Aramaic Papyri of the Fifth Century* (Oxford, 1923), pp. xx–xxiii, with references to the pertinent texts of the papyri. Albright, however, thinks that these names represent hypostatizations of the divine attributes, as found in the works of Philo, cf. *Archaeology and the Religion of Israel*, pp. 168–175. The more common view sees in them deities of Aramaean paganism; Anath is the name of the Canaanite fertility goddess.

55. *Intellectual Adventure of Ancient Man*, p. 296.

56. Albright writes: "It is very improbable that the evolution [of Canaanite religion] which we have indicated had seriously begun when the Israelites conquered Palestine. The sedentary culture which they encountered in the thirteenth century seems to have reflected the lowest religious level in all Canaanite history, just as it represented the lowest point in the history of Canaanite art. Against this religion the Israelites reacted with such vigor that we find only the scantiest traces of it surviving in Yahwism — many of these traces belonging, moreover, to later waves of Canaanite (Phoenician) influence" (*Archaeology and the Religion of Israel*, p. 94).

57. *Ibid.*, p. 114.

58. This theory is defended by Mowinckel, *Psalmenstudien II*, 1922, and Hans Schmidt, *Die Thronfahrt Jahves*, 1927. These two works were not available to me when this article was written. I have employed principally Oesterley, *The Psalms*, I, pp. 44–45, and Hans Schmidt, *Die Psalmen*, on Pss 29, 47, 68, 93–100.

59. Oesterley, *The Psalms*, I, p. 45.

60. Cf. *TS*, 11 (1950), 278–279.

61. So Schmidt and Oesterley; Calès, without accepting a mythological allusion, sees it as "the interpretation of the reign of God from the creation of the world."
62. *Intellectual Adventure of Ancient Man*, p. 141.
63. Ebeling, in Gressmann, *Altorientalische Texte*, pp. 261–262; Stephens, in Pritchard, *Ancient Near Eastern Texts*, p. 392.
64. *Religion of Babylonia and Assyria* (Boston, 1898), pp. 313–314.
65. I accept what appears to be the far more common view of modern interpreters that the locust plague of Joel is an actual event, and not a military invasion allegorically described; cf. Nowack, *Kleine Propheten* (*GHK:* Göttingen; 1897), p. 92 ff.; Marti, *Dodekapropheton* (*KHC:* Tübingen, 1904), p. 111; Lippl, *Die zwölf kleinen Propheten* (*HSAT:* Bonn, 1937), p. 92 ff.; for summaries of the history of interpretation, cf. especially Bewer, *Joel* (*ICC:* New York, 1911), pp. 65–67, and Pautrel, in Pirot-Robert, *Supplément, Dictionnaire de la Bible*, "Joel," cc. 1102–1103.
66. *Religion of Israel under the Kingdom*, p. 93.
67. Tromp, *De Revelatione Christiana* (Rome, 1945), p. 115.
68. Tromp, *loc. cit.;* cf. also Garrigou-Lagrange, *De Revelatione* (Rome, 1945), II, pp. 40–41: "[The miracle] surpasses the activity of entire created nature. . . . The miracle is distinguished 1° from natural events, even the extraordinary . . . 2° from diabolical prodigies . . . 3° from extraordinary divine deeds or effects . . . the miracle is also distinguished from those ordinary divine actions which are called providential."
69. *Inspiration and Revelation in the Old Testament*, pp. 34–39.
70. *Tract. in Joannem* 24, 1 (*PL*, Vol. 35, c. 1593).
71. *Prophecy and Divination* (London, 1938), pp. 391–412.
72. *Ibid.*, p. 411.
73. *The Call of Israel*, pp. 137–172, 180–182.
74. *Inspiration and Revelation in the Old Testament*, pp. 46–47. I have not deemed it necessary to give serious attention to Immanuel Velikowsky's *Worlds in Collision*. I have been assured that the natural science of this book is fanciful; I know that its exegesis is fanciful.
75. Paul Heinisch, for instance, permits himself to say that in the Exodus God made use of the operations of natural forces (*Das Buch Exodus, HSAT:* Bonn, 1934, p. 113); and Dr. Heinisch does not write from rationalistic presuppositions.
76. *The Religion of Israel under the Kingdom*, pp. 185–186.

NOTES FOR CHAPTER 7

1. Is 40:18–20, 44:9–20; Jer 10:1–9 are the clearest examples.
2. Duhm (*Jesaja, GHK*, 1902, p. 301) agrees in substance with Kaufmann, but this is because he regards Is 44:9–20 as a production of late Judaism; earlier Hebrews did not so think of polytheism. Duhm also says (263) that Is 40:18–20 is not directed against heathen religion, but against the worship of the god in the image. Nötscher (*Jeremias, HSAT*, 1934) regards Jer 10:1–16 as an *argumentum ad hominem*. Marti (*Jesaja, KHC*, 1900, p. 304): "The identification of image and god does not touch the essence of polytheism; but there is scarcely any doubt that the ordinary heathen did not clearly distinguish the image and the god." Marti opened up a fruitful line of thought, but did not pursue it.
3. *JBL* 70 (1951), 179–197 (tr. from the Hebrew by Moshe Greenberg).
4. Tallqvist, *Der Assyrische Gott* (1932), p. 112: "The sources do not present a unified picture of the Assyrian god, and even less do they answer the

question of his original essence." Cf. also *ibid.*, p. 40 ff. In 1905 Jastrow could write that it had been convincingly demonstrated that Marduk was originally a solar deity (*Religion Babyloniens und Assyriens*, 1905, I, p. 112), and Langdon could say the same thing in 1923 (*Epic of Creation*, 1923, pp. 32–33); but Dhorme ignores any solar character of Marduk (*Religions de Babylonie et d'Assyrie*, 1945, pp. 139–150).

5. Cf. *TS*, 11 (1950), p. 275 ff.

6. The same opinion is expressed by Alfred Jeremias, *Das alte Testament im Lichte des alten Orients* (1930), p. 39: "[The author of Genesis 1] knew the ancient Oriental conception of the universe. This conception corresponded to the scientific knowledge of the period. But the biblical narrator is not concerned with speculation; rather he contemns it and combats — however tacitly — the mythological formulation of the doctrine, although, as a child of his time, he cannot avoid it entirely." Cf. also Paul Heinisch, *Probleme der biblischen Urgeschichte* (1947), p. 43: "As we may conclude from different expressions in the prophets and the psalms, the epic *Enuma Elish* was known to the Hebrews as it is preserved for us, or in a similar form; it is easily possible that it was present to the mind of our author [of Genesis 1], and that he elaborated his conception in opposition to it." Modern critics, such as von Rad (*Das erste Buch Mose*, ATD, 1950, p. 52), do not admit that the creation account of Babylonia was unknown to the Hebrews before the Assyrian period, or even before the Exile. The creation account of P, according to von Rad, took form early in Israel's history.

7. D. D. Luckenbill, *Ancient Records: Assyria and Babylonia* (1927), II, p. 243.

8. W. F. Albright, *From the Stone Age to Christianity* (New York, 1946), pp. 202–203: "Equally vital to Mosaic religion was the aniconic character of Yahweh, who could not be represented in any visible or tangible form. In spite of the unanimous testimony of Israelite tradition, scholars have made repeated efforts to prove the existence of representations of deity in early Israel. Every effort of this kind has been based on subjective arguments and on arbitrary assumptions which have won only the most limited acceptance even in friendly circles. Of course, it would be equally unscholarly to deny the *possibility* of such images or portrayals in material form. But the testimony of our written sources, plus the completely negative results of excavation, should be evidence enough to prove that Yahwism was essentially aniconic and that material representations were foreign to its spirit from the beginning. We shall show below that there is no basis whatever for the idea that Yahweh was worshipped in bull form by the northern tribes of Bethel and Dan." *Ibid.*, p. 229: "This gross conception is not only unparalleled in biblical tradition, but is contrary to all that we know of Syro-Palestinian iconography in the second and early first millennia B.C. Among Canaanites, Aramaeans, and Hittites we find the gods nearly always represented as standing on the back of an animal or as seated on a throne borne by animals — but never as themselves in animal form. . . . It was, therefore, pointed out by K. Th. Obbink in 1929 that the 'golden calf' must have been the visible pedestal on which the invisible Yahweh stood." Cf. also ZATW, 47, 264–274; Hempel, *Gott und Mensch im alten Testament* (1936), p. 265 f.; JBL, 57 (1938), xviii.

9. The question of the relations of magic and religion is extremely complex; as Frazer has remarked, it is determined by one's definition of religion. Frazer's distinction (which I take from *The Golden Bough*, abridged ed.,

1922, pp. 48–60) is very commonly accepted: the two are distinguished by their conception of the higher powers. To religion these powers are conscious, to magic they are unconscious and impersonal. Cf. Bertholet in *RGG*, III, 1839 ff. Marett (*ERE*, VIII, 245 ff.) is rather highly critical of Frazer's distinction; but he does not altogether identify the two. G. van der Leeuw (*Religion in Essence and Manifestation*, Eng. tr., 1938, p. 547 ff.) affirms their identity, because both magic and religion deal with power, although he admits that magic differs from all other forms of religion.

10. Magic in Assyria and Babylonia is treated recently by Dhorme, *Religions de Babylonie et d'Assyrie*, pp. 254–271; cf. also F. Jeremias, in Chantepie de la Saussaye, *Lehrbuch der Religionsgeschichte*, 1925, I, pp. 572–575; A. Jeremias, *Handbuch der altorientalischen Geisteskultur*, 1929, pp. 410–417. A study of the texts themselves (cf. M. Jastrow, *Religion Babyloniens und Assyriens*, I, pp. 289–392) makes the analysis given in the text abundantly evident. Mesopotamian magic is complicated by the presence of many introductory passages to the magical formulae which are hymns to the high gods. These are often of an elevated tone and content, in direct contrast to the magical formulae which follow. But in Mesopotamia, as in other regions, we rarely find magic and religion distinctly set off against each other; religious beliefs and practices are mingled with gross superstition. But the texts themselves show that the two should not be identified. Once the address to the high gods is finished, the magical atmosphere is evident. The effect is sought not by the impetration of a higher personal power, but by fire and water, by the recitation of set formulae, by the mechanical repetition of determined gestures. The evil effect is to be averted by these material means, which constrain either the demons or the human sorcerer. There is divine activity only in this, that Ea himself is the great sorcerer who has taught men the formulae by which the demons may be overcome.

11. *The Re-Discovery of the Old Testament* (London, 1946), p. 130.

12. Jacques Guillet, *Themes of the Bible* (Notre Dame, Ind., 1961), p. 32 ff.

13. Cf. *CBQ*, 10 (1948), 180 ff.

14. G. van der Leeuw, *op. cit.*, pp. 449–450: "The image of the god is a means of holding him fast, of guaranteeing his presence. . . . By the image of the god it is essentially the *sacrum* that is indicated, the presence of the divine . . . even where fetish or semi-fetish has long yielded place to the human image, it is never a matter of mere external resemblance; for the essence of the god's image consists not in its resemblance to man but in its being filled with power, exactly as in the case of the fetish. . . . The essential factor in the image, then, is power." Edvard Lehmann, in Chantepie de la Saussaye, *Lehrbuch der Religionsgeschichte*, I, p. 88: "Where the divine image was originally made of some animate material, the presence of the god in the divine image was self-evident; and in fact some such identification of the god and his image lies at the base of every form of idolatry." Cf. also Hubert Schrade, *Der Verborgene Gott*, 1949, especially pp. 13–23, and *TS*, 11 (1950), pp. 588–593.

15. A. L. Oppenheim, in Ferm, *Forgotten Religions* (New York, 1950), pp. 73–75: "It should be noted that it was considered an indispensable prerequisite to transform images as well as 'symbols' from dead and unclean matter into the proper seat for the Divine by means of a consecration which changed them into 'living' things, ready for perceptions, sensations,

and even emotions. . . . It has to be borne in mind that — as the cuneiform religious texts repeatedly indicate — the deity actually 'lived,' that is: was kept potent, efficient, and present on its fare." *Id.*, *BA*, 7 (1944), 59: "After having been awakened by a ceremonious assembly of minor deities, the image is furnished water for its morning toilet, then clothed and decked out with sumptuous garments, crowns, etc., according to the requirements of the day's ceremonies; it is served twice or three times a day with a plentiful repast on exquisite and precious plates; it receives the visits of the members of its family or court, and was led on festival occasions through the streets of its town to rites performed in out-of-doors sanctuaries, or carried in a festive cortege to nuptials with its divine spouse. It was not even refused the truly royal pleasure of hunting in its game-cover."

16. Luckenbill, *Ancient Records*, II, pp. 121, 123, 138, 152, 154, 155, 185, 209, 214, 215, 309–310, 311. The same idiom appears in the Amarna letters; cf. *EA*, 55.42–43; 129.49–51; 134.4 ff.

17. Albright (*Archaeology and the Religion of Israel* [Baltimore, 1942], pp. 114–115) notes that no Astarte plaques or figurines have been discovered in any early Israelite levels (Iron I) in central Palestine; on the periphery of Israel, however, they have been found in early levels in some number. In central Palestine they are found frequently in deposits of Late Bronze and Iron II, from the ninth century onward. The type of plaque and figurine described here (115) is found illustrated in the same author's *Archaelogy of Palestine* (Baltimore, 1949), p. 133.

18. Albright, *Archaeology and the Religion of Israel*, pp. 142–155; cf. also G. Ernest Wright, *BA*, 7 (1944), 73 ff.

NOTES FOR CHAPTER 8

1. *Historical Criticism and the Old Testament* (London, 1905), p. 183.
2. *Ibid.*, p. 185.
3. *Ibid.*, pp 186–187.
4. *Ibid.*, p. 190.
5. *Ibid.*, p. 194.
6. *Ibid.*, p. 196.
7. *Ibid.*, p. 201.
8. *Ibid.*, p. 202.
9. *Ibid.*, p. 203.
10. *Ibid.*, p. 204.
11. *Ibid.*, pp. 205–206.
12. *Ibid.*, p. 208.
13. *Ibid.*, p. 211.
14. *Paradies und Sündenfall* (Münster, 1913), p. 602.
15. *Ibid.*, pp. 602–603.
16. *Das Buch Genesis* (*HSAT;* Bonn, 1930), p. 138 ff.
17. *Probleme der biblischen Urgeschichte* (Lucerne, 1947), p. 102.
18. *Civiltà cattolica*, XCIX (1948), 123.
19. *Loc. cit.*
20. *Ibid.*, p. 125.
21. *Le livre de la Genèse* (Paris, 1949), p. 71 ff.
22. *Ibid.*, p. 71.
23. *Ibid.*, pp. 72–73.
24. *Das Buch Genesis* (*GHK;* Göttingen, 1922), p. vii. English seems to lack a

word which properly renders *Sage*. "Saga" in English is limited to heroic and epic narratives. "Legend," almost the standard English equivalent, strictly defined as "a narrative based chiefly on tradition," is an exact translation; but in common use, it seems to me, the word has overtones which have made me hesitate to use it. *Sage*, as Skinner has pointed out (*Genesis* [*ICC;* New York, 1910], p. iii), means things said, as opposed to *Geschichte*, things which happened. The distinction does not lie in the historical reality of the event but in the manner of its transmission. In this paper I employ by preference the terms "folklore" or "popular tradition" (Fr., *récit populaire*).

25. *Ibid.,* p. viii.
26. *Ibid.,* pp. viii–ix.
27. *Ibid.,* p. ix.
28. *Ibid.,* pp. ix–x.
29. *Ibid.,* pp. x–xi. Gunkel writes: "The way in which narratives speak of God is one of the most certain criteria by which they may be distinguished as historical or poetic. Here also the historian does not appear without his philosophy. We believe that God is operative in the world as the imperceptible and hidden cause of all things; many times his work can, as it were, be seized with the hands, in especially great and impressive events and persons; we surmise his power in the marvelous concatenation of events; but he never appears to us as one of a number of operative factors, only as the ultimate cause of all things." This is, at least, an agreeably honest philosophical profession.
30. *Ibid.,* pp. xi–xii.
31. *Ibid.,* pp. xii–xiv.
32. *Civiltà cattolica,* XCIX (1948), 124.
33. *Genesis,* pp. xxvii–xxx.
34. *Ibid.,* pp. xxxi–xxxix.
35. This characteristic has also been pointed out by Bea, who calls it narration in concentric circles; cf. *Institutiones biblicae de Pentateucho* (Rome, 1928), pp. 66–67; *Civiltà cattolica,* XCIX (1948), 126.
36. *Genesis,* pp., lvi–lxxx.
37. *Divino afflante Spiritu,* nos. 35–39 (Eng. tr., NCWC, pp. 18–20); (1948), 319–320, 322–323.
38. Driver, *Genesis* (7th ed.; New York and London, 1909), pp. 54–57; Feldmann, *Paradies und Sündenfall,* pp. 601–605; Gordon, *Early Traditions of Genesis* (Edinburgh, 1907), pp. 161–164; Heinisch, *Genesis,* p. 138; Gunkel, *Genesis,* pp. 29–33; Skinner, Genesis, pp. 94–97; Chaine, *Genèse,* pp. 69–70.
39. Ebeling, in Gressmann, *Altorientalische Texte zum Alten Testament* (Berlin, 1926), p. 134; Speiser, in Pritchard, *Ancient Near Eastern Texts* (Princeton, 1950), pp. 99–100.
40. Heidel, *The Gilgamesh Epic and Old Testament Parallels* (Chicago, 1946), p. 19; Speiser, in Pritchard, *Ancient Near Eastern Texts,* p. 74.
41. Heidel, *The Babylonian Genesis* (Chicago, 1950), pp. 46–47; Speiser, in Pritchard, *Ancient Near Eastern Texts,* p. 68.
42. Erman, *Die Religion der Aegypter* (Berlin, 1934), pp. 24, 44.
43. Ebeling, in Gressmann, *Altorientalische Texte,* p. 136.
44. Heidel, *Gilgamesh Epic,* p. 88; Speiser, in Pritchard, *Ancient Near Eastern Texts,* p. 95.
45. *BASOR,* 96, 18 ff.

46. This has also been noticed by Chaine, *Genèse*, p. 62.
47. *Religion of Babylonia and Assyria* (New York, 1898), p. 475 ff.
48. Heidel, *Gilgamesh Epic*, pp. 21–22; Speiser, in Pritchard, *Ancient Near Eastern Texts*, pp. 74–75, 77–78.
49. *Ezekiel* (*ICC*; New York, 1937), *ad loc.*
50. *Das Buch Ezechiel* (*GHK*; Göttingen, 1900), *ad loc.* Bertholet's opinion in *Hesekiel* (*KHC*; Tübingen, 1897) was the same as that of Kraetzschmar; in *Hesekiel* (*HAT*; Tübingen, 1936) he agrees with Gunkel.
51. *Genesis* (*GHK*; Göttingen, 1922), p. 343.
52. Cooke, *Ezekiel, ad loc.*; Hölscher, *Zeitschrift für alttestamentliche Wissenschaft*, Beih. 39 (1924), 142. Widengren has pointed out some elements of Mesopotamian mythology in Manichaeism which are quite like the story of Ezekiel; cf. *The King and the Tree of Life in Ancient Near Eastern Religion*, pp. 1–19. Steinmann suggests Ugarit as the source of the myth; cf. *Le prophète Ezéchiel* (Paris, 1953), p. 147. Fohrer follows Hölscher, adding parallels from the myth of Dilmun (cf. note 69 below); cf. *ZATW*, Beih. 71 (1952), 236–237.
53. *La connaissance du bien et du mal et le péché du Paradis* (Louvain, 1948), p. 69.
54. An extensive bibliography is found throughout Coppens' work cited above.
55. *Paradies und Sündenfall*, p. 35; *Genesis*, p. 131.
56. *ZATW*, XLIII (1925), 35 ff.
57. *ZATW*, Beih. 34 (1920), 127 ff.
58. *ZATW*, L (1932), 94 ff.; this is identical in principle with the opinion of Gunkel (*Genesis*, pp. 25–26).
59. *Early Traditions of Israel* (Oxford, 1948), p. 94 ff.
60. *La connaissance du bien et du mal*, p. 69 ff.
61. *RSR*, LXVI (1949), 465–480. This article deserves special attention. I have found no other Catholic interpreter who admitted the composite character of the Paradise story to this extent, that he formulated an analysis of its sources. Lefèvre thus divides the account: the history of Eve, 2.4b–7, (8), 9a, 16, (17), 18–25; 3:1–4, (5), 6–21; the history of the garden of Eden, 2:(8), 9b, 10–15, (17); 3:(5), 22–24. Parentheses indicate verses in which the two documents have been fused.
62. Cf. Dhorme, *RB*, XVI (1907), 374. This etymology is mentioned with some doubt by Zorell and Koehler, and seems to be favored by Chaine, *Genèse*, p. 32. It has not, however, been generally accepted.
63. *Genèse*, p. 38.
64. *Timaeus*, 41e, 90e–91d; cf. also *Symposium*, 189c–193d, and A. E. Taylor, *Commentary on Plato's Timaeus* (Oxford, 1928), pp. 258, 635–639, 652–654. G. F. Moore mentions two rabbinical references to the idea that man was created androgynous, and calls it "probably a bit of foreign lore adapted to the first pair in Genesis"; cf. *Judaism* (Cambridge, 1927), I, p. 453. These references would not evince the existence of any such idea among the ancient Semitic peoples.
65. *ZATW*, Beih. 34 (1920), 127.
66. *La connaissance du bien et du mal*, p. 18.
67. *Ibid.*, p. 24.
68. *The King and the Tree of Life in Ancient Near Eastern Religion* (Uppsala, 1951).
69. Speiser, in Pritchard, *Ancient Near Eastern Texts*, pp. 96, 101–102.
70. *La connaissance du bien et du mal*, pp. 92–117.

71. R. de Vaux, in a review of Coppens, denies that the serpent is a "phallic emblem in the precise sense"; cf. *RB, XLVI* (1949), 307. The opinion of Père de Vaux is worthy of the highest consideration: it is with regret that I must say that I do not see how it is possible to counter the evidence which Coppens amasses. Perhaps the difference lies in the "precise sense"; the serpent is certainly a symbol of fertility; cf. Langdon, *Semitic Mythology* (Boston, 1931), pp. 77–78, 90. The serpent is very frequently associated with the nude goddess, sometimes in a position which leaves little doubt about its sexual significance; cf. Albright's reinterpretation of a stele from Tell Beit-Mirsim, *Archaeology and the Religion of Israel* (Baltimore, 1942), p. 189; also his *Archaeology of Palestine* (Penguin, 1949), pp. 96–97; Galling, *Biblisches Reallexikon* (Tübingen, 1937), pp. 223, 227–228; Langdon, *Semitic Mythology*, Figs. 13, 15, 17, 69, 78, 94; Schaeffer, *Ugaritica*, II (Paris, 1949), Fig. 10; Vincent, *Canaan* (Paris, 1914), pl. IX; pl. III, no. 9, Fig. 103

72. Cf. Gordon, *Ugaritic Handbook* (Rome, 1947), Text 68, p. 150; *id.*, *Ugaritic Literature* (Rome, 1949), pp. 15–16; *TS*, XI (1950), 275–282.

73. *ZATW*, XLIII (1925), 35.

74. *Genèse*, p. 49.

75. *ZATW*, L (1932), 108.

76. Langdon, *Semitic Mythology*, p. 39 ff. Cf. the stele of Aleyan Baal of Ugarit (Schaeffer, *Ugaritica*, II, pl. XXIII–XXIV, pp. 121–130).

77. *Genèse*, p. 51.

78. *Genèse*, p. 71.

79. Cf. above, pp. 154–156.

80. To the authors cited already the following may be added, although none of them goes into the question in detail. W. A. Irwin says simply that Ezekiel has used the actual symbolism of the religion and mythology of Tyre as the theme of his oracle (*The Problem of Ezekiel* [Chicago, 1943], p. 221). Walther Eichrodt is content to speak of mythological traits and allusions and of the myth of the *Urmensch* without attempting to identify it more closely (*Theologie des AT*, I [Berlin, 1948], pp. 234, 249). The wisdom of the *Urmensch* is also mentioned by Otto Procksch (*Theologie des AT* [Gütersloh, 1949], p. 476).

81. *Ezechiel* (*HAT* [Tübingen, 1955]), p. 162.

82. Cf. above, p. 154. The material of the myth of Enki and Ninkhursag must be employed with the greatest caution; cf. the critical reviews of S. N. Kramer's *Sumerian Mythology* (Philadelphia, 1944) by Jacobsen (*JNES*, V [1946], 128 ff.) and Witzel (*Orientalia*, XV [1946], 239 ff.).

83. *The King and the Tree of Life in Ancient Near Eastern Religion* (Uppsala, 1951), especially pp. 1–19.

84. *The Ascension of the Apostle and the Heavenly Book* (Uppsala, 1950), pp. 27, 94–96.

85. E.g., Kraetzschmar and Cooke among the older writers, and most recently Fohrer and Marvin H. Pope (cf. below).

86. *El in the Ugaritic Texts* (Leiden, 1955), p. 97 ff. Cf. also Arvid Kapelrud, *Baal in the Ras Shamra Texts* (Copenhagen, 1952).

87. Julian Morgenstern, *HUCA*, XIV (1939), 29–126, cited by Pope.

88. Otto Eissfeldt, *Baal Zaphon, Zeus Kasios und der Durchzug der Israeliten durchs Meer* (Halle, 1932).

89. Pope, *op. cit.*, p. 61.

90. *Ibid.*, pp. 75–81.

91. Most recently, Fohrer, *op. cit.*, p. 159.

92. W. F. Albright, *From the Stone Age to Christianity* (Baltimore, 1946), p. 163.
93. *Genesis* [*GHK* (Göttingen, 1922)], p. 34.
94. Cf. above, p. 155.
95. Procksch, *op. cit.*, p. 491.

NOTES FOR CHAPTER 9

1. *RGG*, IV, 381.
2. Stählin covers myth in the Old Testament and in Judaism on one page (*Theologisches Wörterbuch zum Neuen Testament*, IV, pp. 787–788).
3. *Language and Myth* (translated from the German; New York, 1946), p. 8.
4. *Ibid.*, p. 13.
5. *Ibid.*, p. 35.
6. *Essay on Man* (Garden City, 1956), p. 101.
7. *Ibid.*, p. 102.
8. *Ibid.*, p. 110.
9. *Patterns in Comparative Religion* (translated from the French; New York, 1958), p. 426.
10. *Ibid.*, p. 418.
11. *Ibid.*, pp. 429–430.
12. *ZAW*, 65 (1953), 110.
13. *Ibid.*, p. 122.
14. E. Buess, *Geschichte des mythischen Erkennens* (Munich, 1953), p. 27.
15. *Ibid.*, p. 73.
16. *Ibid.*, pp. 159–162.
17. *The Intellectual Adventure of Ancient Man* (Chicago, 1946), p. 8.
18. *Ibid.*, pp. 11–19.
19. *Myth and Ritual in the Ancient Near East* (London, 1958), p. 279.
20. *Ibid.*, p. 283.
21. *Ibid.*, p. 307.
22. In Brilliant and Aigrain, *Histoire des Religions* 1 (Paris, n.d.), pp. 89–90.
23. G. van der Leeuw, *Religion: Its Essence and Manifestation* (translated from the German; London, 1938), p. 444.
24. *An Outline of Biblical Theology* (Philadelphia, 1946), pp. 115–116.
25. *PEQ*, 88 (1956), 88.
26. *Introduction to the Old Testament* (Copenhagen, 1948), I, p. 241.
27. Cassirer, *Essay on Man*, pp. 84, 94.
28. Cf. above, pp. 85–92.
29. The term "school" perhaps imposes a false unity on this group of scholars. Their views were set forth in three collections of essays published by S. H. Hooke: *Myth and Ritual* (Oxford, 1933); *The Labyrinth* (Oxford, 1935); *Myth, Ritual and Kingship* (Oxford, 1958).
30. It is for this reason that the position of Rudolf Bultmann is not entirely clear and consistent. It is curious that the most discussed and debated article in the history of modern exegesis, "Neues Testament und Mythologie" (1941; quoted here from *Kerygma und Mythos*, Hans-Werner Bartsch), defined myth only in a footnote: "Mythologisch ist die Vorstellungsweise, in der das Unweltliche, Göttliche als Weltliches, Menschliches, das Jenseitige als Diesseitiges erscheint. . . . Es ist vom 'Mythos' also nicht in jenem modernen Sinne die Rede, wonach er nichts weiter bedeutet als Ideologie" (*Kerygma und Mythos*, I [1948], 22). Under criticism Bultmann defended his position by modifying it. In response to Julius Schniewind (*ibid.*, 122) he wrote that myth is a *Denk- und Redensweise,*

where in his first definition he had called it a *Vorstellungsweise;* these two are not exactly the same, as one can see from the summary of the recent discussion of myth cited above, and it was careless of Bultmann to imply that they are. It is even more curious to find him saying later that he does not think the concept of myth is important (*Kerygma und Mythos,* II [1952], 180). He then goes on to place the essence of myth in its opposition to scientific thought; he sets this forth well (*ibid.,* 180–190), but he ends with exactly what he denied he had in his first definition: the concept of myth as an ideology. But B. has committed himself to the position that there is no valid intellectual process except scientific thought; and since this seems to imply that the mythical processes of the New Testament are not an intuition of truth, it is hard to see how anything can be left after *Entmythologisierung.* But the New Testament is much more meaningful for B. than this, and hence his lack of consistency. I am tempted to say that if B. had spent as much space on the definition of myth as I have here we should have been deprived of a piquant controversy.

31. *Op. cit.,* pp. 552–553.
32. *The Philosophy of Symbolic Forms II: Mythical Thought* (translated from the German; New Haven, 1955), p. 45.
33. *Ibid.,* pp. 46–47.
34. *Ibid.,* p. 48.
35. Thorkild Jacobsen has written: "Through and under [the order of nature] he [the Mesopotamian] sensed a multitude of powerful individual wills, potentially divergent, potentially conflicting, fraught with a possibility of anarchy. He confronted in Nature gigantic and wilful individual powers. To the Mesopotamian, accordingly, cosmic *order* did not appear as something given; rather it became something achieved — achieved through a continual integration of the many individual cosmic wills, each so powerful, so frightening" (*The Intellectual Adventure of Ancient Man,* p. 127).
36. Henri Frankfort writes: "The whole man confronts a living 'Thou' in nature; and the whole man — emotional and imaginative as well as intellectual — gives expression to the experience. All experience of 'Thou' is highly individual; and early man does, in fact, view happenings as individual events. An account of such events and also their explanation can be conceived only as action and necessarily take the form of a story. In other words, the ancients told myths instead of presenting an analysis or conclusions" (*ibid.,* p. 6).
37. *RGG,* IV, 366.
38. *ZAW,* 65 (1953), 120.
39. In Brillant and Aigrain, *Histoire des religions* 4, pp. 154 ff., 191 ff. On the cultural myth Cassirer said: "[In culture myths] the question of origins shifts more and more from the sphere of *things* to the specifically human sphere: the form of mythical causality serves to explain the origin not so much of the world or particular objects in it as of human cultural achievements. True, in accordance with the style of mythical thinking this explanation stops at the view that these benefits were not created through the power and will of man but were given him. They are regarded not as produced by man but as received by him in a state of completion" (*The Philosophy of Symbolic Forms II: Mythical Thought,* p. 204). It appears that this form cannot be transferred as described to Gn 4:17–22; 9:20–21; but, as we shall see, the Hebrews always transformed mythical patterns.
40. Cassirer pointed out the social function of myth: ". . . the mythical-

religious consciousness does not simply *follow* from the empirical content of the social form but is rather one of the most important *factors* of the feeling of community and social life. Myth itself is one of those spiritual syntheses through which a bond between 'I' and 'Thou' is made possible, through which a definite unity and a definite contrast, a relation of kinship and a relation of tension, are created between the individual and the community" (*ibid.*, p. 177).

41. R. A. F. MacKenzie, following Gunkel (*CBQ*, 15 [1953], 136).
42. Cf. above, pp. 146–175.
43. Cf. above, pp. 175–181.
44. *RGG*, IV, 382–383, 387–388.
45. *ZAW*, 65 (1953), 111–135. For this tension in the prophets S. B. Frost cites Is 29:1–2; 2:10–17; Am 5:18 ff. (*VT*, 2 [1952], 70–80).
46. E. Jacob, *Theology of the Old Testament* (translated from the French; New York, 1958), pp. 197–201.
47. In S. H. Hooke, *Myth, Ritual and Kingship*, pp. 159–176. On the theophanies cf. also Otto Eissfeldt, *Einleitung in das Alte Testament* (Tübingen, 1956), pp. 37–38, and my own remarks above, pp. 101–107.
48. I collected these passages in *TS*, 11 (1950), 275–282. For a more recent treatment, cf. Widengren in *Myth, Ritual and Kingship*, pp. 170–173.
49. *Op. cit.*, p. 138.
50. Thus reversing an opinion expressed in *TS*, 11 (1950), 282.
51. Cf. Hempel in *ZAW*, 65 (1953), 126–128, and my remarks above, pp. 93–97.
52. Translated by John A. Wilson in Pritchard, *Ancient Near Eastern Texts*, pp. 4–6.
53. In *Alttestamentliche Studien* (Bonn, 1950), pp. 147–149.
54. *Le péché originel dans l'Écriture* (Paris, 1958), pp. 52–53.
55. In Brilliant and Aigrain, *Histoire des religions*, 1, pp. 90–91.
56. *DBS*, VI, 245–246.
57. *Ibid.*, 252.
58. *AAS*, 42 (1950), 577.
59. *Op. cit.*, pp. 189–192.
60. *CBQ*, 15 (1953), 140.
61. *Les sages d'Israël* (Paris, 1946), p. 9.

NOTES FOR CHAPTER 10

1. *The Messianic Idea in Israel*, tr. William Stinespring (New York, 1955), p. 9.
2. *VDBS*, 5 (Paris, 1955), 1168; Klausner, *op. cit.*, p. 10; Otto Procksch, *Theologie des alten Testaments* (Gütersloh, 1949), p. 582.
3. "The Dynastic Oracle: II Samuel 7," *TS*, 8 (1947), 187 ff. [For our readers' convenience, a translation of 2 Sm 7:8–16 is here given.]

    8   Thus speaks Yahweh of hosts:
        It was I who took you from the folds,
           from following the sheep,
           to be prince over my people Israel.
    9   I was with you wherever you went,
           cutting your enemies down before you,
        And I will make your name great,
           like that of the great ones of the earth. . . .
   11b   Yahweh will *make you great*,
          Yahweh will make a house of you.

12 When your days are completed,
and you sleep with your fathers,
I will raise up for your descendants after you,
the offspring of your body,
and I will make firm his kingship.
13 It is he who shall build a house for my name,
and I will make firm forever the throne of his kingship.
14 I will be a father to him,
and he a son to me;
If he acts wickedly I will chastise him
with the rod men use,
with blows the sons of men give.
15 But my covenant-love shall not be taken from him,
as I took it from his predecessor:
16 Your house and your kingship shall endure forever before me,
your throne is set firm forever.

4. Albrecht Alt, *Kleine Schriften* (Munich, 1953), I, p. 357.
5. *Ibid.*, p. 119; A. R. Johnson, *Sacral Kingship in Ancient Israel* (Cardiff, 1955), pp. 12–16.
6. Hugo Gressmann, *Der Messias* (Göttingen, 1929), p. 627.
7. J. de Fraine, *L'aspect religieux de la royauté Israélite* (Rome, 1954), p. 371 ff.
8. *God Who Acts* (London, 1952), pp. 64–65.
9. *JBL*, 63 (1944), 219, 226–227.
10. *Loc. cit.*, 214; Procksch, *op. cit.*, p. 583; Hans-Joachim Kraus, *Die Königsherrschaft Gottes im alten Testament* (Tübingen, 1951), pp. 77, 92–93; Heinrich Gross, *Weltherrschaft als religiöse Idee im alten Testament* (Bonn, 1953), p. 71; de Fraine, *op. cit.*, p. 159; Roland Murphy, *A Study of Psalm 72* (Washington, 1948), pp. 72, 79–80; E. Podechard, *Le Psautier* (Lyons, 1954), II, p. 179.
11. *ETL*, 24 (1948), 354.
12. *Loc. cit.*, pp. 217–218. [Ex 4:22 f: "So you shall say to Pharao: Thus says the LORD: Israel is my son, my first-born. Hence I tell you: Let my son go, that he may serve me."]
13. Procksch, p. 583; Kraus, p. 77; Alt, pp. 132–133. Ps 89 (88): 20–38, CCD translation:
20 Once you spoke in a vision,
and to your faithful ones you said:
"Of a stripling I have made a champion;
over the people I have set a youth.
21 I have found David, my servant;
with my holy oil I have anointed him,
22 That my hand may be always with him,
and that my arm may make him strong.

23 "No enemy shall deceive him,
nor shall the wicked afflict him.
24 But I will crush his foes before him
and those who hate him I will smite.
25 My faithfulness and my kindness shall be with him,
and through my name shall his horn be exalted.
26 I will set his hand upon the sea,
his right hand upon the rivers.

> 27   "He shall say of me, 'You are my father,
>   my God, the Rock, my savior.'
> 28   And I will make him the first-born,
>   highest of the kings of the earth.
> 29   Forever I will maintain my kindness toward him,
>   and my covenant with him stands firm.
> 30   I will make his posterity endure forever
>   and his throne as the days of heaven.
>
> 31   "If his sons forsake my law
>   and walk not according to my ordinances,
> 32   If they violate my statutes
>   and keep not my commands,
> 33   I will punish their crime with a rod
>   and their guilt with stripes.
> 34   Yet my kindness I will not take from him,
>   nor will I belie my faithfulness.
>
> 35   "I will not violate my covenant;
>   the promise of my lips I will not alter.
> 36   Once, by my holiness, have I sworn;
>   I will not be false to David.
> 37   His posterity shall continue forever,
>   and his throne shall be like the sun before me;
> 38   Like the moon, which remains forever —
>   a faithful witness in the sky."

14. Johannes Pedersen, *Israel* (Copenhagen, 1940), III–IV, p. 525 ff.
15. B. D. Eerdmans, *OTS*, 4 (1947), 428.
16. Alt, p. 133; H. J. Kraus, *Gottesdienst in Israel* (Munich, 1954), p. 77.
17. Henri Frankfort, *Kingship and the Gods* (Chicago, 1948), p 341.
18. *Op. cit.*, p. 20 (2 Sm 23:3–5):

> He who rules men with justice,
>   rules in the fear of God,
> Is like the morning light when the sun rises, . . .
>   that makes the grass grow from the earth after the rain.
> Is not my house thus with God?
>   For he has made an everlasting covenant with me,
>   wholly ordered and secured;
> Will he not bring forth
>   whatever I need and want?
>   Ps 132 (131), 11–12:
> The LORD swore to David
>   a firm promise from which he will not withdraw:
> "Your own offspring
>   I will set upon your throne;
> If your sons keep my covenant
>   and the decrees which I shall teach them,
> Their sons, too, forever
>   shall sit upon your throne."

19. A. Robert, *RSR*, 39 (1951), 96; Procksch, p. 595; Gross, pp. 89–90; de Fraine, pp. 275–276.
20. *Op. cit.*, pp. 12–14.
21. *Ibid.*, p. 15.
22. *King and Messiah* (London, 1955), p. 17.

23. *Die Psalmen* (*ATD;* Göttingen, 1950), I, pp. 67–70.
24. *The Psalms* (Dublin, 1953), I, pp. xx, 5.
25. Pedersen, p. 432; Kissane, pp. 7–8.
26. Helmar Ringgren, *ZAW*, 64 (1952), 124.
27. *Die Psalmen* (*HAT;* Tübingen, 1934), p. 204.
28. *ANEP,* §§ 308, 355, 447.
29. Gressmann, p. 25; Ringgren, p. 125; Podechard, p. 170.
30. P. F. Ceuppens, *De Prophetiis Messianicis* (Rome, 1935), p. 417.
31. *Die Königsherrschaft Gottes* . . . , p. 73.
32. M. J. Lagrange, *RB*, 14 (1905), 55.
33. C. R. North, *ZAW*, 50 (1932), 30; the present writer's article in *CBQ*, 10 (1948), 170 ff.
34. *Religion und Kultus* (Göttingen, 1935), p. 56.
35. Gressman, p. 244; Ringgren, p. 133; A. Alt, *Festschrift für Alfred Bertholet* (Tübingen, 1950), pp. 47–48; Volkmar Herntrich, *Der Prophet Jesaja* (*ATD;* Göttingen, 1950), 166.
36. *The Book of Isaiah* (Dublin, 1941), I, p. 112.
37. *Le prophète Isaïe* (*LD;* Paris, 1950), p. 126.
38. Alt, *Festschrift* . . . , p. 29; Herntrich, p. 166.
39. *CBQ*, 10, 170 ff.
40. *RSR*, 36 (1949), 187.
41. *Ibid.*, pp. 200–201.
42. Klausner, p. 77.
43. Gelin, p. 1183.
44. *Israelitisch-Jüdische Religionsgeschichte* (Leipzig, 1933), p. 86.
45. Hans Schmidt (*Der Mythos vom wiederkehrenden König im Alten Testament* [Giessen, 1933], pp. 9–10) thinks this passage is preexilic.
46. *Id.*, *RGG*, 3, 2144.
47. *Theologisches Wörterbuch zum Neuen Testament*, 1, 565.
48. A lack of attention to native Israelite belief vitiates Ringgren's (129) otherwise impressive list of parallels between Israelite and Mesopotamian king ideology, which, he thinks, reached the Hebrews through the Canaanites. The king is elected by Yahweh and proclaimed as His son; rules with justice and righteousness; he communicates the divine blessing of fertility to the land; by divine power he overcomes his enemies, and he shall rule over the entire world. In some features king ideology is the same everywhere, whether in the Babylon of Hammurabi or in the Versailles of Louis XIV. In the text above I have tried to point out the distinctive Hebrew beliefs which lie beneath these superficial parallels. No one thinks the Hebrews invented kingship; but they did incorporate the idea into their own religious beliefs.
49. For the kingship of Yahweh cf. above, pp. 114–116.
50. Kraus, *Gottesdienst in Israel*, p. 77 ff.
51. *ZAW*, 54 (1936), 191 ff.
52. *Ibid.*, p. 171. H. W. Wolff describes messianism as consisting in: (1) royal power: (2) a unique relation with Yahweh; (3) eschatology (171). But Gressmann (270–272) thinks that royal messianism was exclusively political; the transformation of messianism into an ethical and religious ideal was due to the prophets. The messianic hope was eschatological from the beginning (*ibid.*, 230).
53. Joseph Coppens says that the Messiah is not necessarily eschatological; he is first the perfect king according to the image of David (*L'attente du Messie*, ed. L. Cerfaux [Bruges, 1954], p. 35). Walther Eichrodt says that

the covenant of David and the royal Psalms were originally not eschatological, although eschatological traits may have been added in subsequent
redactions (*Theologie des alten Testaments* [Berlin, 1948], pp. 243–
244). Steinmann (295) speaks of messianism in existing kings; Gelin
(1178) speaks of each king as a presumptive Messiah. G. E. Wright (78)
says the royal Psalms are not messianic in the usual sense, but refer to a
future king and portray in ideal form the role which the king is to play
in God's purposive activity. Roland Murphy (177) says that the messianic
era is described in terms of the ancient world. These writers, I believe,
formulate royal messianism more clearly than the writers who place a rigid
distinction between the historical king and the eschatological Messiah.

54. Von Rad, ZAW, 58 (1940), 219–220; Schmidt, *Der Mythos vom
wiederkeherenden König im Alten Testament.*

55. Only when this paper was ready to go to press did I see the English
translation of Sigmund Mowinckel's *Han som kommer* (*He That Cometh*
translated by G. W. Anderson [Oxford: Blackwell, 1956]). Mowinckel here
as usual follows a highly original approach and cannot be classified with
any school. With Gressmann and others he defines messianism as eschatological (3 ff.), but in other respects he is generally in opposition to Gressmann's theses. No genuinely messianic passage is earlier than the fall of the
monarchy (20). His treatment of the Israelite kingship is splendid. He
affirms that the Israelite king ideology is profoundly different from that
of Mesopotamia and Canaan and invokes the same two Israelite beliefs
which I have mentioned, the covenant (70, 82, 89) and the kingship of
Yahweh (143 ff.). The royal Psalms refer to the contemporary monarch,
and it seems that Mowinckel denies that they are messianic only because
of the absence of eschatology: "the Messiah is the future, eschatological
realization of the ideal of kingship" (156). In other respects, his treatment
of the "royal" passages is remarkably similar to that given in this paper.
This makes it all the more surprising that he takes little or no account
of the oracle of Nathan. Mowinckel deserves a full discussion rather than
this brief note; but the note will at least call the attention of the reader
to one of the most stimulating and challenging treatments of the subject
by a modern writer.

NOTES FOR CHAPTER 11

1. Joseph Klausner, *The Messianic Idea in Israel*, tr. William Stinespring
(New York, 1955), p. 9.
2. *Ibid.*
3. Recent surveys of messianism: the papers of Cerfaux, Coppens, de
Langhe, de Leeuw, Descamps, Giblet, and Rigaux collected in *L'Attente
du Messie* (Desclée de Brouwer, 1954); A. Gelin, "Messianisme," in
Dictionnaire de la Bible: Supplément (Paris, 1955), Vol. V, cc. 1165–
1212. The 1956 meeting of the Catholic Biblical Association of America
presented a collection of papers on messianism which appeared in the
Catholic Biblical Quarterly: E. F. Siegman, "The Stone Hewn from the
Mountain (Daniel 2)," 18 (1956), 364–379; R. E. Murphy, "Notes on
Old Testament Messianism and Apologetics," (1957), 5–15; Eamonn
O'Doherty, "The Organic Development of Messianic Revelation," 19
(1957), 16–24; J. L. McKenzie, "Royal Messianism," 19 (1957), 25–52;
R. E. Brown, "The Messianism of Qumran," 19 (1957), 53–82; J. E.
Menard, "*Pais Theou* as Messianic Title in the Book of Acts," 19 (1957),
83–92; Alphonsus Benson, ". . . From the Mouth of the Lion," 19 (1957),

199–212; E. H. Maly, "Messianism in Osee," 19 (1957), 213–225; F. L. Moriarty, "The Emmanuel Prophecies," 19 (1957), 226–233; R. A. F. MacKenzie, "The Messianism of Deuteronomy," 19 (1957), 299–305; Antonine De Guglielmo, "The Fertility of the Land in Messianic Prophecies," 19 (1957), 306–311; R. T. Siebeneck, "The Messianism of Aggeus and Proto-Zacharias," 19 (1957), 312–328. Additional bibliographical material will be found in these articles.

4. The question can be easily pursued in the articles of D. M. Stanley: "*Didache* as a Constitutive Element of the Gospel-Form," *Catholic Biblical Quarterly*, 17 (1955), 216–228; "The Conception of Salvation in Primitive Christian Preaching," *CBQ*, 18 (1956), 231–254; "The Conception of Salvation in the Synoptic Gospels," *CBQ*, 18 (1956), 345–363; "Balaam's Ass, or a Problem in New Testament Hermeneutics," *CBQ*, 20 (1958), 50–56; "Liturgical Influences on the Formation of the Four Gospels," *CBQ*, 21 (1959), 24–38; "The Conception of the Gospels as Salvation-History," *TS*, 20 (1959), 561–589.

5. Cf. above, pp. 228–230.

6. Cf. above, pp. 203–231.

7. Cf. the perceptive article of Martin Dibelius, "Rom und die Christen im ersten Jahrhundert," in *Botschaft und Geschichte* (Tübingen, 1956), Vol. II, pp. 177–228.

8. Cf. D. M. Stanley, "Kingdom to Church," *TS*, 16 (1955), 1–29.

9. H. H. Swete, *An Introduction to the Old Testament in Greek* (Cambridge, 1914), p. 386. Mk 15:28, a contamination from Lk 22:37, is not found in the critical text.

10. Millar Burrows, *More Light on the Dead Sea Scrolls* (New York, 1958), pp. 297–311, J. T. Milik, *Dix Ans de Découvertes dans le Désert de Juda* (Paris, 1957), pp. 83–85; F. M. Cross, *The Ancient Library of Qumran and Modern Biblical Studies* (New York, 1958), pp. 65–66, 165–166.

11. Vincent Taylor, *The Names of Jesus* (New York, 1953), pp. 38–51.

Index of Names

Albright, W. F., 62, 108, 113, 141, 205, 258, 260, 262, 265, 266
Allen, E. L., 254
Alt, Albrecht, 55, 207, 253, 269, 270, 271
Aristotle, 90
Augustine, 124

Barucq, A., 251
Bea, A., 148, 150, 263
Begrich, J., 157, 159, 163, 168, 252
Benoit, Pierre, 63 ff
Benson, A., 272
Bentzen, A., 185, 209, 212
Bertholet, A., 261, 264
Bewer, J., 259
Boman, Thorleif, 43, 251, 252, 253
Brown, R. E., 272
Buess, E., 183, 188, 198, 266
Bultmann, Rudolf, 78, 239, 266 f
Burrows, Millar, 90, 184, 273
Buttenwieser, M., 256

Calés, J., 104, 256
Cassirer, Ernst, 182 ff, 266, 267 f
Cazelles, H., 197
Ceuppens, F., 215, 219, 271
Chaine, J., 148 f, 159, 167, 170, 263, 264
Contenau, G., 255
Cooke, G., 154 f, 264, 265
Coppens, Joseph, 16, 157, 164 ff, 258, 264, 271
Cross, F. M., 273

Davies, G. Henton, 185
de Boer, P. A. H., 252
de Fraine, J., 209, 215, 269, 270
De Guglielmo, A., 273
Deimel, A., 255
Desroches-Noblecourt, C., 257
de Vaux, Roland, 265
Dhorme, E., 255, 260, 261, 264
Dibelius, M., 273
Dillmann, A., 255

Driver, S. R., 255, 263
Dubarle, A. M., 152, 197, 200
Duhm, B., 259
Duhm, H., 105
Dürr, L., 37

Eerdmans, B. D., 270
Eichrodt, Walther, 251, 254, 255, 256 f, 265, 271
Eissfeldt, Otto, 265, 268
Eliade, Mircea, 183
Erman, A., 263

Feldmann, J., 147 f, 157, 263
Feuillet, A., 220
Fohrer, G., 176, 264, 265
Frankfort, H., 183, 207, 257, 258, 267, 270
Frankfort, H. and H. A., 92
Franzelin, J. B., 59, 68
Frost, S. B., 268

Galling, K., 265
Garrigou-Lagrange, M. J., 259
Gelin, A., 203, 212, 218, 221, 224, 271, 272
Gemser, B., 256
Ginsberg, H. L., 257
Gressmann, H., 208, 212, 213, 215, 219, 220, 224, 225, 228, 256, 269, 271
Grether, Oskar, 37, 44, 46, 51, 53, 251, 252, 253
Gross, Heinrich, 211, 215, 269, 270
Gruenthaner, M., 255
Guillaume, Alfred, 126
Guillet, J., 142, 252, 261
Gunkel, Hermann, 100, 149 ff, 155, 180, 182, 192, 255, 263

Heidel, A., 255
Heidt, W., 255
Heinisch, P., 148, 157, 255, 259, 260, 263
Hempel, Johannes, 183, 190, 192, 253, 260, 268

275

Subject Index

Adam, 159
Ammonites, 139
Anger, divine, 116 ff
Apologetics, 71 f, 232 ff
Apostolic witness, 76 f
Ashurbanipal, 144
Assyria, 138 f

Baal, 178 f
Baalism, 137 ff
Blessing, 42, 110

Calf images, 141
Canaanite fertility cults, 107 ff
Canaanite religion, 137 ff
Chaos, 96 f
Church, and the Gospel, 76 f
Corporate personality, 229
Covenant, 207, 226 f, 247
Creation, 195; a continuous activity, 97; myths of, 136 ff; as victory of Yahweh, 193; and wisdom, 98 f
Creative word, 53 f
Creator, Yahweh as, 93 ff
Curse, 42 f

David, 42, 48
Day of Yahweh, 242
Deluge, 194 f; Mesopotamian, 154
Demons, 89
Deuteronomic movement, 55
Dilmun, 154, 163 f
Divination, 141

Eden, 154, 158, 179 f
Elephantine, 258
Elijah, 106 f, 112, 125, 139 f
Elisha, 125
Emmanuel, 219
Enuma Elish, 38, 43, 96, 100, 136 f, 153
Error, theological, 6 f
Esarhaddon, 139, 144
Eschatological messianism, 228 ff, 272
Eschatology of nature, 129 ff

Exodus, 126 f

Faith, 77 f
Feasts, Israelite, 114
Fertility, myths of, 136 ff
Fertility cults, 107 ff, 164
Fetishism, 134 ff
Folklore, 149 ff; and history, 73 ff
Fulfillment, 234

Genuinity of Gospels, 75
Gilgamesh epic, 105, 153 f, 165
Gospel, and the Church, 76 f
Gospels, 235 f; genuinity of, 75; historical character of, 72 ff; sources of, 63

History, as event and record, 78; and folklore, 73 ff; Israelite conception of, 52
Holy ones, 193

Idols, 134 ff
Ikhnaton, 256
Image(s), divine, 113, 138 ff, 261 f; prohibition of, 141 ff; significance of, 143 ff
Infallibility, 5 f
Inspiration, and biblical criticism, 59 ff; and revelation, 67 ff
Intellectual mission, in the Church, 12 ff

Jephthah, 139

King Messiah, 237
Kingship, 226, 271; divine, 114; Israelite, 204, 213
Kingship of Jesus, 239 ff
Kingship of Yahweh, 204, 226 ff
Knowledge of good and evil, 173

Law, casuistic and apodictic, 55; as word of God, 55
Leviathan, 129

Scriptural Index

Page reference indicated by italic numbers

Gn

1	*53, 136 f*
1:1–2:4a	*94 ff*
1:2	*48*
1:3	*51*
1:26–27	*153*
1:26–28	*252*
2:2	*97*
2:4b–25	*94 ff*
2:7	*48, 161*
2:9	*158 f*
2:9–17	*163*
2:10–14	*157*
2:16–17	*160*
2:18–23	*161 f*
2:19	*161, 252*
2:21 ff	*192*
2:23–24	*162 f*
2:25	*162 f*
3	*120*
3:1–7	*168 f*
3:14–19	*166 ff*
3:16 ff	*192*
3:22	*165*
3:23–24	*169*
4:1	*162*
6:4 ff	*192*
6:7	*51*
8:21–22	*114*
9:4	*153*
9:12 ff	*192*
9:13	*122*
12:1	*51*
12:17	*119*
18:14	*124*
20:17–18	*119*
21:2	*109*
27	*42*
27:28	*109*
28:31	*109*
29:20–27	*42*
30:2	*109*
31:7–9	*109*
33:5	*109*
49:24–26	*109*

Ex

3	*51*
4:22	*206*
7:20–8:19	*125*
12:29–30	*252*
15:3	*97*
19:16, 19	*103*
20:3	*140*
34:28	*55*

Lv

26:4	*109*
26:25	*119*

Nm

5:12–31	*42*
24:17	*205*

Dt

1–3	*51*
4:2	*56*
4:13	*55*
4:40	*56*
5:3	*56*
5:7	*140*
6:20–25	*56*
7:13	*109*
8:1 ff	*56*
8:3	*56, 253 f*
10:4	*56*
11:2–8	*56*
11:13–15	*109*
11:26–28	*56*
13:1–5	*56*
13:2–3	*123, 125*
30:14	*56*
32:22	*169*
32:47	*56*

Jos

3:5	*127*
10:11	*104*